NEW MUSIC AND THE CLAIMS OF MODERNITY

For my parents,
Bryan and Fiona

New Music
and the
Claims of Modernity

Alastair Williams

Ashgate

Published by
Ashgate Publishing Limited
Gower House
Croft Road
Aldershot
Hants GU11 3HR
England

Ashgate Publishing Company
Old Post Road
Brookfield
Vermont 05036–9704
USA

British Library Cataloguing-in-Publication data.

Williams, Alastair
    New music and the claims of modernity
    1.Music – 20th century. 2.Music – Theory – 20th century
    I.Title
    780.9'04

Library of Congress Cataloging-in-Publication data.

Williams, Alastair
    New music and the claims of modernity / Alastair Williams.
    Includes bibliographical references and index.
    ISBN 1–85928–368–3
    1. Music – 20th century – Philosophy and aesthetics. 2. Music – 20th century – History and criticism. 3. Adorno, Theodor W., 1903–1969 – Criticism and interpretation. I. Title.
    ML3845.W59 1997
    780'.9'04–dc21   96–45418
                        CIP
                        MN

ISBN 1 85928 368 3

Printed on acid-free paper

Typeset in Sabon by Photoprint, Torquay and printed in Great Britain by Biddles Ltd., Guildford.

Contents

Acknowledgements

An earlier version of the section on Ligeti appeared in Christopher Norris (ed.) *Music and the Politics of Culture* (Lawrence & Wishart, 1989); a condensed form of Chapter 3 was published in Andrew Benjamin and Peter Osborne (eds) *Thinking Art: Beyond Traditional Aesthetics* (Institute of Contemporary Arts, 1991); and the discussion of *Répons* derives from a chapter contributed to Anthony Pople (ed.) *Theory, Analysis and Meaning in Music* (Cambridge University Press, 1994). I am grateful to the editors and publishers for permission to reproduce materials from these earlier publications. Figure 3.1 is reproduced by permission of Faber and Faber Ltd. from Jean-Jacques Nattiez (ed.) *Orientations: Collected Writings by Pierre Boulez*, tr. M. Cooper (London, 1986). A British Academy award funded my postgraduate research; Keele University Music Department financed a trip to Germany; and research leave enabled me to complete the manuscript.

Many people have influenced this book. Malcolm Troup and Eric Clarke motivated me to explore the intersection of music and ideas, whilst Bojan Bujić supervised the doctoral thesis from which this project sprang. Terry Eagleton and Jim Samson provided very helpful comments on drafts of the manuscript, and I benefited from discussing issues with Ken Hirschkop, Tony Pinkney, Robert Samuels and colleagues at Keele. I am also grateful to Christopher Norris and Anthony Pople for supporting my research, while Alan Street provided encouragement at a crucial stage. Paul McFadden set the music examples, with fortitude, and Rachel Lynch, of Ashgate, was a helpful and efficient editor.

Finally, I thank Wendy for her companionship through long years of writing.

Introduction

Adornian aesthetics and later critical theory are used in this study to argue for an expanded understanding of modernism in music. New music as a category refers to a repertoire driven by an historical dynamic to develop new material and techniques; its emphasis on progress is challenged by postmodernist aesthetics, but since these ideas and the cultural practices that embody them are themselves recent and, it is claimed, have superseded modernism, the notion of the new remains operative. Post-1945 new music in the West is characterized by a bewildering array of strategies, many of which apparently bear little resemblance to one another; this book explores the internal dialectics of this repertoire, identifying and pursuing certain recurrent issues and problems. The conviction behind this task is that in an age when the functions and possibilities of art are themselves subject matter for artistic contemplation, philosophical reflection has become an intrinsic part of the medium.

The writings of Theodor Adorno include not only a rich body of work on modernism, but a ground-breaking attempt to understand music in the fullness of its immanent, sociological and philosophical dimensions. Music is undeniably a specific area of creativity with its own stringent and particular demands, but to view it as no more than this is to fail to understand the degree to which it encodes culturally – and historically – sedimented insight and critique. Adorno intensified the interpretation of music as a form of knowledge carrying a philosophical stratum within it: for him, 'to be musical converges with the philosophy of music' (1992a: 149). Recent musicology has recognized that music engages multifaceted discourses, but often regards this perception as a late innovation without acknowledging that Adorno was developing a holistic approach, albeit from a materialist perspective, as far back as the 1920s. Like some contemporary music, musicology is seeking renewal in aesthetic currents, including the confused world of late romanticism, that Adorno realized were blocked by the institutionalization of high modernism.

Part I examines Adorno's portrayal of modernity and scrutinizes his understanding of modernism in music. Parts II and III identify ways in which a modified version of Adorno's aesthetics continues to be pertinent for understanding post-war new music. There is thus a two-way flow: Adorno's ideas are used to unravel the claims of new music; conversely, practices in music feed back into the aesthetic framework, extending it and revealing fresh potential. Adorno's contention that 'the crisis in composition today . . . is also a crisis in analysis' emphasizes the overlap between the two disciplines (1982: 185). It is essential that immanent analysis should inform and complement cultural critique, but in the case of much new music in particular it is also crucial that a considered aesthetic response informs analytical insight. This is clearly the case for music that rejects the kinds of procedures normally addressed by analytical techniques, but the same observation is also pertinent for music which includes familiar elements. Some of the passages by Wolfgang Rihm discussed in Chapter 7, for example, can be understood by means of traditional functions, but provoke questions about the aesthetic meaning of evoking pre- and early-modernist procedures at the end of the twentieth century. From the perspective of critical theory, many of the problems associated with 1950s high modernism, which recent compositions try to avoid, stem from the impoverished aesthetic dimension associated with this music; or, more precisely, from the assumption that pre-compositional procedures would somehow generate their own aesthetic.

My modifications of Adorno's aesthetics are inflected by the second-generation critical theory of Jürgen Habermas and Albrecht Wellmer. Habermas has undertaken a full-scale reworking of Frankfurt critical theory, moving it away from a philosophy predicated on the interaction of subject and object to a medium of intersubjectivity; and Wellmer has attempted to translate Adornian aesthetics into this framework. Chapter 1 concludes by considering the impact of Habermas's turn to communicative action on Adornian critical theory, while developing his understanding of systems-world and lifeworld for use in later chapters. Intersubjectivity is again examined in Chapter 6, where the significance of Wellmer's interpretation of Adorno is examined.

Chapter 6 also touches on poststructuralist theory, within the context of the postmodernism debate, and the affinities between Adorno's work and deconstruction are addressed in Chapter 4, after encountering musical logics of disintegration in Chapter 3. While deconstruction, particularly as practised by Jacques Derrida and Paul de Man, has debunked organicist doctrines of music, it is argued that Adorno's materialist theory also interrogates ideological closure, yet is less inclined to push form towards heterogeneity. Poststructuralist cultural criticism encourages incisive reading and isolates the inflexible areas within Adorno's materialist aesthetic, but his attempts to rethink the relationships between part and whole beyond the imposition of unity remain inspirational.

This study addresses major new currents in music since 1945, but no attempt has been made to give comprehensive coverage; instead, a repertoire has been chosen that confronts key issues directly. The critique gravitates around Pierre Boulez and John Cage as major polar figures from this era because they personify extreme, if related, aspects of contemporary musical thought, though they do not define the boundaries of possibilities available to musicians. Scrutiny of these composers is divided into two periods: one pertains to high modernism and initial encounters with postmodernism, the other to more recent activity. The music and aesthetics of György Ligeti provide another way of negotiating the problems confronted by Boulez and Cage: a developed theoretical awareness enables Ligeti to explore directly the interface between structure and dissolution encountered by these composers and explored by deconstructionist criticism. His music also assimilates the concerns that inform postmodernism's challenge to the tenets of high modernism, but does so without abandoning the latter's aspirations.

Following Chapter 6's scrutiny of postmodernism and contemporary Frankfurt theory, Chapter 7 examines the renewal of tradition, and considers how music can react to the range of coexisting subjectivities and materials at its disposal. Music employing an inclusive range of compositional references questions the role played by advanced material in modernism, thereby reasserting issues identified by Adorno in his writings on Mahler. The study concludes by arguing for an inclusive theory of modernism and by suggesting that musical creativity is intimately linked to the exploration of subjectivity within a global space of simultaneous possibilities.

Part I Modernity

1 Critical Theory and Aesthetic Modernity

Modernity

Kant's three critiques effect a division of modernity into scientific and philosophical knowledge; ethics and law; aesthetics and expression. The two-edged quality of the dynamic force which, to varying degrees, drives processes within these spheres and affirms their separation is encapsulated by Baudelaire as a tension between creation and destruction: something of the past is destroyed in order to create the new.[1] The proximity of these opposing forces is embodied in the refashioning of natural resources essential to modernization, and the inherent instability of the formula is intensified by the profit motive of commodity production. This volatility is revealed in the modes of thought characteristic of modernity and is unremittingly drawn out by Adornian critical theory.

Modernization becomes a recognizable phenomenon with the rise of market economies at the end of the eighteenth century and facilitated the arrival of bourgeois, autonomous art. Artistic autonomy occupies a crucial place in Adorno's aesthetics because autonomous art is able to maintain a distance from the prevalent rationality, but at the same time it protests at the containment of expressive needs within a defined area. The material of art participates in the process of creative destruction, since previous material is partly destroyed in the process of renewal, but artistic invention is also attuned to remembrance of what is lost. The illusion of wholeness found in bourgeois, autonomous art – though challenged by late Beethoven – confirms an ideal of synthesis upon which modernity is founded but rarely achieves. That which cannot be achieved in everyday life can, seemingly, be found in art. Just as the concept should grasp its object, so artistic form apparently contains its content. The other pole of this dialectic is that aesthetic truth content, a distillation of subjectivity under prevailing social conditions, resides stubbornly in the gap between artistic form and the diverse particulars it seeks to control, thereby challenging the chimera of seamless form. The illusion of bourgeois art is more intensely disputed by modernism in two main ways: by a reworking of the relations between form and content, as heard in the pre-serial music of Schoenberg where tonality is subjected to a disintegrative force; and by an attack on autonomy itself, as theorized by Peter Bürger (1984), which is seen in modernist avant-garde movements such as Dada and Surrealism. Against this process, the idea of wholeness is inflated into a quasi-scientific dogma by the innovations of post-Second World War high modernism.

It is the progressive rationality of modernity, which finds aesthetic expression in a limited understanding of modernism, that much postmodernism reacts against. In recent years capitalist methods of production and profit accruement have shifted away from the relatively transparent methods of what is frequently known as Fordism to the occluded strategies of flexible accumulation, which are triggered by the contingencies of the market. Because this process can be understood as an intensification of capitalism, it is questionable whether so-called postmodernity does represent a paradigm shift away from modernity, since both phases are underpinned by similar economic configurations. Nevertheless, this latest phase of modernity is marked by fast reponses to situations and a rapid exchange of information, and it is not far fetched to argue that such a flux of activity is also apparent in the discourse of ideas that characterizes contemporary theoretical debates and aesthetic practices. Pitted against the axioms of modernism, postmodernism asserts itself as an alternative to the fixation on progress and often comprises an eclectic mixture of styles and practices. It is, however, perhaps more fruitful to posit postmodernism as the other side of modernism than as its opposite; to understand postmodernism as a reassertion of earlier aspects of modernism, hitherto submerged beneath the path of historical advancement.

Adorno died before the postmodernism debate became aware of itself as such, but many of its hotly-contested issues find a pre-echo in the contortions of his cultural analysis. The emergence of postmodernism on the theoretical stage has forced us to reconsider what exactly we understand by modernism and modernity, and Adorno's work represents one of the richest seams for such an investigation: his writings constitute a major attempt to understand aesthetic modernity and his projection of philosophical argument into the understanding of modernist art, particularly music, is incisive. It is, therefore, essential to examine his ideas before proceeding to trace the capillaries linking contemporary thought and music. Habermas's critique of Adorno's one-dimensional under-standing of modernity provides a crucial sounding board against which to test developments in critical theory since Adorno's death. From this point, one can examine ways in which Adorno's understanding of modernism and his aesthetics of music might be reworked.

Dialectic of Enlightenment and the Culture Industry

The work of the Frankfurt School during its formative years in the 1930s can be understood as an attempt to enrich the stream of thought, central to the writings of Hegel and Marx, that seeks to establish a critical theory of society rooted in immanent critique. Such a critique aims to scrutinize the conditions and ideals of a society in terms of themselves, without bringing outside values to bear, in order to reveal the ideological distortions often present. Two moments of immanent critique are found in Hegel and Marx: Seyla Benhabib identifies these as 'explanatory-diagnostic' and 'anticipatory-utopian' (1986: 142). The first approach is geared to revealing unacknowledged social assumptions and to releasing their blocked potentials; it functions by detecting contradictions inherent within the norms of a society, diagnosing their causes and seeking fulfilment of existing possibilities. The second moment of critique attempts to understand such immanent crises with regard to individual responses and needs; furthermore, it offers a utopian dimension in the form of a future ideal capable of transcending the current state of affairs. In the critical theory of Hegel and Marx these two moments of critique work alongside each other in an uneasy manner, but become somewhat dissociated in Frankfurt critical theory. For the first-generation Frankfurt theorists (particularly Adorno, Horkheimer and Marcuse), the utopian dimension was of paramount interest; but the second generation (led by Habermas) is preoccupied with diagnostic research and the establishment of normative view points.

The research programme of the *Institut für Sozialforschung* stemmed from the attempt to subject Hegelian-Marxism itself to immanent critique, and broadened the field of enquiry so that it would incorporate cultural and psychological analysis. From approximately 1932 to 1937 research focused on 'interdisciplinary materialism'; this approach was followed by the 'critical theory' of 1937–40; finally attention moved to the 'critique of instrumental reason'. The latter emerged in the aftermath of the war and was to remain a touchstone for the work of Adorno in particular. As is frequently pointed out, these shifts in emphasis away from the ambitious programme of interdisciplinary materialism reflect Adorno's and Horkheimer's attempts to come to terms with three historical experiences that were disastrous to the socialist project: 'The Soviet-Russian perversion of the humane content of revolutionary socialism, the collapse of the social-revolutionary labour movement in all industrial societies', coupled with the growth of fascism in Europe, 'and the socially integrative accomplishments of a rationalization that had penetrated into cultural reproduction' (Habermas 1984: 367).[2] Experience of the third tendency can be attributed to Adorno's and Horkheimer's years of exile in the United States. It was against this desolate background that utopian aspects of critical theory fused with the messianic tradition of Judaism for first-generation Frankfurt school thinkers such as Adorno and Benjamin.

The uncompromising depiction of contemporary society presented in Adorno's and Horkheimer's critique of instrumental reason cannot, however, be reduced entirely to the historical events against which the development of Frankfurt critical theory took place. At an early stage, Adorno detected an affinity between the exchange value system of commodities, based on the equivalence and fungibility of goods, and the identity principles of the philosophy of consciousness. In his inaugural lecture at Frankfurt University in 1931 Adorno had already raised the problem of an identity logic which must exclude the non-identical; an issue that was to occupy him for the rest of his life (Adorno 1977b). *Negative*

Dialectics relentlessly draws attention to the impoverished quality of formations of identity that exclude the claims of the non-identical, or non-conceptual, and this theme pervades the author's last work, *Aesthetic Theory*.

Adorno's and Horkheimer's *Dialectic of Enlightenment* is a key text for first-generation critical theory, but the argument also feeds the later concerns of Adorno's philosophy. The authors maintain that Western rationality is distorted by a narrow pursuit of instrumental and technological ends that shows scant regard for ethical or expressive considerations; and they trace the dark vein that threads its way through the European Enlightenment, mirroring the development of reason and ideals of social freedom with a subterranean history of violence and repression. By harnessing the dark writers of the Enlightenment – notably the Marquis de Sade and Nietzsche – Horkheimer and especially Adorno take the radical step of locating the Janus-faced quality of enlightenment in the non-contradictory premisses of formal logic itself. (Opposition by the Frankfurt school to these axioms of reasoning reached a head in the positivist dispute of the 1960s.) Reason increasingly appears as purposeful manipulation of nature guided by the motor of self-preservation, but loses sight of its own ends and eventually becomes a means-oriented rationality. The environment is divided into non-reflective facts, and the particularity of objects is eliminated by a prevailing mode of equivalence. Awareness that subject and object are mediated, in material terms, is obfuscated by the forces of 'reality'.

Dialectic of Enlightenment attempts to fuse the insights of Max Weber with a Marxist tradition of immanent critique, already heavily indebted to Lukács's theory of reification (and this itself was influenced by Weber). The pessimistic tone of Weber's theory of history is well known: as rationalization moves away from mythical modes of consciousness towards distinct spheres of under-standing, it hypostatizes into institutional systems that undermine the ideal of human autonomy. For Adorno and Horkheimer, Weber's theory provides a good working description of contemporary society, but relies on a 'truncated' conception of rationality that closes down reason's utopian dimension (see Wellmer 1985c: 44). Thus, while incorporating Weber's portrayal of an administered society, Adorno and Horkheimer attempt to show that, from the vantage point of utopian reason, the symptoms are linked closely to dysfunc-tional processes within modernity. Weber's theme concerning the disenchantment of mythical world views is a key issue in *Dialectic of Enlightenment*, especially in the chapter devoted to Homer's *Odyssey* where the argument demonstrates that reason is already cursed by duplicity within the configurations of a mythical outlook. Odysseus recognizes the superior strength of brute nature and is canny enough not to confront it head on: instead, he eludes violent manifestations of the natural world and manipulates them towards his own ends by cunning. He forges an individual identity, at the expense of his own desire, by adapting to the mythical world of which he is afraid.

The conflict that Adorno and Horkheimer tease out of rationality is evident in the Sirens episode of the *Odyssey*, during which the hero, in order to dominate external reality, must repress his inner nature. The lure of the Sirens 'is that of losing oneself in the past' (Adorno 1979: 32); it is the call of a womb-like origin and demands an integrated ego in order to resist it – an 'I' constituted from the fettering of inner nature. The longing for happiness and fear of the self disintegrating into continuous nature are locked and embattled together. Given the physical constraint that Odysseus's ship must pass the Sirens, there are two ways in which the fate exacted by the Sirens can be avoided, one of which Odysseus prescribes for his crew, the other he adopts for himself: the crew have their ears blocked with wax and are instructed to look only straight ahead, thus avoiding the hazard; their captain, meanwhile, is lashed to the mast, and, while fully able to drink in the Siren's song, is incapable, despite his pleas, of satisfying his craving to draw closer to them. In Adorno's and Horkheimer's analysis, the situation of the oarsmen is that of an industrial workforce of whom maximum efficiency is required: in the pursuit of instrumental goals, they are denied and eventually deny themselves distracting experiences outside their lifestyle – the very experiences in whose name the work is often performed. On the other hand, the plight of Odysseus is that of a successful manager who having pursued and achieved instrumental aims, allegedly with the goal of a better lifestyle, is impotent to fulfil them because of his or her own social fixedness. 'The servant remains enslaved in body and soul, the master represses' (Adorno 1979: 35). Adorno regards the dilemma of the Sirens episode, in which pleasure is simultaneously yearned for and denied, as inherent within the 'emotional power of all art music' (1979: 60).

The subtext drawn by Adorno and Horkheimer out of Homer's interplay between myth and epic – in which nature is mastered by adaptation but always at the cost of repression, whether at the level of the self or society – is developed, they argue, into a celebration of power, of the indisputable superiority of the strong over the weak, in the writings of the Marquis de Sade and of Nietzsche at his most nihilistic: the umbra of enlightenment is empowered with a validity equal to that of liberal ideals. In their most pessimistic vein, Adorno and Horkheimer are unable to shake off this heritage; instead, they weakly appeal to the vantage point of a utopian critique increasingly unanchored in present tendencies. This aspect of the authors' work has been keenly criticized by subsequent critical theorists, as will be apparent from the discussion later in this chapter.

The manipulative side of rationality already present in myth, and which can be traced through the history of enlightenment, appears in a particularly barbed form in the authors' analysis of twentieth-century culture and their depiction of the 'culture industry'. The insidious advance of instrumental reason creates the smooth surface of a purposive rationality that administers the public and private sphere, and which is fully capable of engulfing dissent. The culture industry organizes people's free time in ways commensurate with the system of exchange value: fatigued workers who wish to be passively entertained at the end of a day's work are provided for, and end up reappropriating the instrumental means-oriented rationality to which they are subjected during working hours. The invasion of private desire by administered rationality completes the seamless continuum called 'reality'. Human beings are subjugated by their own apparatus of production.

In the bleak outlook presented by Adorno and Horkheimer, modern society is distinguished by slick uniformity: they note that 'even the aesthetic activities of political opposites are one in their enthusiastic obedience to the rhythm of the iron system' (Adorno 1979: 120). Having developed its identity by rejecting mythological and superstitious modes of consciousness, reason returns, iron-ically, to a monolithic world view: the environment appears schematized, or packaged, for the individual by a dysfunctional reason. As Habermas reminds us, this thesis is a variant of Max Weber's well-known vision of 'the ancient, disenchanted gods rising from their graves in the guise of depersonalized forces to resume the irreconcilable struggles between the demons' (Habermas 1987: 110). The return of myth is a theme that must be addressed by any theory of modernism; it is central to Adorno's critique of Stravinsky.

Paradoxically, the homogeneity of the culture industry achieves the total unity sought by high bourgeois art, but at a terrible price: cultural products comply with rigorous formulae designed to ensure that one item is more or less the same as, and hence exchangeable with, another. Adorno and Horkheimer point out that popular cinema, by and large, constitutes a string of familiar situations, tacked together by a flimsy plot, with the intention of initiating standardized responses from the well-trained viewer. This theme underlies Adorno's critique of mass culture in general, including his ill-informed, but not insignificant, condemnation of jazz (Adorno 1967).[3] The moronic inferno thrives on a cult of what appears to be new but is essentially the same. The person or fad that purports to be slightly different from the rest becomes a dominant trend only because at root it is indistinguishable from other products, and thus reinforces the system. The principle of universal fungibility underpins the market-led shift from use-value to exchange-value, which impacts on both the production and reception of culture. Nor is autonomous art immune from this force, since the value of art becomes a measure of the social prestige accrued to it: 'The consumer', Adorno comments acerbically, 'is really worshipping the money that he himself has paid for the ticket to the Toscanini concert' (1978: 278; 1991c: 34).

Truth as Negation: *Negative Dialectics* and *Aesthetic Theory*

As mentioned above, the dissonant portrayal of modernity advanced by Adorno is not determined exclusively by the historical experiences through which he lived; it also emerges from his socially-based critique of transcendental philoso-phy. Much of *Negative Dialectics* is concerned with demonstrating that supposedly unified philosophical systems reveal antinomical aspects when subjected to a critique capable of conveying the extent to which consciousness is mediated by social conditions. *Negative Dialectics* and the posthumously published *Aesthetic Theory* represent the quintessence of Adorno's thought:

alongside a planned work on ethics, these studies would have corresponded to the subject areas of Kant's three critiques. Adorno's wish to rework Kant's systematic approach is characteristic of his critical theory: it seeks to break through the limitations of philosophy's traditional apparatus from the inside.

Negative Dialectics develops from *Dialectic of Enlightenment* the idea that the over-unifying tendencies of philosophy embody an all-consuming passion for self-preservation and the control of nature, for expelling the non-assimilable and inflating the concept to a principle of self-identity. Adorno considers totalizing thought systems to be rooted in the primitive impulse of the hunter to conquer the heterogeneity of the surrounding environment in order to survive, and this untamed urge feeds into an all-subsuming epistemology: 'The system is the belly turned mind, and rage is the mark of each and every idealism' (Adorno 1973b: 23). The fury concentrated in a logic of formal identity becomes directed at those elements of experience resistant to classification: the materially specific is eliminated by the abstract general. Yet phenomena subsumed by such a process have a tendency to haunt the final system. Adorno comments that:

> The name of dialectics says no more, to begin with, than that objects do not go into their concepts without leaving a remainder, that they come to contradict the traditional norm of adequacy (1973b: 5).

This remainder leads Adorno to attack transcendental philosophy, particularly as practised by Martin Heidegger.

For Adorno, Heidegger's outlook obscures the mediation of consciousness by history; an irrational model of a prehistorical authority is invoked, along with the assumption that the conditions of contemporary society cannot be overcome but should be accepted as 'the way things are'. In such a framework the autonomy of the individual is submerged under the generality of Being. Adorno describes Heidegger's conundrum as follows: 'The dialectics of Being and entity – that no Being can be conceived without an entity and no entity without mediation – is suppressed by Heidegger' (1973b: 115).[4] That Being can only be perceived in terms of its difference from entity, but in order to maintain its primal status it must somehow include the notion of entity within itself, is regarded by Adorno as the central paradox in Heidegger's ontology. Adorno unmasks this move as follows: 'The outcome of the definition of entities in *Dasein*, of existents *qua* existents, by the concepts of *Dasein* and existence is that precisely what is not essential in *Dasein*, precisely what is not ontological in it, *is* ontological' (1973b: 117). Adorno thus reveals Heidegger's metaphysics of Being and presence to be dependent on a sleight of hand (*volte*) (1973b: 121–2). Like Adorno, Heidegger seeks in art an alternative voice to a technologically-dominated rationality, but does so transcendentally instead of through material analysis of modernity.

Negative Dialectics is incisive about the mediated quality of the concept: Adorno notes that 'concepts on their part are moments of the reality that requires their formation, primarily for the control of nature' (1973b: 11). But his aim is not to sabotage the role of the concept in philosophy; instead, the task of a critical philosophy is to acknowledge its dependence on concepts, but to elude the false security of viewing the concept as a being-in-itself. Adorno's intention is to inform the abstract qualities of the concept with the particular historical formation of the object: 'To change the direction of conceptuality, to give it a turn towards non-identity, is the hinge of negative dialectics' (1973b: 12). This is not to say, however, that *Negative Dialectics* abandons theory in favour of unreflective praxis: the design of Adorno's philosophy is to attain a mode of rationality in which the attributes of phenomena are not eliminated by the imposition of universal concepts; but conceptual thought ensures that the world is not perceived as a collection of random objects.

Adorno proposes a practice of cognition in which concepts constellate around the object, because a constellation of concepts is less likely to obscure the historical imprint and mobility of phenomena: 'by gathering around the object of cognition, the concepts potentially determine the object's interior. They attain in thinking, what was necessarily excised from thinking' (1973b: 162). Constellation seeks to release the immanent history locked into the object's interior, and hence to lever it from the bed of reification. As Susan Buck-Morss has painstakingly shown (1977: 90), Adorno's understanding of constellation was derived from Benjamin's presentation of the idea in his *Trauerspiel* study. In this work, which concerns itself with a somewhat mystical redemption of phenomena from oblivion by history, Benjamin emphasizes that constellations of ideas are non-hierarchical and discontinuous. Adorno and Benjamin translated this conception into a materialist framework, the emphasis on phenomena fitting well with a philosophy that strives to be faithful to the object. By exploring constellation as a technique, Adorno intended to release the social totality 'as it quite literally *appeared* within the object in a particular configuration' (Buck-Morss 1977: 96), and sought to decipher the 'previous subjectivity' naturalized in objective conventions (Paddison 1993: 35). The unlocking of a constellation is a two-part process: in the first stage, the phenomenon is analytically broken down into components which are understood as ciphers of the socio-historical truth and are interpreted by means of often Marxist or Freudian concepts; in the second stage, the elements are 'congealed into a visible image of the conceptual terms' (Buck-Morss 1977: 102). The concept might unlock the object, but the object at the same time provides a physical image of the concept in a real rather than metaphorical or symbolic way. 'In this sense', Buck-Morss observes, 'constellations were not unlike hieroglyphs, uniting the perceptual and conceptual; the phenomena became rebuses, riddles whose qualitative elements, juxtaposed, were the concepts translated into picture form' (1977: 102). In Adorno's words:

> Cognition of the object in its constellation is cognition of the process stored in the object. As a constellation, theoretical thought circles the object it would like to unseal, hoping that it may fly open like the lock of a well-guarded safe-deposit box: in response, not to a single key or a single number, but to a combination of numbers (1973b: 163).

Examples of the technique can be found in the Wagner monograph, written in 1937–38 not long after the original formulation of constellation as an analytical tool. The discussion of Adorno's Wagner critique in Chapter 2 shows how Wagner's use of the illusory and magical is broken down and analysed through the concepts of phantasmagoria and second nature. In the rearranged constellation of the phenomenon (the magical), Wagner's unified system is juxtaposed with the, not obviously related, seamless continuum of mass culture. Wagner's aesthetic is thereby turned upside down: the magic work of art anticipates the mechanical work of art.

Adorno's predilection for tensioning dialectical thought to its limits, together with the practice of constellation and the syntactical techniques of parataxis and chiasmus, all contribute to the notorious density of his written style. By using language against itself, Adorno attempts to produce configurations capable of dislocating reified thought; in fact many of his ideas are intrinsically bound up with their stylistic presentation. In their search for the ineffable, the attempt to shoot beyond the confines of language, Adorno's writings closely link philosophical interpretation with artistic presentation. It is, then, not surprising that aesthetic issues are such a rich domain for him. The aporetical task of a philosophy that strives 'by way of the concept, to transcend the concept' (Adorno 1973b: 15) finds some sustenance by entwining itself with art and its articulation of the non-conceptual. Adorno acknowledges that the content of *Aesthetic Theory* came to override a standard, ordered presentation of ideas: 'Instead', he comments, 'I have to put together a whole from a series of partial complexes which are concentrically arranged and have the same weight and relevance. It is the constellation, not the succession one by one, of these partial complexes which has to make sense' (1984a: 496).[5] The demand this affinity with aesthetic issues makes of the reader is that, somehow, the components of the constellation must be thought simultaneously.

Aesthetics as a branch of philosophy traditionally concerned with beauty and taste had foundered on the attempt to gain an epistemological purchase on art and eventually stagnated; but when confronted with the tensions of modernist art, it acquires a new vitality in Adorno's hands. He finds support from Pierre Boulez for his contention that the reflective capacity of aesthetics has become inseparable from the techniques of art (Adorno 1984a: 469–70). *Aesthetic Theory* is in essence a theory of modernism, exploring how traditional forms mutate from within; like *Negative Dialectics*, it constitutes both a rejection and a critical transformation of established issues. Just as Schoenberg saw himself as continuing the lineage of Western music precisely by abandoning tonality, so Adorno's negation of classical aesthetics is also an acknowledgement of the past. The categories of aesthetics are given a materialist twist by Adorno, so that questions of beauty and taste become inseparable from matters of truth and ethics, since all are locked into the material of art by socio-historical sedimentation. For Adorno's materialist aesthetic, art provides a cipher of what a non-instrumental rationality might look like.

In a discussion of *Aesthetic Theory*, Albrecht Wellmer has isolated a constellation of truth, appearance (illusion) and reconciliation as the three principal components active in Adorno's philosophy of art (Wellmer 1985a).

Philosophy and art enter into a symbiotic relationship where each is able to articulate an area of thought inaccessible to its partner: art depends on philosophy to judge its truth content, but can follow the inner life of particular impulses in a way prohibited to discursive logic in its present form. Artistic form shares with conceptual thought the capacity to synthesize particulars, but can also countenance resistance to this subsumptive process. Art articulates social tensions and indicates that they might be transformed; philosophy is able to reflect upon the significance of this illumination – though not to translate it – and consequently to turn its own discursive logic towards the pull of the particular as demonstrated by art. In its ability to glance the absolute, bourgeois autonomous art can achieve enigmatically the telos of metaphysics but does not render its insights transparent to conceptual philosophy (Adorno 1984a: 471). Art – especially music – like nature, is discursively mute, touching truth in a non-conceptual and enigmatic way. At the same time, as a human construct, art is obviously very different from nature. In Adorno's words:

> Art imitates neither nature nor individual natural beauty. What it does imitate is natural beauty as such. This puts the finger on the paradox of aesthetics as a whole, which is intimately tied up with the paradox of natural beauty. The subject matter of aesthetics, too, is defined as its undefinability. This is why art needs philosophy to interpret it. Philosophy says what art cannot say, although it is art alone which is able to say it: by not saying it (1984a: 107).

Art alludes to non-coercive logic as an antidote to an all-pervasive rationality; but as an intrinsic part of the Enlightenment heritage and modernism's advance, it is, like philosophy, nevertheless caught up in the whole problem of an identity logic and its exploitative relationship to nature.

Just as instrumental reason dominates the particularity of nature, so artistic form risks subjugating its own specific impulses. But at the same time, much autonomous art appears to be an unconstructed, nature-like object; and it is this illusion, Adorno argues, that is challenged by modernism. Art cannot wholly transcend the circumstance that Adorno identifies in his history of the Enlightenment whereby philosophical abstraction is complicit in the self-perpetuating conquest of external nature, at the expense of inner nature: cultural artefacts both partake in this process of rationalization and retain something of the spontaneity and intuition lost to such a channel of thought. The sensuous qualities of art give voice to a mode of consciousness untrammelled by self-identical reason; yet at the same time authentic art is rigorously rational and conveys something of the social context from which it emerged. Art contributes to Enlightenment rationality in its own way, by encountering both the fear of being dominated by nature and the danger of repressing it.

Art both subjugates nature in the form of an image, but simultaneously transcends this repression by its mode of objective beauty. Further, the autonomous art work presents itself as a self-contained whole, as a being-in-itself unlike the being-for-other of commodity exchange; and this being-in-itself opposes nature through its unified self-determination, but at the same time cannot suppress the nature-like immediacy of its individual moments which transgress any over-reaching totality. Equally, however, if this being-for-itself is undercut by its own individual components, it also reaches beyond itself and reveals the not-yet-being of a nature reconciled with humanity – a being-other-than-itself. Adorno argues that art indicates what nature might be:

> Art is influenced by the fact that nature is not yet what it appears to be; and this condition will last as long as nature is exclusively defined in terms of its opposition to society. Art accomplishes what nature strives for in vain: it opens its eyes (1984a: 97).

In its non-coercive and non-cognate logic, its interaction between the particular and the general, art thus points to an emancipated rationality in a strong utopian sense.

The non-identical goes by many names in Adorno's philosophy: in art it is alluded to by the term 'mimesis', and this idea forms a central plank in Adorno's aesthetic thought. He defines it as the 'non-conceptual affinity of a subjective creation with its objective and unposited other' (1984a: 80). Broadly speaking, mimesis denotes the non-conceptual, particular and sensuous qualities of the object; those aspects suppressed by the coercive force of instrumental reason. Mimesis is not, then, to be understood in the standard sense of the term as representation or imitation; its import is better described as an affinity with something, but the exact meaning of mimesis is dependent on the constellation in which it is used by Adorno. In one sense, it functions as an after-image of the magical and shamanistic, 'which art left behind with the disenchantment of the world, to use Max Weber's term' (1984a: 80). In this capacity mimesis operates as a corrective to an overbearing rationality; yet without mimesis crossing over to the pole of rationality, art would revert to the amorphous form of nature itself. The art work also mimes the conceptual in its form, but unless there is some internal resistance to this mode of mimesis, it becomes indistinguishable from reified conditions of instrumental reasoning; in this case, art loses contact with nature.

The second, though related, meaning of mimesis pertains to the utopian dimension of art: it harks to the reconciliation of rationality with nature. Nature is here to be understood not only as the physical environment but also as our, often pre-verbal, inner nature. Mimesis denotes an affinity with the idea of a non-reified nature that seems to stand in contrast to the conception of second nature as objectified convention put forward by Adorno in 'The idea of natural history' (1984b): nature, as alluded to by mimesis, in Paddison's words, 'is that region to which are consigned those things rejected or repressed by society in its dominant form' (1993: 57). But the crucial point is that this dormant nature can only be expressed in art through mediation of mimesis with the constructional, or rational, pole of the art work. Like Odysseus, art distinguishes and protects itself from the outer environment by adapting itself to it, but, unlike Homer's hero, it also retains the memory of what is lost in the process. Adorno makes the point as follows: 'Tagging along behind its reification, the subject limits that reification through the mimetic vestige, the plenipotentiary of an integral life amid a damaged life where the subject is being reduced to an ideology' (1984a:

171). Mimesis in art refers to an emancipated subjectivity and to the prospect of an openness to the particular. This non-conceptual possibility is encoded within the objective material of emancipated art works.

It is by engaging with objective qualities of the material that the expressive dimension of art emerges. 'Art is expressive', Adorno maintains, 'when a subjectively mediated, objective quality raises its voice to speak: sadness, strength, yearning. A better model for understanding expression', he continues, 'is to think of it not in terms of subjective feelings, but in terms of ordinary things and situations in which historical processes and functions have been sedimented, endowing them with the potential to speak' (1984a: 163). The subjectivity of the artist is objectified by working on the material; the objectivity of the material is rendered subjective because the configurations into which the material is formed release the sedimented subjectivity within it. Expression emerges from the dialectical exchange between these poles; Adorno describes it 'as a phenomenon of interference, a function both of method and mimesis' (1984a: 167). The mediation, instead of diremption, of subject and object is all important in art.[6] If the two poles are separated, Adorno argues, 'a totally objectified work would congeal into a mere thing; a totally non-objectified one would be a feeble subjective impulse, drowning in the empirical world' (1984a: 251). By concentrating on technique and construction, the composer releases the subjectivity objectified in the material.[7]

The truth content of an art work is located in its ability to embody social conditions in a critical manner whilst retaining a distance from reality, through autonomy, and obeying the inner necessity of its material working out. Aesthetic truth is thus dependent on illusion, since this is what distances art from utilitarian rationality, but this striving for wholeness and otherness is undercut from within. Truth content emerges from the interpenetration of an unsullied mimetic sensuousness with an historically-determined rational, constructive principle: the two sides of the dialectic cross over and are realized through each other. The constructive logic of an artefact critical of prevalent social conditions both mimes a dominant rationality, and, as a separate form, mimes instrumental reason's repressed other. Truth, in Adorno's more unyielding statements, is embedded in art to the extent to which it can maintain a mimetic dimension by means of the most advanced state of artistic material. The insistence on an historically advanced stock of material is problematic, since it suggests that only a small selection of art works will have historical validity; in fact, because in his writings on music Adorno can find positive things to say about composers such as Zemlinsky and Schreker who were not obviously in the vanguard, the difficulty is not insurmountable. A more diffuse version of musical material emerges from Adorno's essays on music than the theoretical presentation of his aesthetics would suggest.

The pragmatic orientation of recent critical theory has attempted to redirect the strong strand of utopianism found in Adorno's aesthetics towards a dimension of art capable of re-orienting people's perception of reality, rather than hinting elusively at a redeemed world. One does not, however, have to replace the framework of Adorno's aesthetics in order to draw attention to moments of non-instrumental expression which have transformative potential within present social conditions. In the sense that mimesis refers to the consciousness of needs, Adorno's own dialectic, with its orientation towards the particular, can be used to unearth areas of thought and practice within contemporary subjective creation that are not held fast by the grip of a coercive identity logic. These traces have an affinity with possibilities for direct expression within existing social conditions. The two faces of redemptive critique need not be mutually exclusive: the practical possibilities of art as consciousness-raising are not necessarily crushed by the strong utopian motif of art.

The position of art in the dialectic between nature and its domination by instrumental reason provides an insight into the way art relates to society. In Adorno's words:

> How can works of art be like windowless monads, representing something which is other than they? There is only one way to explain this, which is to view them as being subject to a dynamic or immanent historicity and a dialectical tension between nature and domination of nature, a dialectic that seems to be of the same kind as the dialectic of society. Or to put it more cautiously, the dialectic of art resembles the social dialectic without consciously imitating it (1984a: 7).

Art both embodies and rejects society: it embraces the conditions of society as immanent content, but distances itself from society by means of its formal autonomy. Yet form and content are dialectically related, rendering the exclusion and assimilation of society intrinsically part of each other. The view that art is autonomous – itself determined by the condition of modernity – is normally held to be incompatible with the opinion that art reflects society. Adorno employs a subtle version of both these options, and holds them in extreme dialectical tension.

The appearance of autonomous art is synchronous historically with the emergence of a liberal market economy, and its status is to some extent generated by eluding roles defined by the church or court. This context partly defines art as a commodity, but a commodity with use-value which resists slippage into an economy dominated by exchange-value. The close ties between artistic autonomy and bourgeois economics do not, however, lead Adorno into the all-too-easy dismissal of bourgeois art as a conservative institution, though this aspect is there, along with much else. The material concerns specific to the medium, which autonomy conveys, are sedimented subjectivity and represent the artist's attempt to grapple with historical circumstances. It is on this level of immanent autonomy that art rebels against its status as a commodity and offers a critique of the prevailing social conditions, while intangibly pointing to a better state of affairs. By revealing reality for what it is, instead of simply reproducing it, authentic art alludes to the possibility of a reconciled world. In attempting to decode this cipher conceptually, philosophy encounters politics.

The art work presents itself as something akin to nature, a phenomenon which could not be otherwise, yet it is a human-made artefact. This paradox emerges when art works become entities divorced from their creator: they obey certain immanent laws, capable of determining, to some extent, their historical reception; and they appear to be self-determining autonomous objects, presenting themselves as puzzles for which one needs to search for potential solutions. Adorno regards art works as akin to fairy tales because they convey the absolute but only in the form of a riddle which eludes one's grasp. The self-determining whole to which autonomous art lays a claim is undercut and shown to be an illusion by the individual moments within that totality, since these ultimately refuse to be subsumed under a generality (1984a: 149). If, however, these particulars do not cross over to a pole of construction, if, that is, they attempt to convey the immediacy of nature in themselves, then they too are illusory. This is because what seems to be natural is historically mediated: that which appears to elude the history of rationalization, and its distortions, already contains the same imprint as immanent form.

Art, then, is illusory both in its manifestation as self-determining form and as sensuous immediacy, a contradiction that erupts in the shift from modern to modernist art. Particular moments can no longer be contained by the whole, but instead fragment and undermine a unified conception; in this sense, Adorno's own ruminations about art copy their object. It is therefore no coincidence that Schenker's conception of musical form, which is predicated on the illusion of art constituting a nature-like object, is hostile to a modernism in which the other side of the dialectic asserts itself. Ironically, the seamless whole sought by bourgeois art is realized in a disfigured form by the culture industry, at the time when the original ideal is threatened from within by modernist art. Against this background, an embattled autonomy takes on greater significance as a realm of resistance: it works against a flattened totality by means of its own internal disintegration. For Adorno it is crucial, however, that this disintegrative tendency exists in tension with an integrative impulse, as determinate irreconcilability; that the autonomy of art undertakes its own internal critique instead of being simply abolished.

Artistic autonomy is associated with the illusory quality of art, but Adorno is wary of abandoning the critical distance from reality facilitated by autonomy. This is the issue at stake in his unease with the historical avant-garde movements of Dada and Surrealism; and, partially as a consequence, his disputes with Brecht and Benjamin concerning politically-motivated art. Adorno counters direct intervention by observing that once the critical distance between art and reality is broken down, in an attempt to merge art and life-praxis, then art can only register a gesture of protest and fails to point to anything beyond the prevailing conditions. Notwithstanding this viewpoint, the political disappointments of the historical avant garde are embedded within *Aesthetic Theory*: they contribute to its emphasis on transforming autonomous art from within instead of attacking it from the outside.

Second-Generation Critical Theory

So pervasive is the domination of consciousness by instrumental reason, according to *Dialectics of Enlightenment*, that later theorists have questioned whether Adorno and Horkheimer can evade this distortion in their own critique. For the critical theory of Habermas and his followers, the two authors cannot ultimately avoid the impasse concerning the status of their critique which haunts neo-Nietzscheans. Theories of a generalized nature such as those advanced by Nietzsche and Heidegger, which are grounded respectively in power and Being, purport to offer insights into the essence of reality. Unfortunately, the transcendental status of these concepts elevates them above the level at which they could be rationally disputed: they can only be justified ultimately on the basis that the philosophers had insights into experience denied to normal consciousness. The problem is that the theory becomes entangled in its own validity claims (as Adorno himself argued against Heidegger), and this is precisely the criticism that Habermas levels against *Dialectic of Enlightenment*: for him, the critique becomes entwined with the very relationship between myth and enlightenment under scrutiny, thereby forfeiting any normative validity claims. If instrumental reason and the drive towards self-preservation have become all-consuming false universals, then critical thought becomes so much part of the prevailing rationality (it has, so to speak, to pick itself up by its own bootstraps) that it cannot reveal the emancipatory potential present in existing social configurations through explanatory-diagnostic critique. Instead, he argues, it must resort to a radical anticipatory-utopian critique that negates current circumstances.

For Habermas, Adorno's emphasis on aesthetics as the realm of resistance represents nostalgic hankerings after theoretical purity, and a strategy of hibernation at the expense of the real task of critical theory. Instead of pursuing an explanatory-diagnostic version of immanent critique, Adorno, it is argued, can only weakly appeal to the impulses of a suppressed nature – to be found in the mimetic moments of advanced art – as the other of instrumental reason. In Adorno's attempts to negotiate the aporias within which he works, philosophy becomes a search for style.

> In the shadow of a philosophy that has outlived itself, philosophical thinking intentionally retrogresses to gesticulation. As opposed as the intentions behind their respective theories of history are, Adorno is in the end very similar to Heidegger as regards his position on the theoretical claims of objectivating thought and of reflection: the mindfulness [*Eingedenken*] of nature comes shockingly close to the recollection [*Angedenken*] of being (Habermas 1984: 385).

At the heart of this damning remark from Habermas is his view that Adorno abandoned the possibility of philosophy and science working critically together, and conflated the three validity spheres operative in Kant and Weber. Adorno and Horkheimer, in Habermas's opinion, should have attempted an immanent critique of scientific thought; instead they puffed up instrumental reason into an all-embracing ideology. This alternative approach, Habermas maintains, would have ascertained the type of knowledge science could make a genuine claim to represent, and hence could have decided whether validity claims are distorted within technologically-dominated societies. Habermas is correct to assert that identity as a principle in scientific analysis need not assume the full ideological force that Adorno attributes to it, providing its criteria do not pervade other domains of activity; but a wish to protect genuine validity claims does not require the major theoretical restructuring undertaken by second-generation critical theorists.

As an alternative to a subject-based philosophy of consciousness, Habermas has put forward an intersubjective *Theory of Communicative Action*, which attempts to bypass the aporia reached by Adorno and Horkheimer without collapsing into an outmoded metaphysics or relativism. In Wellmer's words:

> Habermas' basic argument is as simple as it is convincing: the intersubjectivity of communication is as much an integral part of the sphere of mind attached to language as is the objectification of reality in contexts of instrumental action; likewise a symmetrical, communicative relationship between subject and subject is as much a part of this sphere as is an asymmetrical, distancing relationship between subject and object (Wellmer 1985a: 98).

This theory advances some way towards recognizing the role of the non-identical in Adorno: to engage in meaningful communication, social actors must assume common linguistic functions which they share, but at the same time acknowledge the individual identities of one another. Communicative action is not founded on the way in which a solitary subject relates to something in the objective world,

> but the intersubjective relation that speaking and acting subjects take up when they come to an understanding with one another about something. In doing so, communicative actors move in the medium of natural language, draw upon culturally transmitted interpretations, and relate simultaneously to something in the one objective world, something in their common social world, and something in each's own subjective world (Habermas 1984: 392).

Habermas' emphasis on intersubjectivity works alongside an endorsement of what he calls modernity's progressive and non-reversible diremption of metaphysical world-views into the three spheres addressed by Kant: (a) functional rationality – natural and social science, philosophy; (b) moral-practical rationality – law, politics; (c) aesthetic-expressive rationality. He argues that all three function within the medium of language.

A major feature of Habermas's *Theory of Communicative Action* is the distinction drawn by him between lifeworld (*Lebenswelt*) and systems-world, the former term referring to areas of social life, cultural formation and the needs of individuals (retaining something of the direct perception found in Husserl's usage), the latter denoting domains of professional expertise. Specialized systems complement the lifeworld because without forms of systemic integration, the delicate structures of the lifeworld would become overloaded by the demands of industrial society. Steering media, such as economics and information technology, achieve a certain degree of autonomy and are considered to be impaired languages with their own validity claims, so they do not tax the communicative functions of natural language. System integration does, however, presuppose rationalization of the lifeworld and should remain rooted in its needs; what has happened instead, Habermas argues, is that the lifeworld has become depleted by increasingly autonomous systems. The condition that Adorno and Horkheimer attribute to the pervasion of instrumental reason is understood by Habermas as colonization of the lifeworld by systems integration; but, according to him, though this is the configuration of the two areas that has emerged from consumer society, it is not the only formation possible.

Habermas's attempt to regenerate the interdisciplinary project of 1930s critical theory by means of communicative action is not without difficulties of its own. In Benhabib's view, Habermas's at least partial move away from the third person perspective of society as a transsubjective subject, in favour of a communicative first and second person perspective, is crucial, though she is less sanguine about his vision of modernity. Regrettably, the project loses sight of the utopian-transfigurative dimension of critique that functions alongside the explanatory-diagnostic version for Hegel and Marx, and which distinguishes the work of Adorno and Horkheimer, not to mention related figures such as Benjamin and Bloch. In other words, Benhabib argues, Habermas's theoretical impetus has become so tied up with current social conditions, it has rendered itself ineffective as a means of transforming these constraints. Benhabib concurs with the Habermasian critique of Adorno, but her own assessment of Habermas's theory draws attention to a tendency for the particular to be subsumed; in effect, offering a belated vindication of Adorno.[8] Benhabib's conclusion is that Habermas's stress on validity claims and social norms makes it hard for his theory to address 'those qualities of individual life histories and collective life forms which make them fulfilling or unfulfilling' (Benhabib 1986: 328).

The Adornian impasse, which Habermas seeks to circumnavigate, still clearly represents a severe challenge to a theory of communication. Habermas's contention that Adorno's work is predicated on the idea of a reconciliation with nature, which is more properly thought of as 'the structure of life together in communication that is free from coercion', is insensitive to Adorno's attempts to turn conceptual thought towards the subjectivity encoded within the material world (Habermas 1983: 107). The immanent status accorded by Adorno to the concept is transferred by Habermas to the linguistic rules considered by reconstructive sciences to be present in all members of the species. But it is questionable as to whether anything in ordinary language impels speakers to enter into discourse, so Habermas's theory lacks a volitional component that could be motivated to overcome distorted communication. Despite second-generation critical theory's claim to re-address issues of democracy and politics, and its pragmatic emphasis on the need for specialized systems to cope with steering media such as money, communicative action remains as marooned in theory as Adorno's negative dialectic.[9] It is unclear how the considerable shift in consciousness required for Habermas's ideas to bear fruit would come into being.

For Adorno, the whole problem of the identity logic addressed by art cuts across modernity's three validity spheres; it is because art is excluded from functional and practical reason, while using and being implicated in modes of reality derived from these spheres, that it has such critical significance for him.[10] Indeed, the dialectic of construction and mimesis maps the dialectic of law and desire. With his almost visceral fear of irrationality, Habermas rebuffs attempts to understand society/politics in aesthetic terms as neo-conservative, and dismisses Adorno's concentration on the aesthetic as a strategy of quietism. It seems essential to Habermas's formulations that cultural and expressive areas of knowledge are not allowed to leak out of their proper area of discourse with any force; this is why the particular, emphasized in aesthetic discourse, tends to be eradicated in favour of the general in his reconstruction of critical theory. If Adorno's philosophy of art is considered, as it demands to be, as anything more than a strategy of hibernation, then it is in this area that his thought provides the most problems for a theory of communicative action which has had little to say about aesthetic needs, beyond a generalized recognition of the resistance of the lifeworld to imposed administration. Habermas's distinction between systems and lifeworld remains useful; but Adornian theory provides crucial insights on the distortion of the latter by the former.

Adorno's diagnosis of modernity remains perspicacious: the culture industry, even when perceived as a dysfunctional systems-world imposition, is still a massive social force, and art continues to be taxed by dialectics of the general and the particular, construction and mimesis. The dominant trend of conformism in much popular music continues to love 'the expression of longing more than happiness itself' (Adorno 1992b: 50), often generating stereotypical reactions instead of initiating a reception that would stimulate people to contemplate change in the lifeworld. The strength of Adorno's musical insights resides in his capacity to trust the social distillation he finds in music and to place it on a level of perspicuity equal to that of philosophy. An emancipated rationality, for Adorno, would involve neither coercion nor opposition, in his words: 'Utopia would be above identity and above contradiction; it would be a togetherness of diversity' (1973b: 150). This is a weak hope, but the unlikelihood of a utopian breakthrough does not prevent one from seeking social forms with a trans-formative capacity. Adorno's own attempts to release the mediated subjectivity within objects offer a form of resistance against false identity, and his writings on music along with other cultural artefacts do not always confirm the stranglehold of instrumental reason he describes on a theoretical level. In some discussions Adorno is able to look for instances of non-identity which, although they relate to a central problem, express themselves in diverse ways.

Notes

1. Harvey 1989: 16–17 describes the conflicting forces of creation and destruction in modernity.

2. Habermas is here paraphrasing from Helmut Dubiel, *Wissenschaftsorganisation und politische Erfahrung* (Frankfurt, 1978).
3. This essay is in part a reply to Benjamin's optimistic appraisal of the potential for contemporary art in *The Work of Art in the Age of Mechanical Reproduction*. See Benjamin 1969.
4. Translation modified.
5. This description is attributed to Adorno in the Editors' Epilogue to *Aesthetic Theory* (Adorno 1984a: 496). Paddison discusses the passage in relation to the 'open structure of *Aesthetic Theory*' (1996: 52–3).
6. See Paddison 1993, chapter 3, for an informative discussion on the topic of mediation in Adorno's aesthetics.
7. Bernstein's discussion of the crossover between technique and mimesis in Van Gogh's painting of the peasant woman's shoes is illuminating (1992: 215).
8. Bernstein 1987 makes this point.
9. See Schmidt 1979 for a comparison of Habermas's universal pragmatics with Adornian critical theory.
10. See Bernstein 1987, 1989 and 1992.

2 Alienated Music: Beethoven to Schoenberg

The Beethoven Critique and Nineteenth-Century Music

Adorno's writings on music form an integral part of his diagnosis of modernity: in this medium he locates an immanent material working-out of the themes that pervade his socio-philosophical edifice. Beethoven and Schoenberg constitute the main anchor points for Adorno's philosophy of music: Beethoven marks the entry into modernity, but it was not until the innovations of Schoenberg that the implications of Beethoven's artistic challenge were fully realized. By the age of Beethoven, music had become part of a fully-fledged aesthetic sphere, a status reflected in Beethoven's independence as a composer and enhanced by the marked autonomy of his works; but their proximity to philosophy in making a strong claim to knowledge challenges the containment of music within an aesthetic sphere defined by beauty and taste. Adorno regards the ideal inherent within sonata form as a temporal dynamic: like a narrative, the material presented in the exposition works out latent and unexpected aspects of itself (its non-identity) in the development section; the same material then returns in the reprise having recognized and assimilated its non-identical components. One thus experiences the recapitulation as the resolution of a temporal event and re-hears the original material in the knowledge of its fulfilled potential. Middle-period works, such as the *Eroica* Symphony or the *Waldstein* Sonata, strive for a non-coercive reconciliation of the particular (the motivic unit) with the whole (the overall form), in a process comparable to the way in which Hegelian philosophy builds a dialectical synthesis.

Adorno considers that in his late style Beethoven ventured beyond the Hegelian system by refusing to impose a false unifying scheme over non-reconcilable musical elements; in effect, challenging narrative unity. The some-times abrupt transitions between sections are illustrative of this resistance, as is the 'unmediated juxtaposition of callow aphoristic motifs and polyphonic complexes' in the late quartets (Adorno 1976a: 123). By following the objective impulses of the material where they lead, this music challenges the assumed prevalence of subject over object. Beethoven's late style achieves a degree of objectivity through emphasis on detail. Embellishments take on an immanent dynamic of their own, bearing witness to the fragile unity in which they previously operated. Adorno is famously short on empirical detail for this type of observation, but one can imagine the sort of comparison he had in mind. The Adagio Cantabile of the Quartet Opus 18, Number 2, provides an example of a movement in which embellishment is rife and, in a sense, constitutes the music, though it works within a frame of phrases, harmony and rhythm defined by reference to the basic melody. The Piano Sonata Opus 111, by contrast, uses 'ornaments' as an integral part of the material: the rumbling trill in the first movement, bars 16–17, and the line of trills leading into the close of the work achieve a concreteness which defies mere decoration. Kretschmar's Adornian analysis of the same sonata in Thomas Mann's *Dr Faustus* discusses the chains of trills and the vocal-like embellishments, cadences and other conventions which throw off the illusionary appearance of art (Mann: 56). These elements, it is argued, reveal the illusion of a supposedly non-coercive whole instead of adorning it.

Central to Adorno's understanding of the late style is his essay 'Alienated Masterpiece: the *Missa Solemnis*', one of the few detailed discussions of a piece of music undertaken by him. Adorno's critique explores the enigma of the work: its uncertainty and false totality are compared unfavourably with the compositional daring of the late quartets, but Beethoven's own assessment of the music as his greatest work is taken seriously. In Adorno's view, the austerity of the Mass setting registers the ideal of a self-legitimating subject buckling under enormous pressures:

> It [the human idea] calls upon positive religion for help whenever the lonely subject no longer trusted that it could of itself, as pure human essence, dispel the forward surging chaos of conquered and protesting nature (Adorno 1976a: 120).

This positive religion appears not only in the text but in Beethoven's use of archaic and formal contrapuntal methods, associated by Adorno with a pre-Enlightenment, theological world-view. By contrast, the process of thematic development and the dialectical principle of sonata form – normally considered to be characteristic of Beethoven – are linked with the temporal thrust of historical transformation, which to this work appears more destructive than creative. Thematic-motivic working, in Adorno's opinion, is nearly eliminated by the archaic model upon which Beethoven draws, though, as Dahlhaus mentions, there is a level of submotivism in the *Missa* that associates it with other late works (1991: 196). Adorno argues that the unfathomable quality of the *Missa* lies in the way that its human tone, which would usually be associated with Beethoven's dynamic techniques and the ideal of an autonomous subject, pseudomorphically adapts to an alien form. The music, he continues, is shrouded in a 'taboo about the negativity of existence, derived from Beethoven's despairing will to survive' (1976a: 119). The human tone, which is evident when the *Missa* 'addresses or literally conjures up salvation', is cut off in those expressionless passages that correspond to a prevalence of death and evil in the text, notably in the Agnus Dei, with the result that 'despair and yet anxiety of having that despair become manifest' (1976a: 119). Beethoven challenges the union of subject and object posited in the bourgeois appearance of freedom – and upheld in the illusion of aesthetic synthesis – but fails to find solace in the ontological order of an earlier music (Adorno 1976a: 122). In effect, the music touches upon the condition of modernist art.

In other late works a withdrawn subjectivity is characterized more by fragmentation and the transformation of functions within music than by a negative prohibition on expression, and Adorno speaks in Benjaminesque terms of the broken forms and abrupt transitions that prevail in Beethoven's late works as allegory (Adorno GS 17: 15). When drained of their original meaning, the symbols explored by Benjamin in *The Origin of German Tragic Drama* take on new relationships; likewise, the embellishments of late Beethoven – sapped of subordinate functions – are free to form new configurations. The resistance by particular elements against total integration in late Beethoven anticipates the insight, deriving from Baudelaire through the *art pour l'art* movement to critics such as Derrida and de Man, that works of art aspiring to organic wholeness cannot exclude impulses which will undermine that goal. Adorno's focus on this aspect of the late style stems, however, from a philosophy which strives to reveal the imbalance between concept and object, and from an aesthetic theory which argues that artistic fragmentation is an index of a society whose forms of cognition and ethics are impoverished by exclusion of the aesthetic. Adorno, unlike some practitioners of deconstruction, does not abandon the hope that the particular and the general might become porous to each other within a non-subsumptive rationality. The particular, as registered through mimesis, refers to an intuitive and expressive level of knowledge, threatened by a means-oriented subjectivity; it is this repressed experience, which asserts itself in art's pull towards the particular, that challenges the illusion of a seamless form. The means by which Beethoven prefigures an emancipated subjectivity emerges from the interlocking of a mimetic strand with the constructional method. In a statement that encapsulates his own philosophical project, Adorno contemplates the glimpse of utopia in late Beethoven.

> This illuminates the anomaly, that late Beethoven is referred to at the same time as both subjective and objective. The crumbling (*brüchige*) landscape is objective, the light in which it uniquely glows, subjective (Adorno GS 17: 17).[1]

It is the subjectivity of the composer, working with the historically derived, objective material (itself a sedimentation of previous subjectivity), that releases the mimetic from the music and posits a permeable dialectic of subject and object beyond coercion, or, within the art work, beyond a contrived illusion of wholeness. Likewise, the task to be undertaken by a responsible philosophy, as described by Adorno in the closing paragraph of *Minima Moralia*, is 'to contemplate all things as they would present themselves from the standpoint of redemption: knowledge has no light but that shed on the world by redemption' (1974: 247).

Adorno's critique of late Beethoven emphasizes the degree of objective hardening in the music but fails to register that some of the flourishes and cadenza-like passages in the late works have an improvisational feel to them, revealing a softening of formal restraints, in addition to, or instead of, the supposed fragmentation of the whole. Beethoven may be hinting at the possibility of coherence through means other than organic wholeness, and he is perhaps indicating that a totality of structural relationships is not always a central concern. Nonetheless, Adorno's Beethoven critique remains powerful; it is at fault more for its unrelenting world-historic approach than for being intrinsically wrong. Dahlhaus accuses Adorno of imposing his philosophy of history, which, it is claimed, drags everything into the dialectic of enlightenment and the whole problem of a self-identical logic, onto Beethoven's music (1979a: 174). This aspect of Adorno's approach is problematic, though not intractable, because it frequently generates one-sided or extreme conclusions; but Dahlhaus's viewpoint is insensitive to the possibility that Beethoven's music may have been formative for Adorno's philosophy. Beethoven represents the quintessence of Adorno's thought because his compositions are able to express and to work through internal experiences within formal constraints, and yet to place the particular in a larger frame. The problem lies less in Adorno's understanding of Beethoven, than in the extent to which the degree of artistic rigour located there becomes the standard by which Adorno judges subsequent culture. It is unjust to imply, as Adorno often does, that music is necessarily regressive or repressive if it does not meet the challenge presented by Beethoven's achievement.

In Adorno's view, this demand was met by Schoenberg, but a socio-philosophical view of music history that emphasizes the authenticity of one path creates problems. Dahlhaus traces two divergent aesthetics in nineteenth-century music (1989: 8–15):[2] one strand refers to Beethoven's instrumental music and the notion of music as a text, to be understood in the manner of a literary or philosophical document; the other is associated with Rossini and the idea of music as an event, for which the score merely functions as a performance recipe. It could be argued that Adorno rigidly adopts the music-as-idea model and applies it remorselessly to music conceived in another mode, Rossini's music constituting the impulse found in the wider arena of popular music today. This viewpoint does highlight Adorno's tunnel vision, but encounters problems with his sophisticated understanding of immediacy in art. Dahlhaus's assertion that Rossini's art is a music of the moment, which makes no claim to knowledge, employs a narrow definition of musical text and implies, unconvincingly, that music dependent on the vagaries of performance cannot project a mode of subjectivity. Even apparently immediate and contingent music takes place within a social context, and, whether conceived of as event or idea, it is relevant to ask if a music engages its social situation.

No doubt Adorno does not advance a panoptic view of nineteenth-century music because to do so would be to emphasize the general over the particular; an overview does nevertheless emerge in his discussion of this repertory. Adorno accedes to the commonly-held viewpoint that nineteenth-century music is to a large extent a response to, even a critique of, the achievements of Beethoven. Later composers, it is suggested, seized upon the model of a self-determining whole characteristic of the composer's middle-period works and inflated the idea into a doctrine of organicism, instead of pursuing the objectivity of the late works. The paradox, however, is that when subsequent music sought to give voice to subjective feeling, it became rigid, thereby losing the techniques of thematic working that were so admired in Beethoven. The cyclic and repetitive forms of nineteenth-century music frequently create an impression of spatial time, and by doing this they abandon the pursuit of temporal progress, despite this repertoire being habitually associated with the struggle of the individual.[3]

Adorno finds the most extreme, though related, responses to the dilemmas of nineteenth-century bourgeois aesthetics in the music of Wagner and Mahler: the former, Adorno argues, fuses the archaic and the modern in mythology, the latter exposes symphonic form to its own shortcomings. A mixture of these two responses is found, in varying proportions, in all Adorno's portraits of nineteenth-century composers. Adorno comments that '*Weltschmerz*, the break between the aesthetic subject and reality, had been the posture of musical spirit ever since Schubert' (Adorno 1992b: 85);[4] the extent to which music manifests or obscures this situation is, for him, a measure of its truth content.

Like many other critics, Adorno is simultaneously fascinated and repelled by Wagner, but for him these two tendencies exert themselves in a tension between anticipations of both modernist music and mass culture: advanced tonality paves the way for Schoenberg's innovations, while manipulation of the listener emphasizes the illusory quality of art and pre-echoes the seamless continuum of the culture industry. Adorno's fixation with the Beethovenian idea of music developing through time is at the heart of his critique of Wagner. He compares Wagner's technique of motivic transformation with Beethoven's method of thematic working:

> In Beethoven, the isolated occurrence, the 'creative idea' [*Einfall*], is artistically trivial wherever the idea of totality takes precedence; the motiv is introduced as something quite abstract in itself, simply as the principle of pure becoming, and as the totality emerges from it, the isolated motiv, which is submerged in the whole, is concretized and confirmed by it. In Wagner the over-inflated creative idea denies the triviality that adheres in it by virtue of its status as a prelinguistic gesture. The penalty it must pay for this is that it is itself denied by the development that it proves unable to generate, even though it unceasingly claims to sustain that development and provide it with a model. The seemingly unified totality, which owes its existence to the extirpation of the qualitatively individual, turns out to be mere illusion, a contradiction raised to the level of the absolute (Adorno 1981: 51).

The other side of Adorno's critique of Wagner's motivic working is that, especially in the later *Ring* music dramas, the failure of a developmental logic inadvertently creates a modernist, allegorical technique. In the case of *Götter-dämmerung*, these aspects are conveyed in the tension between the all-consuming current of the music, which draws malleable motives into the web, and those motives which have retained their rigidity from earlier in the cycle, producing 'allegorical brittleness' (1981: 45). He omits to mention that a distinction between fluid and defined motives is also found in *Tristan* and *Parsifal*, though here it feeds into a musico-dramatic principle as a more deliberate compositional procedure. Adorno is prone to generalize his theory of allegory in Wagner, but when used selectively it is able to illuminate the composer's dismantling of convention:

> Beneath the thin veil of continuous progress Wagner has fragmented the composition into allegorical leitmotivs juxtaposed like discrete objects. These resist the claims both of a totalizing musical form and of the aesthetic claims of 'symbolism', in short, the entire tradition of German idealism. Even though Wagner's music is thoroughly perfected as style, this style is not a system in the sense of being a logically consistent totality, an immanent ordering of parts and whole. But this very fact is not without its revolutionary implications. In art, as in philosophy, the various systems strive to create a synthesis out of diversity. In the process they let themselves be guided by an existing, but now questionable, totality whose immediate right to exist they dispute even while they indirectly reproduce it (1981: 48).

The notion of allegory expounded here registers the inconsistency between Wagner's musical technique and his aesthetic ideals; further, it reveals modernist fragmentation at the heart of a late-romantic, organic sensibility. Adorno is saying that Wagner both emulates and undercuts the ideal of totality.

While this may be true, Dahlhaus is surely right to argue that Adorno's analysis of Wagner is overly indebted to Lorenz's schematic portrayal of the composer: it is the illusion of Lorenz's schemes that Adorno often breaks open, not necessarily the actual compositional technique (Dahlhaus 1970: 141). Adorno's insight is weakened by his reliance on a symphonic ideal, against which leitmotivic organization appears to be nothing more than failed motivic development.[5] With his aversion to spatial tendencies, Adorno does not seem to grasp fully that Liszt and Wagner are frequently more concerned with thematic transformation than development. Their themes are often self-contained and, though retaining a core identity, can radically transmute themselves within limited confines. The fluid exchange of identity and difference within a defined space has more progressive potential than Adorno is prepared to envisage, and thematic transformation can certainly be understood as something other than empty repetition or generalized allegorical fragmentation of the whole. The motivic webs of the mature Wagner cannot be convincingly dismissed as unsuccessful developing variation (see Dahlhaus 1970: 144).

Adorno's Wagner study responds to Benjamin's envisaged *Arcades* project, which finds an exciting fusion of old and new in the phantasmagoria of modern life. In a famous exchange of letters over this study, Adorno argues that Benjamin failed to mediate the individual features of Parisian life he describes through the total social process (1977a: 129). Adorno's study of Wagner, in contrast, attempts to unmask conditions of commodity production that inform the composer's ideology. Adorno analyses the illusionary and magical elements of Wagner's music dramas by referring to their commodity-like appearance: in seeking to offer an illusory world as an alternative to everyday reality, it is argued, Wagner's phantasmagoria actually reproduce the characteristics of commodity exchange whereby an artefact seeks to occlude its production by human labour. Phantasmagoria – 'the outside of the worthless commodity' (1981: 85) – is an intensification of illusion, it seeks to hide the construction of art so that it appears to be natural, and hence ahistorical.[6] Deriving from the German Romantic tradition of magical scenes, in phantasmagoria 'music pauses and is made spatial, the near and the far are deceptively merged' (1981: 86). In a sense it anticipates the space-time compression that is such a familiar experience in modern life, and Boulez uses the term 'phantasmagoria' in a positive sense to distinguish techniques of fusion and illusion from analytical types of configuration.[7] Boulez's interest in the phenomenon suggests that it amounts to more than the deception that Adorno finds in Wagner. Indeed, the fire music that closes *Die Walküre* furnishes Adorno with an example of phantasmagoria, but this passage can be understood as an exploration of illusion, rather than simply an example of it, and the apparently seamless surface is generated by diversified, not uniform, techniques of repetition.

On the level of the *Gesamtkunstwerk* and its appropriation of myth, the obfuscation of phantasmagoria, according to Adorno's argument, becomes expanded to a second nature, which presents as 'natural' the reified conditions of society. The seductive characteristics of phantasmagoria, whereby characters can 'function as universal symbols by dissolving into the phantasmagoria like mist' (1981: 89), anticipates the elusive advertisement, and the *Gesamtkunstwerk* (notably the transformation scenes in *Parsifal*) foresees film techniques and the passive assimilation of mass culture in general – 'the birth of film out of the spirit of music' (1981: 107). The complete cosmos of an emancipated art music beckons the self-perpetuating system of mass culture: in a devastating irony, mass culture cynically attains the totality traditionally sought by bourgeois art – 'The magic work of art dreams its complete antithesis, the mechanical work of art' (Adorno 1981a: 109). Adorno's critique of Wagner attempts to show that the culture industry is not simply the other of bourgeois art, but he acknowledges that Wagner's music dramas are not subsumed by the elision, and detects moments in which the music breaks through its aesthetic environment. Such instances are found, Adorno contends, in those jagged passages of *Tristan*, Act III. When Tristan curses love he negates the possibility of reconciliation through love in a disfigured world, and, significantly, the music following the words '*Der furchtbare Trank*' (that potion so dread) anticipates the emotional climate and sound of Schoenberg (1981: 156): an alienated subjectivity seeks refuge in objective techniques of construction, the mimetic breaks through the restrictions of form. Elsewhere Wagner fails to unlock the embrace of his own mythology, but such twists of the dialectic are more abundant than Adorno concedes.

Published in 1960, the Mahler monograph was written relatively late in Adorno's career. In describing Mahler's ability to turn a reified language against itself and to find new possibilities within the worn-out material, Adorno's conception of musical material and form becomes broader than it had been in earlier writings such as *Philosophy of New Music*. In particular, Adorno demonstrates that the radical quality of Mahler's music is not always dependent on the criteria of advanced material and thematic development, which had been touchstones for much of Adorno's earlier writing on music. Mahler uses the outward shell of traditional tonality and its forms, but his expressionism and anticipation of modernist alienation are achieved by breaking open and pseudomorphically transforming reified material and forms. Genres such as the ländler and the march are brought within the sphere of high art, preventing the language from falling into standard patterns; and Mahler's aesthetic appeals against the split between high and low culture, his use of popular and folk music breaking the flow of musical logic. As Adorno puts it: 'A foreigner speaks music fluently, but as if with an accent' (1992a: 32).

Folk-derived melodic material and many of Mahler's original themes do not easily break down into motivic units capable of being transformed into something else; instead, they form *Gestalten* that retain an underlying identity through transformations (1992a: 87). Adorno uses the term 'variant', as opposed to variation, to describe Mahler's technique of thematic manipulation, and by doing so he demonstrates greater sensitivity to Mahler's innovations than to Wagner's motivic webs. Beethoven transforms motives by building thematic complexes from them; by contrast, Mahler's themes maintain an overall shape and recognizable characteristics but are modified within by variants. Adorno describes the technique as follows: 'The concept of the theme as a given, then to be modified, is inadequate to Mahler. Rather, the nucleus undergoes a treatment similar to that of narrative element in oral tradition; at each telling it becomes slightly different' (1992a: 88). Mahler does not therefore renounce temporality, but Adorno argues that he detects something reified in the traditional idea of development since it is reliant on the notion of the given and what it becomes; for Mahler, there is not a given as such. Nevertheless, there is a certain fascination with images of pre-capitalist Europe and *Urphänomen* (1992b: 90). Adorno acknowledges traces of sentimentality in the old-German images utilized by Mahler, but also argues that instead of constituting a reified second nature they are constrained to 'a movement that is finally that of the history that rapt immersion in the images would so gladly forget' (1992a: 47). As Adorno notes, 'themes that are seen to emerge from a collective world of images are reminiscent of Stravinsky' (1992a: 89). But he is insistent that for Mahler 'duration is dynamic' whereas Stravinsky's practice of arranging shapes brings time to a standstill (1992a: 89).

Mahler's music challenges conventional theories of form, not only because it is fractured but also because it uses fields of fulfilment and disintegration that, while contributing to the whole, are themselves 'formal entities as characters' (1992a: 45). Talking of the collapse in the Funeral March of the Fifth Symphony, Adorno comments that 'the dynamics of the catastrophe section are themselves also a character, a quasi-spatial field' (1992a: 45–6); likewise, transitional and linking materials, which sometimes assume the character of a chorale, are not simply subsumed by the overall form but instead project characteristics of their own. Much of Adorno's own account of Mahler is devoted to trying to read the character of these fields. Adorno compares Mahler's symphonies to novels in distinction from the dramatic unfolding of the classical symphony: they present characters whose story is to be told. The 'principle of permanent modification' gives prominence to the development, but the latter does not, because of the novel-like form, stand in dynamic contrast to static elements in the exposition (1992a: 95).

The form of novels written contemporaneously with Mahler's symphonies also informs, Adorno argues, the notion of recapitulation in Mahler. In Adorno's critique, Mahler struggles with a problem already evident in Beethoven's late style (see Dahlhaus 1979a: 175).[8] The difficulty of the reprise in Beethoven stems from its reliance on affirming what is already there; the narrative tendencies in Mahler's music address this problem by associating the recapitulation with an almost Proustian sense of recollection: 'Through the variant his music remembers things past and half-forgotten from a great distance, protests against their absolute fruitlessness and yet pronounces the past ephemeral, irrecoverable' (1992a: 94). The long gaze at a past that seemed to offer the promise of happiness is, Adorno argues, the creative kernel of *Das Lied von der Erde* and the Ninth Symphony: the idea of breakthrough, attributed by Adorno to Mahler's early symphonies, 'becomes sublimated' in these late works, he contends, 'into the memory of a past life as of a utopia that had never existed' (1992b: 91). As an idea, this shares an affinity with the status of mimesis in Adorno's philosophy: the music's longing to burst through its aesthetic confines registers Adorno's desire for cognition and ethics to be permeable to individual fulfilment.

Adorno's espousal of the music of Mahler carries something of a polemic; it responds to the criticism that Mahler's music is overblown (an attitude partially responsible for the lack of interest shown in Mahler earlier this century). Adorno's reply to this objection is twofold: firstly, he explores the paradox 'that he [Mahler] succeeded on the terrain of the large-scale symphony at a time when such works had already become impossible' (1992b: 89); secondly, Adorno acknowledges the sometimes forced metaphysics in Mahler and is critical of the way in which the Eighth Symphony succumbs to the ideology of the art work as religion, as an affirmation of illusion. One wonders how Adorno would have responded to the present use of Mahler as an orchestral showpiece and a launch pad for conductors, in a way that is unimaginable in the case of atonal Schoenberg. The music, to a large extent, resists this impulse, but some of the elements of mass spectacle identified by Adorno in Wagner are also present in Mahler; whatever its quality, this music cannot completely evade the ability of consumerism to assimilate even potentially disruptive material. In such an environment, Mahler's agonized attempt to elicit some metaphysical meaning from a fragmented world risks becoming hypostatized.

The current valorization of Mahler, together with the music's nostalgic reaching back and its anticipatory modernism, places his conception of construction and material in a complex constellation. The radical aspect of Mahler's music lies, to a large extent, in its capacity to convey, by traditional harmonic means, the expression of alienation and the disintegration of organic wholeness so central to modern experience; his tonal chords, writes Adorno, are 'the cryptograms of modernism' (1992b: 85). Mahler achieved through shock and allegory the perception of crisis for which Schoenberg eventually required a reorganized musical syntax. Adorno acknowledges that Mahler reached for, and anticipated, the techniques of Schoenberg, but also uses him to highlight the inadequacies of the later integral serialism: Mahler, he says, already realized that unity is 'undermined as soon as it ceases to unify a plurality. Without a dialectical counterpart it threatens to degenerate into an empty tautology' (1992b: 94).

Like Benjamin's unfinished study of nineteenth-century Paris (the *Arcades* project), Adorno's understanding of nineteenth-century music functions as a pre-history of modernism. From the point of view of Adorno's redemptive critique, much nineteenth-century music is trapped in its own static vision; but from the perspective of a continual process, chromatic harmony extends into modernism and, when combined with the intense motivic working derived from Brahms, triggers the density of construction found in Schoenberg. In late Beethoven Adorno detects a resistance within the material to the unity of an idealistic system; the allegory identified by Adorno in Wagner is generated, inadvertently, against the extreme continuity and organicism that the music tries to convey; by contrast, the music of Mahler is broken 'through and through' (1992b: 83),[9] the interaction of the particular and the whole generating a constant field of tension. Mahler's ability to summon new life from disintegrating materials is an issue of great aesthetic importance, to which Adorno returns in his writings on Berg. It is surely significant that the Mahler renaissance occurred in the 1960s and 1970s, contemporaneous with the emergence of postmodernism.

Dialectic of Modernity: Schoenberg and Stravinsky

Philosophy of New Music forms a core text amidst Adorno's extensive musical writings, and provides a theoretical model for his approach to music criticism by tracking instrumental reason into the interstices of modernist music. *Philosophy of New Music* is dependent on philosophical issues that are worked out theoretically elsewhere (it was written as an extended appendix to *Dialectic of Enlightenment*), but it does succeed in presenting a thoroughgoing critique of modernity in which Schoenberg and Stravinsky embody the two extremes of new music. As the previous discussion of nineteenth-century music indicated, the historical development of compositional techniques provides Adorno with an immanent example of the whole process of Western rationality. He argues that previous subjectivity is embedded within the material a composer works with, but the objective substance requires new configurations, invented by the subjectivity of the composer, to release its expressive potential.[10] The material encodes an ensemble of interconnected practices, ranging from socio-economic configurations and lifeworld conditions to influences of genre and form, which both exerts an influence on and is reconfigured by the composer. Taking his cue from Max Weber's *The Rational and Social Foundations of Music*, Adorno understands musical material to embody a rationalization of nature and detects a dialectic of enlightenment in the historical advancement of this appropriation. The blind and opaque object – the Kantian thing-in-itself (*Ding an sich*) – is rendered increasingly transparent by the process of rationalization; correspondingly, the strangeness of the material is reduced by technical advancement. Adorno's argument is powerful: he is able to reveal the dialectic of enlightenment to be a problem, both logical and expressive, that has been both the motor and demise of Western music in its attempts to find a satisfactory synthesis of expression with the technical manipulation of musical material.

In the work of Schoenberg, the expressive impulse and the striving for technical mastery both reach an extreme and have great significance for each other. Adorno does not spell it out, but Schoenberg represents a meeting place, together with Brahmsian thematic working, for the different experiences of fragmentation identified in Beethoven and Mahler. The early tonal works, such as *Gurrelieder* and *Pelleas und Melisande*, obviously display the influence of Mahler to a considerable degree and there is even something of the Mahlerian grotesque in *Gurrelieder*. With the accelerated disintegration of tonality in the Second Quartet and the First Chamber Symphony, among other works, the experience of loneliness in Schoenberg approaches the objective inwardness that Adorno identifies in late Beethoven, though, as we have seen, this tendency is by no means absent in Mahler. In the expressionist works of Schoenberg, Adorno finds the culmination both of nineteenth-century heightened expression and the inner loneliness of late Beethoven.

Adorno argues that the construction of *Erwartung* emerges from the intensity of its mimetic impulse (1984a: 65), the intersection creating a seemingly unbridled emotional surge and a striking spontaneity despite the notorious complexity of the score. Paradoxically, however, it was precisely this type of *tour de force*, in which particular compositions were forced to establish their own musical syntax instead of relying on the general system of tonality for a context, that led Schoenberg to create the potentially stifling system of serialism. In Schoenberg's struggle to invent a musical medium that would simultaneously enable more freedom and greater discipline, Adorno detects a dialectic that goes right to the heart of Enlightenment rationality. The uncompromising quality of Schoenberg's protest is embodied in the organization of his musical material: the expression of subjectivity through extreme objectivity is able to convey the condition of an autonomous subject in the face of administered society. On the other hand, however, the sovereign control over musical resources facilitated by serialism comes close to epitomizing a rationality that can only advance through an increasing domination over nature. Despite the immanent necessity of serialist methods, Schoenberg at his best succeeds despite rather than because of the system. Adorno puts the dilemma as follows:

> The question that twelve-tone music directs the composer towards is not, how can musical meaning be organized, but rather: how can musical organization become meaningful? (1973a: 67).[11]

Nevertheless, in the assimilation of his ideas to be found in Thomas Mann's *Doctor Faustus*, Adorno does attribute a utopian dimension to serialism in the form of a second mimesis, or, a breakthrough beyond construction. In *Doctor*

Faustus it is posited that the concentrated quality of a medium constructed out of objectified subjectivity, in which every note matters, means that technical rigour is already embedded in the material, leaving the composer free to compose in a purely expressive manner.[12]

> Just by virtue of the absoluteness of the form the music is, as language, freed. In a more concrete and physical sense the work is done, indeed, before the composition even begins, and this can now go on wholly unrestrained; that is it can give itself over to expression, which, thus lifted beyond the structural element, or within its uttermost severity, is won back again. The creator of *Fausti Weheklage* can, in the previously organized material, unhampered, untroubled by the already given structure, yield himself to subjectivity; and so this, his technically most rigid work, a work of extreme calculation, is at the same time purely expressive (Mann 1968: 468).

Despite this optimism, Adorno is well aware that the dividing line between construction as pure expression and control subsumed by objectivity is a very fine one: on the one hand, he contends that the rules of serialism are in fact those which a sensitive composer working in an atonal idiom would anyway observe, since they correspond to an immanent force within the material; on the other, he argues that a technique which mimes technological control, both abandons the illusion of art's resemblance to nature and simultaneously inflates it to a dogma of integration that mimes a second nature. Serialism certainly did create the conditions for a type of composition in which the compositional act became one of realizing the intervallic qualities contained within the pre-chosen row; and it did contribute to an aesthetic that reinstated the aesthetic illusion of artistic autonomy under the banner of quasi-scientific objectivity. The totalizing tendency identified by Adorno in serialism touches on the other major theme of *Dialectic of Enlightenment* and *Philosophy of New Music*: the return of all-embracing mythologies.

In the same way that Adorno reads commodity capitalism as a mythological world view deterministic of people's modes of thought, so he hears the music of Stravinsky as essentially a package of tricks, masquerading as progress but actually reinforcing a repressive, brutal reality in which the individual is crushed. Although Adorno does not specifically make the connection, an acute example of the antithesis drawn between the two composers is contained in their respective portrayals of human sacrifice. The 'dance around the golden calf', from Schoenberg's *Moses and Aaron*, is a subjective and dramatic response to irrational barbarism, but the sacrificial scene from *The Rite of Spring* is an indifferent commentary: the music takes the part of the crowd, the mass mentality that determines the fate of the individual. *The Rite of Spring* and other ritualistic works by Stravinsky are associated, in Adorno's mind, with the experience of fascism: the very nature abused by instrumental rationality now returns as an atavism harnessed to technological domination. At the opposite extreme to Schoenberg and his school whose destruction of tonality was in keeping with tendencies within tonality itself, Stravinsky was reduced to shock tactics that rely on unexpected combinations of colour and material, ill-suited to an unfolding musical logic. Adorno argues that Stravinsky's play of meaning and his eradication of subjective expression in favour of a dazzling exterior constitute an infantile protest against authority and harness an underlying irrationality; likewise, apparent attacks on traditional music can only work within the assured context of that music itself, affirming more than disrupting the established order.

In an effort to reconstruct Adorno's Stravinsky critique, James L. Marsh has attempted to reverse many of Adorno's judgements, asking of *Histoire du soldat* why it should be infantile rather than childlike, schizophrenic rather than playful, or regressive rather than progressive (Marsh 1983). It is more likely, however, that *Histoire* occupies a forcefield defined by these terms and does not side irrevocably with any of them. A childlike response to the world, unsullied by the reality principle, is at the heart of Adorno's aesthetic thought, yet he realizes that such innocence cannot avoid social mediation. The condition Adorno's writings on art aspire to emulate is close to the characterization he gives of Berg: 'He successfully avoided becoming an adult without remaining infantile' (1991a: 34). Adorno also recognizes a double-edged sword in the invocation of play in art: 'Play in art', he comments, 'represents both a renunciation of instrumental rationality and a regression behind it' (1984a: 437). The problem is that while play eludes a purposeful rationality, it risks succumbing to an invariant order through the repetition and reproduction of reified forms. Both sides of this equation are meshed together in Stravinsky's music: the end result is neither unambiguously regressive nor progressive.

The primitivism of Stravinsky's Russian period shares features with the contumacy of the historical avant garde, and Adorno touches upon Stravinsky's association with this aesthetic when he compares the 'second language of dream-like regression' in *Histoire* with the 'surrealists' dream-montages made of everyday remnants' (1973a: 183).[13] In Peter Bürger's well-known reading, avant-gardism refers to movements such as Dada and Surrealism – to which Stravinsky was close in the 1920s – that attempted to break art as an institution (Bürger 1984). Bürger contends that Stravinsky's technique is not one of parody, but of alienation: just as Max Ernst estranges the *fin-de-siècle* bourgeois interior by 'giving his humans beast-of-prey heads, so Stravinsky alienates the forms of entertainment music' (Bürger 1985: 120). Adorno was not far from such an interpretation in an earlier essay, 'The Social Significance of Music', where he talks of *Histoire* using a type of objectivism in which the aesthetic illusion of familiar material is exposed (1990: 227), and compares the music favourably with Weill's ability to illuminate the commodified status of *Gebrauchsmusik*. Nevertheless, montage and its surrealist associations proved a complex issue for Adorno, and he never found a fixed place for this technique in his aesthetics of music. The difficulty, for him, is that the form of a montage is derived from external arrangements of the components, instead of emerging from a process immanent to the material. The conundrum in the case of Stravinsky is whether he affiliates himself with the reality principle by taking a popular form such as the waltz or whether, like Mahler and Berg, he estranges the social form. There is no easy answer to this puzzle because Stravinsky is capable of registering affiliation and resistance within a single work. Speaking of the way in which 'four shattered old-fashioned march formulae are stitched together and reconstituted into form by the same force that had disintegrated them' in the third of Berg's Three Orchestral Pieces, opus 6, Adorno compares Berg's employment of fragments with Stravinsky's formulations:

> While the Stravinsky of the *Soldier* and the Satie of the *Cinq grimaces* allowed such fragments to stand, bald and as inflexible as a mask, Berg's humanity discovered in them the moving force of their decomposition and translated that into the moving force of composition . . . Under the glass plates of form, large as a house, in the wild distorted motley array of orchestral planes, those fragments awaken to a second and catastrophic significance (1991a: 74–5).

Determinate irreconcilability, which is what Adorno finds in Berg, is generated by an immanent impulse, instead of destroying one. Whether Stravinsky consistently destroys the inner life of his fragments is, however, questionable.

The avant-gardist interest in montage and ready-mades carried over into Stravinsky's neo-classical works, and he acknowledged as much with regard to the composition of *Oedipus Rex*, referring to 'much of the music as a *Merzbild*, put together from whatever came to hand' (Stravinsky 1961: 27). Adorno again views Stravinsky through the lens of surrealism when in a later essay he reconsiders his own earlier appraisal of neo-classicism: instead of reviving obsolete forms, Adorno argues, Stravinsky reduced the models to 'bric-a-brac and remaindered goods' (1992b: 156); the hastily assembled dream images 'duplicate the statues in Max Ernst's *Femme 100 Têtes*, which tumble among the living beings and whose faces are frequently missing as if they had been erased by the dream censorship' (1992b: 156). By detecting some affinity between Surrealism and neo-classicism Adorno does, at least, bring the latter into the frame of modernism, whatever his ambivalence about Surrealism itself; and seen as a modernist strand, instead of an anti-modernist movement, it becomes harder to judge neo-classicism *in toto*. The critical issue is whether individual artefacts simply reproduce a closed system or whether an internal dynamic generates new meanings from materials used.[14] In fact, the whole neo-classical label is awkward because certain works such as the *Symphonies of Wind Instruments* resist classification. Despite its dependence on ritual and its use of block textures, this work is inward looking and Stravinsky himself regarded it as 'devoid of all the elements which infallibly appeal to the ordinary listener and to which he is accustomed. It would be futile', he continues, 'to look in it for any passionate impulse or dynamic brilliance' (Stravinsky 1936: 156–7). Stravinsky's play with forms from the past must however in the last analysis be deceptive for Adorno because while it saps aesthetic illusion it offers, in compensation, the illusion of transgression. Adorno comments that 'he [Stravinsky] was able to produce his tricks and to explain them at the same time, something that only the most pre-eminent magicians can allow themselves' (1992b: 146).

Stravinsky evinces a particularly powerful fusion of modernism and the archaic, his version of allegory in the Russian works emerging as a marriage of ritual and folk music with an ascetic avant-gardism. Coming from a Russian tradition, which had consciously sought to distinguish itself from central European dominance, Stravinsky was able to convey from the outside the dismantling of organic unity that was achieved as an internal process at the centre. Methods of construction drawn from the diverse experiences of pre-revolutionary Russia are catapulted into the depersonalized second mythology of modernism. At its best, Stravinsky's Russian period avant-gardism fractures central European idealism and convention from the outside and injects an older stratum of consciousness, reflected in the rawness of sound, which finds a certain familiarity in the distant and intangible steering media of modernity: peasant music, ritual and folk stories on the margins of society suddenly discover resonance in the cosmopolitan centres.[15] By putting these ingredients, drained of much of their original meaning, in a radically different configuration, Stravinsky constructs an Adornian-type constellation, although it registers the shattering of unified space rather more than it constitutes a rethinking of part and whole. The Janus-faced problem posed to interpretation of Stravinsky is whether these configurations of old and new fuse to confirm a second-nature rationality, or whether the archaic components illuminate the mechanisms of modernity. Adorno is, however, sympathetic towards Bartók's radical folklorism and suggests that it touches the nerve-centre of modernism, arguing that 'he [Bartók] refutes the fiction of formal objectivity and goes back instead to a pre-objective, truly archaic material, which, however, is very closely related to current material precisely in its particular dissolution'. 'Radical folklorism', Adorno continues, 'in the rational through-construction of his particular material is, consequently, amazingly similar to the practices of the Schoenberg School' (1990: 238). Yet Stravinsky's mercurial games and quirky play of masks, which parody the European tradition, prevent the music, he insists, from assuming a single expression that would enable it to emulate Bartók's achievement. This position is not entirely convincing: it could equally well be contended that Stravinsky's refusal to occupy a single stance prevents his music from lapsing into a rigid objectivity.

The repeated and juxtaposed cells of Stravinsky's Russian period, Adorno contends, provide a vehicle for articulating the repetitive networks of commodity production and the pre-given; but the other side of this technique, which Adorno fails to perceive, is that the same mechanisms at times engineer a direct collision between the lived spaces of pre-industrial repetition and the emptiness of mass production. That is, Stravinsky registers modernism's protest at aesthetic confinement by invoking the subjectivity of a different social space, and one that was not entirely synchronous with the development of modernity. It is in sections of large-scale rhythmic repetition that Stravinsky risks folding a psychic energy into a machine-like collectivity. Famous passages such as the 'Dances of the Young Girls' and the 'Sacrificial Dance' from *The Rite of Spring* do, however, seem to confront repetitive identity head on and look at ways in which it can be dislocated: in the first example, through irregular placing of accents, in the second, by uneven placing of the repeated rhythm. Here, repetition is not so much a vehicle for motivic transformation as the medium of the music itself.

Stravinsky's primeval world may indeed open out onto the panorama of mass production, but he does, at least, find ways of revealing areas of experience that are not synchronous with that continuum. In addition to decoding, as Adorno does, the extent to which Stravinsky's music is determined by an underlying social ideology, it is also possible to detect within it a consciousness of physiological and ecological time, disruptive of instrumental rationality. Adorno himself touches upon this mimetic strand in Stravinsky when, in a discussion of the composer's orchestration for wind and percussion, he comments that 'the voices of his instruments are like animals whose very existence seems to express their names' (1992b: 168).

Adorno's emphasis on a single historical path for music, dependent on historically advanced material, is problematic. Dahlhaus portrays his philosophy of history as the core problem in the discussions of Beethoven, Wagner and Stravinsky: a single history of society along with – in the cases of Wagner and Stravinsky – a view of musical time predicated on Beethoven and Schoenberg, it is argued, obscures the particular techniques used in compositions. Certainly, Adorno's judgements are often one-sided, but this weakness is not a problem intrinsically bound up with the employment of a philosophy of history in understanding music; it has much more to do with the lack of differentiation within the particular philosophy of history used by him. An understanding of musical material as sedimented history need, *contra* Dahlhaus, be neither politically determinist nor a mask behind which to hide 'subjective' judgements (Dahlhaus 1987: 14), since subjects can debate the strands embedded in a text and compare them with individual and collective experiences. Dahlhaus proposes that historical information is insightful about music when justified by the 'intrinsic, functional coherence of a work', but contends that theory cannot consistently cross the gap between 'internal, aesthetic observations and external, documentary ones' (1983: 32). Consequently, this approach places aesthetic considerations firmly in a sphere of their own and cuts them off from matters of ethics and truth, since the latter are not susceptible to provisional invocation, when convenient. Regrettably, Dahlhaus's argument sacrifices Adorno's insight that it is precisely in internal technical musical problems that history is encountered. It is certainly true that Adorno's account of instrumental reason and his dependence on the idea of developing variation – in *Philosophy of New Music*, at least – load the dice against Stravinsky so that his static sonorities are viewed as regressive in comparison with Schoenberg's motivic technique; but a wrong judgement does not in itself constitute a reason to exempt static techniques from historical scrutiny, it creates an opportunity, rather, to reconsider how spatial articulation operates within history. If compositional technique is detached from wider history, then it is likely to be perceived as solely physiologically-derived and hence ahistorical; the whole thrust of Adorno's theory of second nature, by contrast, is to demonstrate how material conditions impinge on such understandings. Without a philosophy of history, and a concomitant theory of mediation in musical material, the whole edifice of Adorno's aesthetics would collapse; modernism's challenging of traditional

aesthetics, its pull away from integration and its quest for theoretical understanding could be understood only by a pale explanation of technique.

Adorno's understanding of modernism is enriched by Harvey's analysis of the
spatial articulation intrinsic to modernity. Harvey argues that the historical
geography of modernism reveals 'tensions between internationalism and nationalism, between globalism and parochialist ethnocentrism . . . Modernism looks
quite different depending on where one locates oneself and when' (1989: 24–5).
The possibility of related events happening simultaneously across large geographical spaces transforms traditional conceptions of space and time, undermining the sense of coherent, successive events in time that underpins narrative
techniques and the notion of an unfolding temporal logic in music. The process
of time-space compression produces an internationalist homogenization of space,
but an awareness of spatial configurations also has a more progressive potential:
it can alert us to the spaces – and spaces within spaces – that people inhabit and
to the spatial simultaneity of very divergent global experiences.[16] Awareness of
the simultaneous existence of heterogeneous social spaces blunts any insistence
on a single advanced historical material; instead, one is confronted with a sense
of multi-layered and internally differentiated history, each layer pursuing its own
course through time. Such a model provides an insight into the differentiation of
modernist musical materials in both a geographical and social sense, and attunes
the ear to spatial configurations within music. In a similar vein, Andreas Huyssen
has seized upon Bloch's notion of *Ungleichzeitigkeiten* to designate the non-
synchronisms of artistic practices on different, though ultimately related,
historical trajectories (Huyssen 1986: 187; Bloch 1977), the approach recognizing stylistic differences without promoting diversity as an end in itself.

A differentiated history of musical material leaves intact the integrity of
Schoenberg's achievement, but acknowledges that the *Ungleichzeitigkeiten* that
thread their way throughout Stravinsky's oeuvre are not absent in Schoenberg's
music and ideas. The most progressive aspect of Schoenberg is normally
considered to be his innovative use of pitch, though works such as the two sets
of piano pieces Opus 11 and 19 undertake a dissolution of metre and pulse more
radical than that found in Stravinsky. The conception of motivic working,
phraseology, rhythm and metre, however, is often still that of the nineteenth
century; indeed, in his later essay on *Moses and Aaron*, Adorno criticizes
Schoenberg for maintaining quasi-linguistic intonations linked with tonality,
which are associated with the bourgeois individualist's belief in genius and the
great art work which will withstand the test of time (1992b: 242). Adorno
therefore acknowledges, though with a negative connotation in this instance,
that historical non-synchronism can be found between the components of
the music itself. It may well be that one of the radical and prophetic qualities
of Stravinsky's music is that it consciously utilizes the non-synchronism
of constituents and styles as a technique.

In Adorno's aesthetics artistic truth content emerges from the mediation of
subject and object in the material and form of the art work, the decline of

subjectivity lamented by Adorno taking place within a music history that carries the core of negative dialectics within itself. The emphasis on the material of music embodying socio-philosophical truth is appropriate to Beethoven's depiction of a broken metaphysical world, though, even here, more of an allowance could be made for historical currents moving at different speeds. Rethinking Adorno's music philosophy with regard to the reassessment undertaken leaves his Schoenberg critique intact but not unscathed; after all, Schoenberg is very much locked within the same forcefield as Adorno. Mahler and Schoenberg can be heard anew within the framework presented by Adorno, but this scheme should be expanded to include an active awareness of the conflicting currents in modernism.

It is Stravinsky and other composers whose music does not aspire to philosophical knowledge who suffer the most damage from the tenets of Adorno's theoretical approach, and who might stand to gain from being placed within a more open theoretical context. Debussy is problematic for Adorno, since his music attempts to elude the Austro-German tradition but is historically progressive; nevertheless, if Adorno misses the full significance of Debussy, he is able to demonstrate the precarious situation of an aesthetic of art for art's sake. Perhaps predictably, Adorno takes a more sympathetic approach to hedonism in Austro-German music, as embodied by the figure of Franz Schreker. Writing in 1951, at the peak of high modernism, Adorno concludes from a discussion of Schreker's conception of melodic line that 'we have to revaluate many things which previously appeared to be of minor importance' (1992b: 135); furthermore, in a comment of wider significance, he postulates that 'material and consciousness do not necessarily move in a straight line along the same track as the new music' (1992b: 135). Awareness of the diversity available in musical material takes on a geographical dimension in Adorno's opinion of Janáček, whose music is judged to be progressive, though divergent from the Austro-German tradition, because the idiosyncratic use of accents derived from the Czech language has a disorienting effect upon its tonal language but resists a narrow nationalism (1973a: 35). Adorno's comments on Bartók and Janáček, in the context of the Schoenberg versus Stravinsky framework, and on Schreker and Zemlinsky elsewhere (1992b), also indicate the possibility of a perspective in which non-synchronous historical paths co-exist. These thoughts are suggestive of a critical theory that seeks to re-entwine the making of history with the social production of space (Soja 1989: 11), and understands experiences of time and space to be created by different processes of social reproduction (Harvey 1989: 204). Diverse modernisms become indexes of different social spaces, but they all refer to an underlying process of modernity.

Adorno's theory of modernist art takes issue with Lukács's defence of realism, but *Philosophy of New Music* and Adorno's aesthetics in general owe an unacknowledged debt to *History and Class Consciousness*. In this text Lukács offers a piercing critique of the effect of industrialization on our perception of time, arguing that when humankind is subordinated to the machine:

time sheds its qualitative, variable, flowing nature; it freezes into an exactly delimited, quantifiable continuum filled with quantifiable 'things' . . . in short, it becomes space (quoted in Roberts 1991: 84–5).

Extending this argument and applying it to the music of Wagner and Stravinsky, Adorno locates an essentialism, which posits an unchanging world order, when development of material accedes to static sonority: that is, the injustices of a particular political and economic situation are translated into the natural order of invariant material organization. If Adorno's doctrine of advanced material sometimes renders him insensitive to geographical differentiation, his adherence to temporal (historical) process in music makes him often unreceptive to spatial articulation. While an uncritical mode of spatial thought is certainly not desirable, spatial organization may, nevertheless, give voice to those unchanging physiological constraints of human life which can enter into relationships with dynamic possibilities of change. In *Philosophy of New Music* Adorno is distrustful of repetition and stasis, but in other writings, particularly the later ones, shows a broader tolerance towards these characteristics: the essay on 'Analysis and Berg', written in 1968, includes a discussion of Berg's employment of 'fields of static tension [*Auflösungsfeld*] as a formal device throughout a composition' (1991a: 38). Yet, while acknowledging the correlation with Debussy, Adorno is still keen to distinguish the dynamic element in Berg from the sense of the 'already established' in Debussy: 'Berg is a link in the German tradition of "developing variation" to the extent that he not only produces that result, the fields of static tension, down to their differentials, but structures and presents the process of becoming, their dissolving, as the essential content of the composition' (1991a: 38n). At a later stage Adorno contemplates modernism's disruption of the 'conventional ordering of time' (1984a: 34) and, while doubting that art can 'shake off the invariable of time', he argues, perhaps in deference to Stockhausen's idea of moment form, that 'it is more useful to regard time as a moment rather than as an *a priori* assumption of music' (1984a: 34–5).[17] Static and spatial aspects of musical thought are criticized strongly at one stage in Adorno's career and only fleetingly examined later, but their intersection can be addressed by his own technique of immanent analysis of the object (indeed, the practice of constellation, though designed to release sedimented history, is spatially conceived). Drawing on Benjamin's distinction between empty time of the present and full time of the present, one can distinguish between an empty, mechanistic experience of space – as alluded to by Lukács in the reference above – and a non-subsumptive experience of space in music. Instead of space being considered synonymous with reification, one can envisage a social articulation of spatial experience whereby the non-coercive interaction between subject and subject, subject and object – a sense of the constructed space of social relations – opens up a critical response to the dead space of empty repetition and image.

Philosophy of New Music portrays Schoenberg as a heroic failure in his attempt to maintain the autonomy of the subject in an administered world; Stravinsky, by comparison, appears as the successful man of the moment, but one who failed to protest at the annihilation of the subject. The dialectic that Adorno posits between these two figures embraces the problems encountered by a modern subjectivity seeking to avoid either metaphysical or relativist solutions. The depth of feeling sustained in Adorno's discussion of Schoenberg indicates a personal affinity with the composer's search for valid aesthetic expression; correspondingly, Stravinsky, at times, merely becomes a sop for the forces of irrationality in twentieth-century culture. The section which closes the discussion of Schoenberg in *Philosophy of New Music* is as much a portrayal of Adorno's philosophical stance as a commentary on modern music: new music, he says, 'has taken upon itself all the darkness and guilt of the world. . . . It is the true message in the bottle (1973a: 133).[18]

Ultimately, Adorno's analysis, in socio-philosophical terms, of the crisis in material at the beginning of the twentieth century is of more significance than the precise conclusions he draws from it about individual composers. In David Roberts' opinion, Adorno's distinction between the authenticity of Schoenberg and the inauthenticity of Stravinsky is of less importance than the underlying cognizance that the two approaches represent alternative responses to the same crisis: Schoenberg's attempt to invent a new order from within and Stravinsky's parodying of the past and tradition from without both point to the neutralization of conventional technique (1991: 93). Musical material did not reach the absolute stage of indifference suggested by Roberts, but the attempt to reinvent material did lead to the two main paths of twentieth-century art: on the one hand, the development of totally integrated languages, on the other, the reinvestment of material or form with a hidden latency. Although both approaches have held sway throughout the twentieth century, loosely speaking, the former route can be traced to the rigidity of high modernism and the latter path to the outbreak of postmodernism as a recognizable phenomenon. One does not have to share Roberts' conviction that the dialectic should be translated into an ahistorical mode of contingency in order to recognize that the two halves cannot be held apart as right or wrong, progressive or reactionary. The fluidity of relations in much Stravinsky releases the possibility of rethinking the intersection of part and whole, and he introduces the potential for manipulating complex sound objects; Schoenberg, for his part, maintains the capacity for combining intense expression with intricate construction.

Notes

1. My translation.
2. See Kramer 1995: 46–51 for another discussion of Dahlhaus's 'twin styles' view of nineteenth-century music history.
3. See Subotnik 1991 for a discussion of Adorno's depiction of stasis in nineteenth-century music.
4. Translation modified.
5. Dahlhaus makes this point (1970: 144).
6. Adorno 1984a: 150 talks about aesthetic illusion becoming phantasmagoria.
7. See Chapter 5.

8. Dahlhaus is here discussing the finale of Mahler's Sixth Symphony.
9. Translation modified.
10. For a detailed account of Adorno's understanding of musical material, see Paddison 1993.
11. Translation modified.
12. For a good account of second immediacy in *Doctor Faustus*, see Christa Bürger 1990.
13. Translation modified.
14. This point is made by Peter Bürger 1985: 120.
15. For a wide-ranging discussion of the relations between myth, modernism and monopoly capital, see Eagleton 1990: 316–25.
16. For an informative account of early modernism in music that examines the 'shaping role of geography' together with its temporal and spatial impact, see Samson 1991: 43.
17. Also quoted in Paddison 1993: 34.
18. Translation modified.

Part II High Modernism and After

3 Construction and Indeterminacy: Boulez and Cage

High Modernism

Modernization in the West after the Second World War drew upon many of the principles of production and wealth accumulation already established before the war; nonetheless, economic growth in the post-war years was linked to a social space more integrated than before. The standardized conditions of production were intended to create a modern, disciplined assembly-line worker, and, as Harvey observes, Fordist theories of manufacture had recognized that mass production entails mass consumption, with the consequence that both sides of the process need to be held in place by 'a new kind of rationalized, modernist, and populist democratic society' (1989: 126). 'Postwar Fordism', Harvey continues, 'has to be seen, therefore, less as a mere system of mass production and more as a total way of life' (1989: 135). This period also saw an increased internationalism among capitalist countries, based upon the rationalization of production and sales in major construction industries. The other side of this capitalist market was state investment in transport, public utilities and communications systems to provide for the workers who would support the production system.

The rationalist and functionalist principles of high modernism are particularly evident in the architecture of this era, achieving their most extreme form in Le Corbusier's conception of machines for living, which envisaged people carrying out particular functions in designated places: His *Unité d'Habitation*, Marseilles, (1946–52) – an eighteen-storey block, raised on concrete pillars – for example, was intended to house a shopping centre and exercise facilities for its 1,600 inhabitants. The ideas of Le Corbusier and of Mies van der Rohe are representative, in a specific form, of the principles that fuelled post-war urban regeneration; one side of this process expressing itself in the clean lines of buildings designed to be symbolic of corporate power, the other in the tower blocks for housing the working class (for which the *Unité d'Habitation* constitutes a prototype) that have become famous targets for postmodernist attack.

It is indicative of the brave new world of reinforced concrete that the dominant power interests were able to appropriate some forms of older modernist art. These artefacts, which Soviet dogma considered to be degenerate, became in the West symbols of the liberal freedom denied in communist countries. The New York Museum of Modern Art embodies the institutionalization of modernism, but the acceptance of abstract art on the walls of banks also characterizes this condition. Indeed, the phenomenon leads one to question whether abstract art is inherently more resistant to institutionalization than representational art.[1]

High modernist music, with its emphasis on the new, on construction, rationality, integration and, above all, abstraction, in many ways endorses the fundamental impulse of the first three decades of post-war Western society. Babbitt's famous analogy between contemporary music and scientific investigation as research areas for experts is symptomatic, suggesting, in effect, that music should mime specialized systemic languages without recourse to the concrete experiences of the lifeworld (Babbitt 1978). Nevertheless, serialist-related techniques have never achieved the public acceptance accorded to, say, the neo-classical Stravinsky, despite constituting – by means of institutional power – the dominant aesthetic of post-war new music. High modernist music shares the euphoric rationalism prevalent in the era of its production, but clings to the idea of alienation found earlier in the century. The estrangement experienced in the face of Babbitt's institutionalization of music is, however, far removed from the expression of impoverished subjectivity in an administered world envisaged by Adorno. Without making this distinction, alienation in art is often attacked by postmodernists on the premiss that the distancing effect sustains high art as a remote and elitist institution. Serialism's relation to the establishment is not, however, so transparent: for Luigi Nono, serialism was a language in which he could express anti-establishment protest. Because music does not have the obvious practical dimension of a medium such as architecture, it could take high modernist principles to an extreme that clearly shows, and sometimes explores, the fault lines in an overriding rationalism.

The main landmarks in the development of integral serialism are well known: the composers associated with the early years of the summer courses held at Darmstadt were keen to expand upon the achievements of Webern, extending the serial organization applied to pitch to the other components of music. This project had been partially achieved by Messiaen's *Mode de valeurs et d'intensités* (1949), in which the composer employs 'modes' of pitch, duration, intensity and attack, but reached fulfilment in Stockhausen's *Kreuzspiel* (1951) and Boulez's *Structure 1a* (1951). Early work in the electro-acoustic studio at Cologne expanded this desire to maintain absolute control over the components of music into quasi-scientific explorations of the physical properties of sound; the primary aesthetic is succinctly summed up by Eimert's vision of a 'real musical control of Nature' (Eimert 1958: 10).

This principle, with its emphasis on a single, integral, compositional procedure, almost advocates the domination of nature which so appals Adorno and

Horkheimer in *Dialectic of Enlightenment*. It is, then, perhaps not surprising that the lecture 'The Ageing of the New Music', presented by Adorno at the Stuttgart Week of New Music in 1954, is scathing. The kernel of Adorno's criticism of the high modernist obsession with technique is that the objectivity of the musical material becomes a fetish or goal in itself: instead of innovation being driven by a need for mediated, subjective expression, it is propelled by a desire to hide behind prefabricated material; the substance itself is imbued with a specious meaning rather than meaning emerging from the constellations that the composer actually constructs out of it. Translated into Habermas's terminology, Adorno is arguing that high modernist construction imposes a closed system on lifeworld needs, instead of the latter functioning as a resource for technical innovation. The force of Adorno's argument is powerful but, like the critique of popular music, it is weakened by his failure to discuss in specific terms the repertoire to which he is referring.

In a reply to Adorno's article, Heinz-Klaus Metzger accuses Adorno of relying on vague impressions, and questions whether he took the trouble to examine pertinent scores. Trenchant though Adorno's arguments are, Metzger indicates correctly that they are too generalized and fail to take into account differences between individual composers, or self-awareness on the part of musicians of the predicament represented by highly rationalized methods of composition. Metzger quotes at length a passage from 'The Ageing' in which Adorno refers to the tension between non-tonal material and techniques of musical articulation derived from tonal music (Metzger 1960: 68–9), and in which he has the following to say about Schoenberg's compositional techniques:

> Thematic construction, exposition, transitions, continuation, fields of tension and release, etc. are all scarcely distinguishable from traditional, especially Brahmsian, techniques, even in his most daring works (1988: 101; Metzger 1960: 68).

For Metzger, Adorno's suggestion that Schoenberg's traditional techniques of articulation offer compositional defences against prefabricated material lies in stark opposition to the axiom of a 'constructive consistency that subjects all material strata to the same laws', advocated by him in *Philosophy of New Music* (quoted, Metzger 1960: 73). It would be more accurate to say that Adorno perceives a tension between traditional techniques and non-tonal material that cannot be easily resolved, and indicates that new music needs to find its own equivalent for the older forms of articulation.

Adorno's later 'Music and New Music' returns to the issue, with the argument that rigid technical control in new music, which breaks down traditional categories, derives its strength from 'whatever forces had organized all older music, frequently from behind the facade of tonality' (1992b: 258). The implication is that new music can reinvent techniques used by, though not exclusively associated with, tonality; but Adorno proposes a return neither to traditional techniques nor to their associated bourgeois categories,[2] advocating instead a greater permeability between technique and social consciousness in new music, and suggesting that constructional rigour should emerge out of expressive necessity, from the 'density of experience', not from a fetish of technique (1988:

107). For him, then, the internal difficulties that integral composition experienced can be attributed to rationalism and axioms of identity dominating qualities of mimesis and non-identity; a viewpoint that resonates with post-modernist critiques of high modernist abstraction, without abandoning the idea of material distilling experience.

Before scrutinizing the dissent from within systematic composition encoded in Boulez's Third Piano Sonata, it is worth examining *Structure 1a* from *Structures*, the flagship of integral serialism, in order to see how the contradictions of an all-embracing rationality manifest themselves. *Structure 1a* represents an extreme effort by Boulez to extend serial procedures to all the components of music. By predetermining his materials and the operations to be performed on them, Boulez relinquished a large part of the constructional process to automatism, and was then able to make creative decisions with the somewhat crude mass of sound. As is well known, Boulez used the note-succession from *Mode de valeurs et d'intensités* as his basic series, from this devising a grid for the forty-eight permutations of the series – the prime, inversion, retrograde and retrograde inversion in each of their twelve transpositions. This grid was then used to determine a duration series: by taking a demisemiquaver as the smallest component, matching the value 1 on the grid, Boulez built up an additive duration series culminating in a dotted crotchet for the value 12, a particular transposition of the pitch series therefore corresponding numerically to a specific permutation of the duration series. The criterion for doing this was to generate a structural isomorphism between the components of pitch and duration, even though, as Ligeti has pointed out, this linkage is arbitrary: the note series maintains the same intervallic features when transposed, but there is no equivalent to transposition for the duration series; in his words, 'what were originally mere indications of *arrangement* [pitch transpositions] are now used as indications of *value*' [duration permutations] (Ligeti 1960: 40).

This integrational process is continued with the choice of dynamic levels, again divided into twelve, which range from *pppp* (1) to *ffff* (12). This scheme is another arbitrary decision, since there is no particular reason why aural perception of twelve pitches should map onto a twelve-fold division of dynamics. Boulez tacitly acknowledges this point by using only four derived series of dynamics which, unlike the pitch series, include repetitions that favour differentiated changes: for example, *mp–f–mf*, and these – as Ligeti mentions – are also modified in places for the sake of clarity. The attempt to serialize types of attack – twelve gradations ranging from 'staccatissimo' to 'legato' – is even more problematic, especially given the limited range of possibilities on the piano, and there is considerable overlap and potential for confusion between the realms of attack and intensity. The difficulty is again acknowledged: Boulez only uses ten types of attack in four derived series.

The cumulative texture evinces a complete dissolution of counterpoint and harmony: the vertical simultaneities are largely coincidences, with the exception of those occurring at the beginning of sections. Another problem produced by the system is that the greater the number of threads, the more the duration series are reduced to an overall rhythm that is likely to exclude long durations – Boulez addresses this matter by exerting control over the density of simultaneous strands. This second level of decision-making also applies to register, tempo and the duration of fermatas in relation to preceding and succeeding tempi. Boulez uses fixed registers so that repeated notes occur at exactly the same pitch, forming knots – to use Ligeti's term – in the texture and also avoiding octave doublings in the thicker webs, the resultant preponderance of one register over another additionally facilitating large-scale articulation between sections.

According to Ligeti, in *Structure 1a* Boulez renounced the vestiges of expression that linger on in the serial music of Webern, and produced an extreme version of what is implicit in the highly rationalized technique of that composer: 'beauty in the erection of pure structures' (Ligeti 1960: 62). There is a certain austere beauty in the way particular sonorities or constellations of notes gleam through the texture, but this is limited to individual moments which elude the larger-scale identity sought by the constructional principles. Such a beauty hardly aspires to the second immediacy that Adorno considered might emerge from rigorous construction, the result being closer to a demonstration of Adorno's observation that 'constructivist figuration has a tendency to rattle badly because it is achieved at the expense of individual impulses, ultimately of the mimetic moment itself' (1984a: 224). *Structure 1a* reveals itself to be a thesis in automatism and chance that is tempered when it threatens to contradict itself or undercut its own principles. In the words of Ligeti:

> Interacting decisions lead unavoidably to automatism, determination creates the unpredictable; and *vice versa*, neither the automatic nor the accidental can be created without decision and determining (1960: 61).

The key issue dredged by Ligeti from *Structure 1a* is the way in which identity and difference intersect. The constructional identity of the music exists only as an abstract idea, and Boulez's endeavour to make the organization of the pitch grid interlock with other components is, in essence, arbitrary: order and disorder map onto each other. Fully automated serialism accommodates the principle of universal equivalence, whereby every object is measurable against, or substitutable for, another. Though material resists the equivalence foisted on it by a system insensitive to its inner life, if there is little determinate tension between individual elements and the form, the result is capricious: control and indeterminacy overlap, miming a logic of indifference.

In all fairness, Boulez himself is acutely aware of the contradictions and problems inherent in *Structures*, referring to the collection as a 'document' or 'what Barthes might call a reduction of style to the degree zero' (1976: 55). The serial manipulations function as a base line from which to start composition.

> In *Structures* you can follow the process of reintroducing personal invention; it is very clear, though not perhaps to everyone because I later deliberately muddled things by not printing the pieces in chronological order, so as to give an anti-evolutionary impression of the whole (1976: 56).

This desire to start again from scratch is also expressed, though in a different way, by Ligeti's *Atmosphères* (1961): Boulez takes serial procedures to their limits and begins to reintroduce invention, Ligeti adopts as his starting point the thick sonority produced by rampant serialism and refines it. The experience of *Structure 1a* was obviously a turning point for both composers. Boulez came to react strongly against the intellectual environment of *Structures* and echoed many of the points raised by Adorno in 'The Ageing', but it is not clear whether the article was an active ingredient in this reconsideration. Boulez acknowledges that wrinkles of non-identity cannot be squeezed out of the system, that they will appear as the interjections of chance; thus if extreme serialism amounts to, in Boulez's words, 'cutting a slice of chance', one solution is to explore that avenue by actually using chance (1971: 25). This option was spelt out in Cage's lecture, 'Indeterminacy', given on his first visit to Darmstadt in 1958.

Boulez strongly resisted the path to indeterminacy, but the impact of Cage's innovations certainly spurred him to formulate his own ideas on freedom and control in composition. This issue is at stake throughout the whole of Boulez's subsequent infatuation with Mallarmé and is tackled directly in the essay 'Alea', where the pursuit both of extreme objectivity and of extreme arbitrariness are judged to be equally mistaken. He is scathing of attempts to grant the performer considerable freedom to make random choices, since these amount to shifting the compositional decision-making process from the composer to the interpreter; thereby delaying an inevitable and intrinsic part of the compositional act. Instead, Boulez argues that modification of the text by a performer should be implied by that text, and this 'interpretative chance' should be embedded 'like a watermark' (1964: 46). This view finds a practical outlet in the Third Piano Sonata, where he tries to create an environment in which the limited compositional decisions to be taken by the performer are framed by characteristics of the material and chance is used within defined parameters. Boulez is well aware of the implications chance procedures have for the autonomy of music, and is anxious to stem their full flow:

> The 'finite' quality of western art, with its closed circle, is respected, while introducing the element of 'chance' from the open circle of oriental art (1964: 51).

The substance of this statement is that Boulez wishes to protect autonomy from collapsing into heteronomy, but rejects the notion of art as a fixed and immutable object and hopes to align the disintegration of illusion with an attribute of another culture. Whatever the feasibility of such an art form, there is an implication in the idea that he is frustrated by the illusory property of autonomy, but recognizes that critical distance is dependent upon it.

Certainly, Boulez has accepted another part of Adorno's argument: extreme automatism, whether generated by a system or by chance procedures, threatens to erase the subject; and he understands that the composer's subjectivity, when engaged with technique, produces a creative tension, as opposed to indifferent indeterminacy.

> The less one chooses, the more the single possibility depends on the pure chance encounter of the sound objects; the more one chooses, the more what happens depends on the coefficient of chance implied by the subjectivity of the composer. It is the more

or less loose play of this antinomy which will excite interest in any passage of a work composed in such a way (1964: 48).

But Boulez's conception of advanced material is more absolute than Adorno's formulation of the idea. At this stage, Boulez, like Heidegger, attempts to stand outside the antitheses of identity and non-identity: material is understood, almost transcendentally, as something capable of containing its own tension. From an Adornian perspective, of course, this tension is a sedimentation in musical material of an historical stage of social rationalization: there is no transcendental viewpoint in philosophy nor any state of musical material able to contain it. Boulez's mistake as a theoretician, though less so as a composer, was the attempt to buttress the disintegration of modernist form from a non-existent outside instead of working within the contradiction. But the extent of Boulez's theoretical activity at this time demonstrates a growing awareness that artistic activity is linked to aesthetic understanding; indeed his writings have followed a line of development extending from rigorous concern with technical musical matters to wide-ranging aesthetic discussion and interest. Robert Piencikowski's introduction observes that this tendency is already present in the early essays contained in *Stocktakings from an Apprenticeship*:

> Technical problems occupied the front of the stage – and it was the questions raised by the means of giving them concrete realization that led to that of their aesthetic validity. In a word, one passed from the stage at which technique made do with an indefinite aesthetic, to the stage at which it is the aesthetic, made conscious by necessity, that will determine the technical means (Boulez 1991: xv).

Boulez's continual search for an advanced material capable of circumnavigating the aporias of high modernism has led him to absorb an active and self-reflective aesthetic dimension into his music.

Boulez's Third Piano Sonata

The Third Piano Sonata is undoubtedly a musical entity in its own right, but it is embedded within a complex of ideas more preoccupied with the possibility of an advanced musical language than with the existence of an individual work. The Sonata represents a landmark not only in Boulez's oeuvre, but in the language and concepts of post-war music because it involves a sustained attempt to incorporate the dialectic of control and freedom within the material itself. The whole aggregate of ideas is enriched by the influences of Joyce and Mallarmé, an earlier literary modernism being used both to loosen and to revive a flagging high modernism in music.

The Sonata is dubbed – following Joyce – 'a work in progress', and is envisaged in five movements, or *formants* as the composer calls them. The term *formant* is intended to convey, in Boulez's words, the idea of a form 'understood as a specific fixed structure, which is, however, movable as whole: thus the *formant* in itself is fixed, and as an entity it allows no intrusion into its homogeneous structure, but its place within a work may vary' (1976: 81). The sequence of the five envisaged *formants* is mobile: *Constellation/Constellation-Miroir* forms the immovable central kernel and the other four formants gravitate around it in two concentric orbits, giving a total number of eight permutations in which the *formants* can be arranged for performance (see Figure 3.1).

Boulez intended to create a mobile form whose structure would stem directly from properties of the musical material, this resolve leading him to an idiosyncratic development of serialism that Stahnke (1979) terms late serialism and Trenkamp (1976) calls post-serialism. The method of serial proliferation used in the second *formant*, *Trope*, is outlined in *Boulez on Music Today* (1971: 73–4). Example 3.1 demonstrates that the basic series is divided into four groups: (a), (b), (c) and (d), which contain, respectively, 4, 1, 4 and 3 notes. Group (a) holds two generative intervals, the semitone and the 4th, 'which will create the vertical and horizontal relationships (E–F/B–F♯; E–B/F–F♯); the connecting intervals are the augmented 4th and the whole tone (F–B; F♯–E)' (1971: 73). Groups (b) and (d) can be combined to form a four-note group, (b/d), which corresponds to (a) transposed down a minor 3rd and in a different permutation, giving vertical relationships of the augmented 4th and the whole tone (G♯–D/C♯–E♭), and horizontal, or connecting, relationships of the semitone and the 4th (G♯–D♯/D–E♭; D–C♯/E♭–G♯).[3] Group (c) 'is composed of two isomorphic elements, minor 3rds (G–B♭/C–A) observing globally the transposition of a whole tone (G–A/B♭–C)' (1971: 73). This group also contains the semitone and 4th characteristic of groups (a) and (b/d), generating an obscure symmetry that is weakened by the fact that (b) and (d) can be separated (that is,

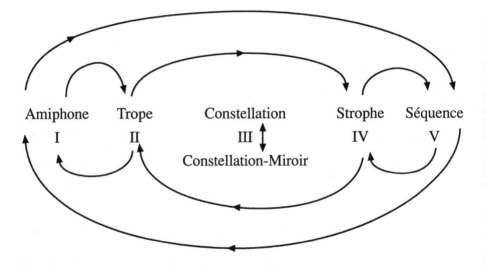

Figure 3.1 (Boulez 1986a: 153)

Example 3.1: basic series used in *Trope*

Boulez on Music Today, © Schott Musik International GmbH. Reproduced by permission.

troped) by (c). The linking intervals, or dividing lines, between the four groups are tone, semitone and 4th; these increase the homogeneity of the series but blur the boundaries between groups. The distinction between homogeneity and heterogeneity in the series is therefore based on whether certain qualities are drawn out instead of others.

In *Trope* Boulez uses the basic series to generate four 'privileged series'. These are derived from the four permutations of the basic series: (a), (b), (c), (d); (b), (c), (d), (a); (c), (d), (a), (b); (d), (a), (b), (c). Each of these permutations can be extended to produce alternating statements of the series in retrograde-inversion and prime orderings – the first and last cells of each sequence overlapping with its neighbours (see Example 3.2). The four privileged series extend the play of identity and non-identity inherent within the basic series. The isomorphism between the basic series and the privileged series which proliferate from it is, however, abstract: neither the altered permutations of elements within over-lapping groups, nor the retrograde-inversions are particularly easy to recognize aurally, but the high density of tones, semitones and 4ths does lend a certain homogeneity to the whole battery of material.

Trope's title refers to the practices of monodic extension in Gregorian chant, and it is divided into four fragments which Boulez calls 'developments': *Texte*, *Parenthèse*, *Commentaire* and *Glose*. The *formant* may begin or end with any of these, but having chosen a starting point, the performer must follow the cyclical order of the remaining three developments. *Commentaire* is, however, mobile, with the result that there are alternative placings for one or both of *Commentaire* and *Glose* in each of the four permutations. The developments trope one another and within the developments themselves Boulez also introduces secondary tropes, either working them into the 'text' or placing them in parentheses. *Trope* expands upon the premiss that the grouping of individual elements within the basic series and the permutations of these groups supply the connections between the material and its flexible form; indeed there is a troping group (c) that matches the mobility of *Commentaire*. Table 3.1 shows the possible orderings given by Boulez of the developments in *Trope*, alongside potential arrangements of the series groups. There is thus a correlation, on an abstract level, between the eight permutations of the series groups and the eight envisaged arrangements of both *Trope*'s developments and of the Sonata's *formants*.

Table 3.1

1/   TPCG   TPGC
     abcd   abdc

2/   PCGT   PGCT
     bcda   bdca

3/   CGTP   CTPG
     cdab   cabd

4/   GCTP   GTPC
     dcab   dabc

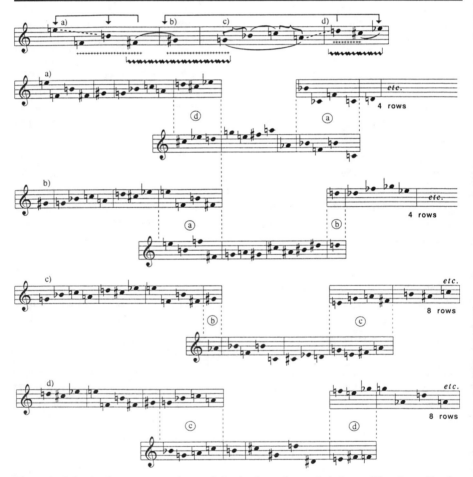

Example 3.2: the four permutations of the basic series and their proliferations (Boulez 1971: 74)

Example 3.3: 1st privileged series

© Universal Edition Ltd. Reproduced by permission.

In an exhaustive study of *Trope*, Manfred Stahnke has shown that each development is based around one of the four privileged series. In *Texte* and *Parenthèse* the serial procedures and their derivations, though disguised, are possible to follow. The material of *Commentaire* and especially *Glose* is, however, so remote from its origin that it is questionable whether the music is serial at all.

   Texte is partitioned into thirteen sections: each one comprises a permutation of the groups, (a), (b), (c) and (d) – defined by interval – of the basic series and its transpositions. The thirteen sections also correspond with the thirteen groups of the 1st privileged series (shown in Example 3.3), and the appropriate notes for

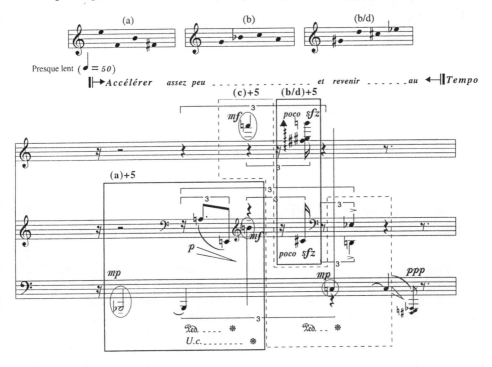

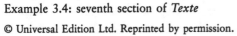

Example 3.4: seventh section of *Texte*

© Universal Edition Ltd. Reprinted by permission.

each group from the privileged series are made prominent by techniques such as duration or placing. Example 3.4 shows the seventh section of *Texte*: it has the group ordering (a), (c), (b/d), it transposes the basic series by +5 semitones and its central pitches are B♭, F, B and C (circled in Example 3.4). The interlocking of groups is fairly convoluted: (a) and (b/d) form defined partitions, but (c) cuts across them in both register and succession. The four central pitches of the privileged series are emphasized by means of duration and dynamics; they also etch the three strata of the section.

The majority of the auxiliary notes in *Texte* occur between sections, serving as both transitions and breaks; in Derridean terms, one might call them hinges or folds. These embellishments can be reduced to twelve-note sets (Stahnke has

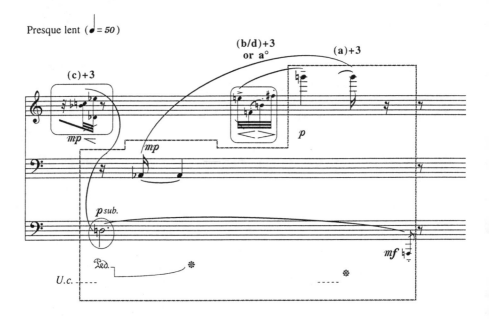

Example 3.5: twelfth section of *Texte*

identified four such collections in *Texte*), but many of the notes are not directly related to the underlying serial scheme and others connect with it in an ambiguous fashion. Initially, the auxiliary notes constellate around central pitches from the privileged series and echo aspects of the main section: in the first section, for example, the framing grace notes outline the opening 7th, but by section 8 auxiliaries have crossed the partitions, though they are within the serial order and pre-echo the pitch organization of the main section. In section 12 (shown in Example 3.5) functions are more ambiguous: the opening group of auxiliary notes frames the set and constellates around the central pitch, D (twelfth partition of 1st privileged series, see Example 3.3), yet it is also group (c) +3. The next nest of auxiliary notes occurs inside the section and constellates around the G, which is not a central pitch. This nest functions as group (b/d) + 3, but because of the transposition is also (a) at its original pitch and ordering; thus distinctions between the main event and its embellishment are blurred, though the meticulous pedal marks are designed to prevent non-auxiliary notes from becoming completely obscured. In vintage Derridean fashion, the frame and its content merge, the inside and the outside overlap. Despite the crossover of functions, stability is maintained here by the fact that the auxiliaries do not cut in as a separate order but, instead, are absorbed into the serial context. When the auxiliaries do operate outside the series elsewhere in this development, they generally use the intervals that define the series: tone, semitone and 4th.

In *Parenthèse* the inessential notes – the tropes – are, as the title suggests, expanded into bracketed interpolations, marked *Libre*, which make up the bulk of the piece, and any of these can be omitted at the performer's discretion. The *Tempo* sections constitute a single statement of the 2nd privileged series, almost entirely in the correct sequence, but the succession is cut into by the interjections of the *Libre* passages (see Example 3.6). The *Libre* sections are also based on the 2nd privileged series but in a considerably more complex way than the *Tempo* sections: Boulez uses the four overlapping parts of the series as four separate entities which are superimposed as well as juxtaposed. The groups are so interlocked and spread out by this process that they lose their identity, only the characteristic intervals providing a vestige of the series. Boulez has allowed the chaotic tendencies inherent within the serial framework to cut across an ordered exposition in a very direct way. The symmetry of the series is interrupted by a chaotic version of the same series – though only the analyst will observe this nicety – thereby rendering *Parenthèse* a bare statement of identity and difference, but the interplay of transparent and dense textures makes the dialectic of order and chaos perceptible.

The use of interlocking sub-series, taken from the privileged series, is widespread in *Commentaire*. The *Tempo* and *Libre* sections in this formant do not each belong to separate organizations, nor are they self-contained statements of a series; instead, they are parts of the same morphology. Stahnke identifies three structural layers in this movement, but acknowledges that the highly ramified second one may be generated by anonymous configurations rather than by any intention on the part of Boulez. On the first structural level, in Stahnke's analysis, the 3rd privileged series is defined, in a highly cryptic manner, by the number of times its pitches occur; on the hypothetical second stratum, irregular configurations of pitch collections, which could belong to the 1st privileged set, are placed over the 3rd privileged series; on the third level, the complete transpositions of the basic series are used, though they do not occur in any of the privileged series. Except as a frame for the composer or a conundrum for the analyst, the serial order of *Commentaire* is meaningless, since the music functions by means of gesture and is articulated by the least defined components

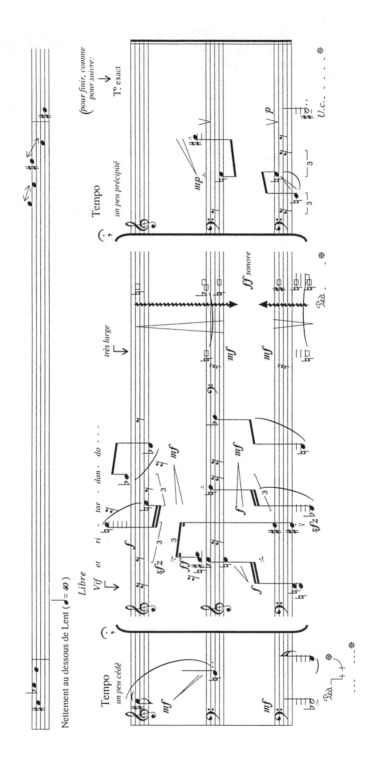

Example 3.6: end of 2nd privileged series and of *Parenthèse*

© Universal Edition Ltd. Reprinted by permission.

of the medium: intensity, texture, timbre and tempo fluctuation. The effect is of a temporal flux of points and blocks of sound (the ingredients of *Constellation-Miroir*), defined by the precise pedalling – surely the influence of late Debussy. The deep trills at the end of *Commentaire* elicit an enjoyment in sound for its own sake, and constitute a climax in *Trope*. Such moments are mediated by technique, but have an affinity with intuitive and non-cognitive knowledge, suggesting that the least calculated events in this music are of the greatest mimetic significance.

Glose does not employ the complex overlapping layers found in *Commentaire*, but its derivation from the 4th privileged series is extremely obscure: the series is defined by its absence. In the opening twelve notes of the first section, the F is repeated three times, the G twice and the D, C♯ and E♭ of group (d) are absent. Such a basis for construction obviously leaves the composer a considerable amount of freedom to make creative decisions. Like *Texte*, *Glose* can be divided into sections – twenty-five of them – but the boundaries are considerably less defined. In many ways the texture of *Glose* resembles that of *Texte*, but, one might say, the paint has run a little: a ghostly outline of the first section of *Texte* can be seen and heard in the first section of *Glose* and much of its writing resembles the auxiliary note passages from *Texte*, though the actual auxiliary notes in *Glose* are bands of clusters defined by little more than contour. The music feels as if *Texte*'s embellishments have moved from the margins to the centre, and juxtapositions of raw sonorities in this music pertain to the disorder latent in *Texte*, but it is a disarray managed by Boulez's superb ear for colour. As Stahnke observes, the overall sound quality of *Glose* is less forbidding than the remainder of *Trope* because it uses tonal intervals such as 3rds and 6ths, along with occasional motivic fragments, which wipe out the serial micro-structure and dilute the all-purpose serial sound.

Stahnke demonstrates that a passage from structured logic to creative decay also takes place in the rhythmic organization of *Trope*. Boulez abandoned the integral serialist ideal of deriving the morphology of pitch and rhythmic domains from the same series, but he nevertheless maintained the possibility of a correspondence between the two. The rhythmic construction of the Third Piano Sonata is based on complex derivations from a primary cell (Stahnke 1979: 80), and the splitting of the basic pitch series into four groups is echoed by the ordering of rhythmic elements.[4] *Trope* is characterized by an alternation of highly organized rhythmic cells with improvisatory-like cells, but the primary units do exert a grip on their supplements. The sections wedged between the isomorphically organized units mainly comply with Boulez's notion of a time bubble: an event 'where only the proportions of the macro-structures are defined, giving the whole range of durational properties, from the most precise and complex definition to the most summary of statistical phenomena' (1971: 58). In all these developments the durational relationships are actually more complicated than those notated, due to changes in tempo, sometimes reached over a span of time, and potential inaccuracies in performance. In *Glose*, however, Boulez uses two methods of temporal articulation to make the organized rhythmic areas and time bubbles collapse into each other. The first applies accelerating and decelerating tempi; the second employs passages in which the tempo is defined and the overall duration of the section controlled by it is given, but relations within the segment are of undefined proportion.

Rhythmic organization in *Trope*, like the pitch scheme, is based upon an isomorphic symmetry that is allowed to collapse. The suggestion that *Glose* is to some extent *Texte* in a state of disintegration is borne out in the rhythmic domain, since there are significant correspondences between the rhythmic proportionings used in the two developments. Nevertheless, in *Texte* the overlapping rhythmic layers and the time bubbles are not particularly easy to tell apart, and *Glose* compounds the situation because, even on the level of textual analysis, the time domains are interlinked. The decay of the rhythmic system is not, however, unique to this specific order, any more than the disintegration of the pitch organization is peculiar to the particular series used: both processes are possibilities within any quasi-serial treatment of rhythm and duration.

Boulez may have chosen a serial matrix that was likely to break up, but the latent disorder manifest in this piece is present in most serial procedures. In *Texte* and in the tempo sections of *Parenthèse* the isomorphic intervallic qualities of the series are, arguably, discernible, but the wider possibility of disintegration lies in the general threat of a meaningless jumble of notes and is not linked in any meaningful way to the inbuilt instability of group (c). Likewise, the juxtaposition of order and chaos in *Parenthèse* is not intrinsically tied to the specific instance of ordered series being troped by itself, since the correlation between mobile ordering of the developments and the permutation of groups within the basic series is little more than arbitrary. Stahnke contends that 'the score, whether liked or not, contains the thesis that a series inside an open logic leads itself to absurdity' (1979: 78); and, one might add, *Structure 1a* embodies the corollary that a completely serial logic also generates incongruity. The difference, in the case of the Third Piano Sonata, is that Boulez averted absurdity by making compositional decisions in what amounts to an atonal idiom: *Glose* demolishes its own structural logic but is the most coherent development in *Trope*; it has the most success in breaking through the synthetic mobility, and the looming chaos is controlled by the composer's creative handling of temporal articulation. *Glose* is meticulously composed, yet has an improvisational feel to it and is generated from a material that has dissolved its external organization; this is what Adorno means by a pull towards the particular in modernist art. If Boulez does achieve a second immediacy here, as Adorno and Mann envisaged in *Dr Faustus*, it is by dissolving an integrated structural approach instead of by emerging on the other side of one. In *Trope* Boulez creates a feeling of spatial association but at the expense of the multi-dimensional coherence he sought; short-term processes, based on textural affinity, are gained at the cost of the progressional logic that serialism once endeavoured to provide.

The third and central *formant* of *Trope*, *Constellation/Constellation-Miroir*, is intended to be played either forwards or in retrograde. The score is printed in red and green ink: green for the groups marked *points* and red for those marked *blocs*. There are three areas of *points*, two of *blocs* and one, *Mélange*, that mixes the two types of sonority. The sequence of the sonority fields is fixed, but within each one there are alternative but defined routes. Boulez compares the mobility in this *formant* to that inherent within a map of an unknown town (an image that stands in stark contrast to the postmodernist emphasis on a familiar urban space surrounding the subject): one's choice is limited by the layout of the streets but one can decide which route to take within those boundaries (1986a: 151; 1976: 82). This formalist representation of space ties in with Boulez's 'conception of the maze in a work of art [as] one of the most considerable advances in Western thought' (1986a: 145), and his stated wish to escape a model of departure and arrival in music (1986a: 144). Such considerations expand the intellectual field of the Third Piano Sonata beyond the techniques of construction used.

Material and Disintegration

In his need to explore creatively the interaction of determinacy and indeterminacy, Boulez draws sustenance from the aesthetic of Mallarmé's projected *Livre*. The extent of the *Livre*'s influence on the Third Piano Sonata is unclear; it may have introduced large-scale mobility into a nearly completed score, since, as Nattiez points out, Scherer's edition of the *Livre* was published in March 1957 and the Sonata was premiered in the following September (Nattiez 1993: 23). The significance for Boulez of the publication was, in any case, immense: he experienced the *Livre* as a 'revelation' and as 'final proof of the necessity for poetic, aesthetic and formal renewal' (Boulez 1986a: 144). Whatever the sequence of compositional events, there is certainly a correlation between Scherer's observation that 'the book, total expression of the letter, must gather a mobility directly from the letter' (quoted, Boulez 1986a: 148), and Boulez's attempts to generate correspondences between the ordering of serial components and the mobile form of the work. Whether, however, the Sonata is composed in Adornian fashion – bottom up, from the particular to the form – is questionable because, although *Glose* approaches this ideal, it is furthest from the *formant*'s constructional principle.

Boulez divulges that 'literary affiliations played a more important part than purely musical considerations' in his conception of the Third Piano Sonata (1986a: 143), and, appropriately, his discussion of Joyce and Mallarmé is pitched on a level that raises a whole complex of issues pertaining to the possibilities of modernist art. In Boulez's view, Mallarmé and Joyce pushed the frontiers of modernism into areas that music hitherto had failed to explore: in the most advanced texts of these writers the art work becomes self-reflective, examining its own procedures and pondering its purpose. Boulez wants to bring this self-knowledge to music, so that the score becomes a text, conceived as a commentary on itself by means of tropes, grafts and constellations; it dwells on its own strategies and alludes to the possibility of its own disintegration.

Boulez's Joyce-inspired desire to create an anonymous art work – impersonal, self-reflective and independent of its creator – for all its radicalism, simply takes on as self-reflective content what Adorno decodes as the condition of bourgeois, autonomous art: the object is divorced from its artist, it traces its own trajectory through history and triggers an active dialectic between its own immanent qualities and the prevailing social circumstances. A work with this knowledge actively encoded within itself derives strength from its extreme autonomy, but also draws closer to theory and attracts attention to the historical condition of its existence. A fetish of autonomy was already a problem for Mallarmé because he failed to envisage that the material world could be both outside and inside art: that is, closed off by autonomous form, but encoded within the material. He followed the self-referentiality of art to an extreme where the art work and its medium turn in upon themselves and implode: the vigorously excluded materiality of existence floods in at the last moment. Mallarmé explores the inconsistency that so many deconstructive readings examine: on the one hand, he espouses, in an extreme way, the nineteenth-century ideology of the absolute in art and even uses music as a metaphor for this; on the other, he is conscious of language's capacity to undercut such a vision. In a sense, Mallarmé's understanding of this aporia is closer to Adorno's perception than to Paul de Man's, since, for the poet, it is not just language that undermines the absolute but also the phenomena which linguistic self-referentiality seeks, in vain, to exclude. Nevertheless, Derrida's reading of Mallarmé's *Mimique* demonstrates the interplay of inside and outside that is such a strong theme in deconstruction, and draws out Mallarmé's unwanted discovery that 'when a literary text refers to or mirrors itself, it necessarily also refers outside itself' (Carroll 1987: 101).

As a theoretician, Boulez opened a flow between critical reflection and compositional practice, but failed to acknowledge the power of the deconstructive force unleashed in his own work to undercut the contrived system of mobility. The composer must intervene to prevent the multiple possibilities inscribed within the work from collapsing into the unordered outside world. Boulez's dilemma, which echoes Mallarmé's attempt to encode art as a private religion, touches, in a strange crossover, on the historical avant garde's attempt to destroy idealism in art and to collapse art into life. This short-circuit was not lost on Adorno who comments:

> The chaotic moment and radical spiritualization coincide in their rejection of shiny comforting notions of what life is all about. This establishes a rarely recognized affinity between highly spiritualized art, such as poetry in the tradition of Mallarmé, and the dream confusion of surrealism (1984a: 138).

Whether one attacks autonomy from the outside or implodes it from the inside, the net result is fragmentation. At its extreme, neither procedure is sustainable: an external attack on autonomy becomes an empty gesture; disintegration from within can only be taken so far before it collapses into the chaos of the outside that it is trying to hold at bay.

The overlap between *art pour l'art* and avant-gardism returns in the relations between Boulez's controlled use of freedom and Cage's chance procedures: while

Boulez tries to contain the dialectic within the material, Cage anticipates and precipitates a postmodern jettisoning of highly constructed art. Boulez's strategy involves a paradoxical double manoeuvre: he recognizes the instrumental, fetishistic tendency of high modernism, as evinced by integral serialism, yet attempts to solve the problem by means of a sufficiently advanced material; he tries to ontologize the paradox, so to speak, to transcend the extremes of identity and non-identity by making their interplay an intrinsic quality of the material, rather than something that emerges in the work. Put in the language of semiology, Boulez concedes the capacity for signifiers to break away from the intended signification of integral serialism, but, paradoxically, tries to create a level of signification that would control this difference; a difference that, from Derrida's point of view, is endemic to signification, and, from Adorno's perspective marks a turn towards non-identity in a specific historical condition of musical material. Boulez's formulation of the problem attempts to upgrade an over-determined material, which has been brought to the limits of its own feasibility, into a super-material that will engulf its own paradox. Adorno, in *Vers une musique informelle*, envisaged a third way between 'the jungle of *Erwartung*' and the 'tectonics of *Die glückliche Hand*', in which sections would be 'placed in a dynamic relationship, comparable to the relationship of subordinate clauses and main clause in grammar. Boulez's work', he continues, 'with so-called parentheses, an idea that goes back to Schumann, probably points in this direction' (1992b: 311–12). The problem, however, with Boulez's realization of this idea is that the parenthetical quality of the music is inscribed in the material at such an abstract level that it does not reveal itself as a logic of associative alternatives: particularity is inscribed within the system instead of generating a life of its own.

The chaos encountered by the rigorous rationality of the Third Piano Sonata is, in Adornian terms, inherent within the endless substitution generated by universal fungibility and its associated identity logic. The interaction of controlled organization with mobile forms does, then, have cognitive and ethical implications, and pertains to the more general social prospect of formulating a coherent mode of construction that does not repress the specific. The challenge, both for music and for social forms, is to achieve a non-subsumptive logic, but this task is something to be faced anew in each creative act and is not likely to be accomplished in advance by a developed musical syntax. The idea of mobile complexes generating an overall constellation is seemingly redolent of Adorno's understanding of his own critical theory, as practised in *Aesthetic Theory*. Both works put forward intersections of ideas that cannot be reduced to one stable configuration, but the differences between approaches are crucial: Adorno's technique is designed to release the history and subjectivity within the constellation, whereas Boulez's flexibility derives from something predetermined within the system. The contingency that Boulez channels through open forms is potentially receptive to the demands of the particular; but if mobility is harnessed by a compositional system instead of crossing through it, the music will map onto standard discourses and lose its sense of otherness. The more integrated an art work, the nearer to pure form it becomes, the greater the likelihood of its components being perceived as entities apart from the system; but these will be comprehended indifferently unless they participate in an active forcefield. In the Third Piano Sonata the potential tension between material and form is weakened by the synthetic quality of the material, with the result that extreme autonomy stands close to extreme heterogeneity, instead of generating what Adorno calls determinate irreconcilability.

The Sonata stands on the brink of its own impossibility and even crosses it if we take into account its unfinished state and the composer's inability, so far, to find a way of realizing his vision of the fifth *formant*, *Séquence*. Yet Boulez has wrested some victories from the aporia in which the work resides: his extraordinary ear for texture and spacing produces moments of sensuous beauty in this music. His mistake was to try to build mimesis, through mobility, into the system: mimesis actually emerges from the inner life of sounds and establishes its own momentum; it is found in those moments of estranged immediacy, distinguished by their sheer sound quality, that are facilitated but not defined by the Sonata's underlying systematic logic, since they are able to establish secondary relations. Boulez brought serialism to the brink of chaos in *Structure 1a*, but in the Sonata he intervened as a composer so that a potential obliteration of meaning becomes a multiplicity of meaning. Perhaps unintentionally, Boulez registered that interpreters, or 'readers', may decode the music in ways other than those built intentionally into the compositional system, generating mimesis by interactive process. Thus, instead of being simply mis-heard, the music opens creative possibilities.

Cage

John Cage represents a curious link between the historical avant-garde movement – embodied in a friendship with Marcel and Tenny Duchamp – and the second avant garde of New York postmodernism. His early avant-gardism is evinced by a predilection for noise and environmental sound, drawing upon the ideas of the Futurists, and is fed by the American experimental tradition. But until, and sometimes during, his use of chance procedures in the 1950s, Cage's preference for raw sound was tempered by a concern for control and organization which, though already idiosyncratic, was commensurate with the rationality of European high modernism. The interest in organized noise is apparent in the *First Construction in Metal* (1939), where pitched and unpitched percussion are combined with the broad frequency sounds of thunder sheets and glissandi on the strings of an open piano. A close-knit method of organization, based on durations, is used: sixteen units – each of sixteen bars in the proportion 4, 3, 2, 3, 4 – are followed by a nine-bar coda. On the micro level, the cells that mark the proportional divisions are defined by changes in instrumentation; the larger-scale proportional divisions are marked by tempo and sonority changes. Much of this particular scheme is audible, though the derivation from the number sixteen is an arbitrary restriction for the composer. In a manner akin to integral serialism, Cage used a predetermined compositional scheme; but the serialist fetish of pitch organization is abandoned and the material is not bonded to the method (form). A load-bearing proportional scheme that repeats its identity on two levels generates a neutral way of placing diverse phenomena within a network of equivalence.

The composer has characterized the development of his compositional technique as follows:

> Chromatic composition dealing with the problem of keeping repetition of individual tones as far apart as possible (1933–34); composition for the dance, film and theatre (1935–); composition with rhythmic structures (the whole having as many parts as each unit has small parts, and these, large and small, in the same proportion) (1939–56); intentionally expressive composition (1938–51); composition using charts and moves thereon, (1951); composition using chance operations (1951–); composition using templates made or found (1952–); composition using observation of imperfections in the paper upon which it was written (1952–); composition without a fixed relation of parts to score (1954–); composition indeterminate of its performance (1958–) (quoted in Francis 1976: 7).

The range is not quite as diverse as it seems – several techniques described are different ways of generating chance procedures – yet it demonstrates that the composer perceived some distinct changes of method in his development. These alterations were not always marked by a clear dividing line: composition with rhythmic structures, according to this plan, extended into the first five years of chance music. What is explicit, however, is the impetus towards ever more depersonalized methods of construction, and this tendency is realized in the transition from placing entities in a form to allowing elements to discard form.

The Concerto for Prepared Piano (1950–51) evinces a palpable transition from organized rhythmic structure to chance procedures. In the first movement only the sound aggregates for the orchestra are arranged on a chart; in the second movement piano and orchestra have a chart each; in the third movement the two instruments are combined on a single chart. The presence of the *I Ching* as a decision-making tool in the third movement is apparent in the parity of sound and silence. Cage says of his use of charts:

> All this brings me closer to a 'chance' or if you like to an *un-aesthetic* choice. I keep, of course, the means of rhythmic structure feeling that it is the 'espace sonore' in which [each] of these sounds may exist and change. Composition becomes 'throwing sound into silence' and rhythm which in my Sonatas had been one of breathing becomes now one of a flow of sound and silence (Nattiez 1993: 78; my emphasis).

Cage's desire to make an unaesthetic choice, like Adorno's *Aesthetic Theory*, recognizes that the traditional aesthetic categories of beauty and taste are inappropriate to modern art. The difference is that Adorno reworks these categories, through materialism and modernism, whereas Cage simply drops them, with the result that his creativity cannot comprehend the forces that made traditional aesthetics irrelevant.

Pritchett points out that the Concerto is built from twenty-three units – each of twenty-three bars – which are arranged into seven sections of varying length: 3, 2, 4; 4, 2, 3; 5 (1988: 56). Over this structure Cage superimposed a three-movement concerto plan, each movement corresponding to one of the three larger divisions of the seven sections. The sound collections used in this work derive from the composer's experiences with the prepared piano: depressing a single key on this instrument will not necessarily produce a single frequency, but may, as the composer indicates, generate an 'aggregate of pitches and timbres' (Cage 1968: 25). The chart for the orchestral part of the first movement of the Concerto indicates associations between the chosen aggregates and the fourteen instruments or instrumental groups; the orchestral score was constructed by making moves of 'down 2, over 3, up 4 etc.' about the chart (Nattiez 1993: 93).

Cage constructed the single chart used in the third movement from the two distinct charts employed for the piano and orchestra in the second movement, making decisions by tossing three coins and consulting the I Ching. Though the actual procedures used are complicated, the principle is straightforward: the combinations of heads and tails produced by throwing the coins translate, in accordance with the I Ching, into a strong, stationary line, a weak, stationary line, a strong line moving towards a weak line and vice versa. By associating the orchestra with a strong, stationary line and the piano with a weak, stationary line, Cage was able to fill the cells of the single chart with the corresponding cells taken from the separate piano and orchestra charts. For lines moving to their opposite, Cage composed cells combining piano and orchestra. By again using the I Ching, he then constructed procedures for moving about the charts, and these included the possibility of selecting empty cells which transcribe into the silences characteristic of the third movement. In this movement the underlying rhythmic structuring is obscured, but it is by undermining the organization of pitch and harmony that Cage achieves the erasure of history, habit and subjectivity that he sought. Cage comments on these depersonalized methods of construction as follows:

> By making moves on the charts I freed myself from what I had thought to be freedom, and which actually was only the accretion of habits and tastes. But in the Concerto the moves brought about the new freedom only in so far as concerned the sounds (Nattiez 1993: 94).

The next stage, obviously, was to apply chance procedures to the other components of music, and that is exactly what Cage undertook in Music of Changes. This four-volume piano work bears comparison with Structure 1a. Like the latter, the material of the Music of Changes was predetermined by charts, but in contrast to Structure 1a, the charts were interpreted by chance techniques. Music of Changes is linked to earlier works by the use of an 'espace sonore' and by a predetermined array of sounds. The rhythmic structure is based around a sequence of numbers – 3, 5, $6\frac{3}{4}$; $6\frac{3}{4}$, 5, $3\frac{1}{8}$ – which form a lopsided symmetry when read forwards or backwards. On the micro level, this number sequence determines the number of 4/4 bars within each unit; on the macro level, the number of units within each section. The fractions in the sequence are not, however, realized completely accurately on the macro level: the last sequence of Volume 4, for example, should, strictly speaking, involve fractions such as an $\frac{1}{8}$ of $\frac{3}{4}$ of a bar.

There is a much greater congruence between the charts and the *I Ching* in *Music of Changes* than there was in the Concerto: Cage used the sixty-four hexagrams of the *I Ching* as a model for his grids. Each hexagram – again constructed by translating coin throws into lines – corresponds to an element from a chart, though in fact only the durations chart has sixty-four elements, including silences with allocated lengths; the others contain blank or immobile (unchanging) elements. Charts were constructed for sounds, durations, dynamics, tempi and density of superimposed events, the sounds used ranging from single pitches to complex objects that include auxiliary notes. Unlike Boulez, who, in *Structure 1a*, tried to organize attack and intensity separately, Cage combined them on a single chart, according to a system whereby only sixteen numbers produce changes; the others maintain the status quo. Despite this control there is, nevertheless, an unrealistically big dynamic range extending from *pppp* to *ffff*. Boulez, to a large extent, corrected the contradictory and unplayable markings produced by his dynamics and accents charts; Cage leaves them to the performer to sort out: Example 3.7 shows massive dynamic changes taking place within the space of brief events. Problems of density were confronted by both composers: Boulez controlled the number of serial threads in *Structure 1a*, while Cage modified the thickness of texture by using super-imposition charts to regulate the density of events. Because the durations were derived by means of cumulative fractions, they were not easily represented by conventional notation: Cage's solution was to express duration in terms of the horizontal distance between notes, the basic unit for this scheme being $2\frac{1}{2}$ centimetres which correspond to a crotchet. Very complex duration patterns are thus generated that cannot be reproduced accurately in performance.

In the account of his compositional development given by Cage in 'Composition as Process', he argues that the structural number sequence was useful but ultimately became indeterminate and hence unnecessary (1968: 20, 22). But, despite the formidable battery of chance procedures employed in this music and the disintegration of the number sequence as a meaningful method of articulating proportion, *Music of Changes* is a highly determinate score. Little is left to chance on the written page – though the sheer difficulty generates variability in performance – and the overlaps with *Structure 1a* are remarkable, both scores exhibiting comparable extremes of register, texture and dynamics. Cage's music is, however, the more fragmented: it contains many more silences and lacks the contrapuntal flow and density of the twelve-tone threads in *Structure 1a*.

The underlying number for Boulez is twelve, for Cage it is sixty-four, but though the number twelve corresponds to the serial organization of the pitch material in the case of *Structure 1a*, when applied to the other components, it approaches the abstraction of *Music of Changes*'s underlying sixty-four. There is, nevertheless, a much closer correlation between Boulez's charts and the actual

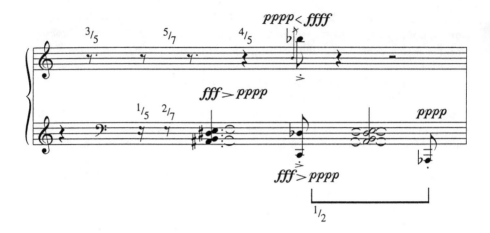

Example 3.7: *Music of Changes*, Volume 2, bar 77 (proportional duration scheme not included)

Edition Peters No. 6256

music than there is in Cage's case, because, unlike Cage, Boulez did not 'transcribe' the charts by chance techniques; indeed, Cage's highly systematized method of making chance decisions is so remote from the resulting music as to be more of a compositional discipline than the basis of a meaningful framework. Cage does not attempt to imbue his musical language with the same degree of historical necessity that Boulez craves, but accounts of Cage's compositional development do nevertheless indicate a logical unfolding of possibilities. Cage also evinces a strong idealism in his assertion that 'The essential underlying idea is that each thing is itself, that its relations with other things spring up naturally rather than being imposed by any abstraction on an artist's' part' (Nattiez 1993: 96); a statement that recognizes the crisis in traditional notions of art, but simultaneously devalues subjectivity in music. Cage's emphasis on the particular opposes Boulez's fascination with the system but also diffuses the creative tension between form and object. In the absence of such determinate irreconcilability, compositional procedure cannot prevent the listener from finding relationships of a more than provisional nature in the music, whatever the composer's intention – even granting that the sounding score is irrelevant to him. The two compositions touch at the extremes: Boulez's all-pervasive structure of identity is unable to exclude the chance surface configurations generated by local detail, and Cage's all-pervasive structure of chance and extreme particularism cannot shut out inferred identity. Both texts strive for an anonymity in which the organizational procedures work out their own consequences, and both represent extreme examples of compositional systems, with all their attendant problems.

Cage concludes from *Music of Changes*, in an exaggerated statement, that 'it is thus possible to make a musical composition the continuity of which is free of individual taste and memory (psychology) and also of the literature and "traditions" of the art' (1968: 59). He thereby describes exactly the fetish of pure objective construction, which eliminates subjective impulses, that Adorno finds objectionable in pre-compositional schemes. It is, of course, difficult for Cage's philosophy of non-intentionality that he actually tried to achieve this depersonalization, and it is hardly without significance that, despite his denial of history and tradition, he should have written an automated work at the same time as Boulez. The Cage of 1951 purveys a peculiar blend of postmodernist ideas and rationalist high modernism: the postmodernist, or avant-gardist, dimension appears in Cage admitting noises to the *Music of Changes* (a tendency more pronounced in the other important chance piece of this time, *Imaginary Landscape No. IV*, which 'accepts as its sounds those that happen to be in the air at the moment of performance' [Nattiez 1993: 95]); the high modernist aspect is reflected in his organizational procedures. But this is a homespun rationality, replacing the historical rationalism of serialism with idiosyncratic methods of organization; and Cage's negation of compositional responsibility eliminates the possibility of releasing the subjectivity embedded within the objects he discovers. In a striking contradiction, his technique mimes the indifference of instrumental rationality towards individual expression and needs, but simultaneously attempts to realize the mute otherness of objects.

Cage makes a strong distinction between compositions constructed by chance procedures that are, nevertheless, determinate, and those that are indeterminate in performance; but the margin between the two is not large, and is crossed the moment chance-based operations are handed over to the performer. When Cage made that step, and developed an interest in environmental sound, obsessive organization quickly gave way to a plurality or even a jettisoning of structures. In 'Composition as Process' Cage traces a trajectory 'from ideas of order towards no ideas of order' (1968: 20), and, having concluded that structure was not necessary in *Music of Changes*, the composer carries on to discuss a type of composition which is 'characterized by process and which is essentially purposeless' (1968: 22). In such music, chance procedures penetrate the performance of the work instead of being used solely as a compositional tool, and the score becomes more a set of instructions for performance than a representation of sounds.

Variations IV (1963) is, according to the composer's instructions, scored for 'any number of players, any sounds or combinations of sounds produced by any means, with or without other activities'. The score comprises nine transparencies and a set of instructions: seven of the transparencies are marked with a single point, the remaining two with a single circle. In conjunction with a plan of the performance space, a map is drawn up by the following procedures:

> Place one of the circles anywhere on the plan. Let the other circle and the points fall on the plan or outside it. Taking the placed circle as center, produce lines from it to each

of the points. (straight lines.) The second circle is only operative when one of the lines so produced (one or more) intersects or is tangent to it.

The piece comprises the sound events that occur along the trajectories of the lines, but these need not be actively produced and may result from a passive act, such as merely opening a window or door; a performance of *Variations IV* may coexist with any other performance and participants may wander from one component to another.

Variations IV envisages a literal multitextuality, since other activities not only enter its space but potentially take place simultaneously. It also heralds, in a limited sense, the prospect of the 'reader' as an active decoder of text, since the score is a set of instructions for an unpredictable event; but performers are discouraged from bringing their own experiences to the work by the distancing effect of the operations, which harbour the composer's distrust of subjectivity. The text encourages the bizarre prospect of intersubjective exchange, as envisaged by Habermas (see Chapter 1) and Wellmer (see Chapter 6), in an area between production and reception, but without sustenance from the lifeworld, since the procedures replicate the apparently inscrutable forces that control our lives. Drawing attention to the penetration of system integration into 'material' may indicate the absurdity of an administered life, but in this case assumes that participants have access to no other experience of subjectivity.

Cage hears the commercial recording as a variation on *Variations IV*, since, he says, 'the original piece dealt with space and space alone. And it didn't have anything to do with the sounds which happen in that space' (Cage 1976: 133); he complains that the recording eliminates the spatial aspect, so that the jumble of sounds appears to emanate from the same place inside the building, with its components equidistant. Cage describes the fundamental characteristic of *Variations IV* – when properly performed – as 'sounds coming from a distance, with a very small number of sounds coming from the spot where the audience was located and with clear distinctions of intensity. Sounds from the audience', he continues, 'should have seemed overly intense compared to those coming from greater distances' (1976: 133). The tranquillity and silences experienced in authentic performances were, according to him, lost on the recording.

Cage's notion of *Variations IV* seems to be of an acoustic environment in which place and direction are associated with sound, the work addressing the idea of simultaneous possibilities within a space. The concept of sound objects is illuminated by a comment made in a discussion of *Music for Piano*: Cage talks about 'a composing of sounds within a universe predicated upon the sounds themselves rather than upon the mind which can envisage them coming into being' (1968: 27–8). A rampant particularism is proposed that releases sounds from determinate association with one another, asking us to hear them for what they are; but the aesthetic endorses what Adorno calls natural history: a fragmented culture – itself an historical construct – is deemed natural. It would be mistaken to call Cage's emphasis on the naturalness of sounds mimetic, in the Adornian sense, because the objects are not distanced from a synthetic environment and its inbuilt mode of rationality – they are frequently the far from neutral sounds of an urban and industrial environment – nor do they become expressive by mediation through a logic of construction. Cage's stance does seek to address the immediacy of sound that high modernism had threatened to obliterate; but instead of establishing a dialectic of construction and mimesis, he attempts to collapse identity and organization into the unfettered spontaneity of sound objects, as if his source materials were not already culturally mediated.

Adorno observes of Cage's Piano Concerto that 'its only meaning and internal coherence is to be found in its rejection of every notion of coherent meaning, [it] presents us with catastrophe music at its most extreme' (1992b: 257).[5] This comment, which closely echoes its author's analysis of Beckett's *Endgame* (1991b), finds in the release of sound from meaning not, *pace* Cage, emancipation, but a crisis in subjectivity. The *Concert for Piano and Orchestra* may portray the situation of the subject after the end of the subject, but does so with indifference. If Cage's procedures reveal the administered world to be absurd, they scarcely indicate how that environment might be reconfigured, since art's illusion of being a self-contained object is so thoroughly undercut that the aesthetic artefact becomes barely distinguishable from the rest of the world.

In his Third Piano Sonata Boulez took the paradoxical step of trying to pre-empt the contingency sometimes produced by serialism, by embedding open form within the qualities of the material. Cage's approach to the duality of control and chance is more drastic: in *Music of Changes* he brought extreme order and extreme chance face to face with each other. By following the logic of his own procedures, he then extended chance operations to the performance of music, rendering it indeterminate, and thereby abandoning the organizational procedures that had generated chance methods. The correspondence between Boulez and Cage demonstrates clearly how Cage's postmodernist jettisoning of autonomy and his emphasis on the reception of art over its production stems from a strong shared interest – or so it seemed – in high modernist procedures. The overlap between *Structure 1a* and *Music of Changes* proposed above is endorsed by Boulez's enthusiasm for this piece over others by Cage: the detailed chart manipulations generate an affinity with his own work, despite the employment of chance procedures (Nattiez 1993: 133). Boulez was fascinated by Cage's use of sonic aggregates, or sound complexes, at an early stage; particularly as they appeared in the works for prepared piano. It was this shared preoccupation that brought the two composers closest together, and eventually pushed them furthest apart: close, in that Boulez hears the sound complex as a neutral component that makes traditional harmonic direction obsolete and thereby necessitates quasi-serialist organization capable of varying the timbre, duration and dynamics for each event (Boulez 1991: 135); far, because for Cage these sounds seek an identity of their own that relinquishes structural control. The tension between these two understandings of the sound object emanates from what Adorno identifies as the pull towards the particular in modernist art. As will be seen in Chapter 6, the difference becomes acute in *Roaratorio* and *Répons*, two later works by each composer. *Roaratorio*'s layered events generate complexes that are torn between their own individuality and the neutral mass of sound; Boulez's interest in a syntax of sound objects remains active in *Répons*, but here the complexes assert their own space and particularity, while engaging in the logic of the composition. The two composers' musical concerns were poles apart by the time these works were composed; and it was, of course, the issue of whether chance should be controlled that separated them. At stake, ultimately, in this dispute is the autonomy of art.

In a more extreme sense than Boulez, Cage breaks down the distinction between the inside and outside of the work, composer and performer, performer and audience, by emphasizing the reception of a text over its production. Throwing the responsibility for interpretation onto the performers and audience, makes Cage initially appear the more enlightened composer, especially when this openness is compared with the circumscribed choices granted to the performer of Boulez's Third Piano Sonata. Indeed, he anticipates 'readers' more active than Adorno's production-based aesthetics usually envisage, but the crossover between the outside and the inside of art is already a mainstay of Adorno's aesthetics and Cage, in effect, tries to collapse one side of the dialectic, formal autonomy, into its other, socially-sedimented material. He breaks the frame of autonomous art and releases its contents into the outside world, swapping the outside for the inside, instead of, like Adorno and Derrida, exploring how the two dimensions intersect each other. Unfortunately, by attempting to eliminate subjectivity from music, or at least from its production, Cage weakens the potential for engagement with the shards of a reified system that he releases. Boulez's comment that 'he [Cage] had a beneficial influence to the extent that he helped to burst the fetters of 1950s discipline' perhaps registers Cage's greatest achievement as an historical intervention (quoted in Nattiez 1993: 23). Nevertheless, in felicitous circumstances the life histories and collective experiences that performers and audiences bring to Cage's events may be touched by the estranged objects they encounter.

Notes

1. This point is made by Peter Bürger 1985: 122.
2. Elsewhere Adorno speculates that 'highly rational and transparent principles of construction' might 'invalidate basic bourgeois categories' (1990: 225).
3. Pitch-class sets (a) and (b/d) share the same prime form, 4–6, in Allen Forte's list.
4. Boulez's techniques for generating rhythmic cells and layering derive from the principles outlined in 'Possibly . . .' (Boulez 1991), but he does deviate from his own rules. In this article Boulez is preoccupied with a basic structural isomorphism in pitch organization, which is retained – at least on an abstract level – through convoluted transmutation.
5. It is unclear from the term 'klavierkonzert von Cage' whether Adorno is referring to the Concerto for Prepared Piano or the *Concert for Piano and Orchestra* (GS 16: 483). I take him to be discussing the latter work.

4   Modernism Inside Out

Music and Deconstruction

Adorno died in 1969, leaving his *Aesthetic Theory* unfinished. In 1967 the Parisian philosopher Jacques Derrida published three works – *Speech and Phenomena*, *Writing and Difference* and *Of Grammatology* – which were to have an enormous impact, not only on French philosophy, but also on the understanding of texts and institutions in a much wider sphere. These books, in conjunction with his subsequent prolific output, have been presented by Derrida, and interpreted by his followers, as representing a radical break with the tradition of Western metaphysics; a tradition that Derrida, in keeping with his Heideggerian background, understands as inextricably bound up with notions of origin and presence. Though couched in different terminology, Derrida's deconstruction of metaphysics, which is undertaken by exploring the rift between intention and meaning in text (understood as a broad range of human activity), bears much in common with Adorno's vigilant practice of exposing the heterogeneous qualities of experience repressed by systems of thought aspiring to absolutist status. It is, however, inadequate to regard Adorno as a deconstructionist *avant la lettre*: meaning, for him, is couched in terms of a philosophy of concept and object; in Derrida's case, meaning is formed within a system of semiotic difference.

Deconstruction's recognition that the instability within a network of signs can be used to turn the discourse against a dominant reading is of significance for much of the music discussed in this book. As demonstrated in Chapter 3, Derrida's insight that the limits of Mallarmé's thought are enclosed in the very folds of his own text has a parallel in Boulez's Third Piano Sonata. The paradoxical overlap between serialism and indeterminacy, whereby arbitrariness seeps into total determinacy and determinacy leaks into chance procedures, is mirrored by the transition from structuralism to poststructuralism. Structuralism is an interpretative method and serialism is a constructional technique; they are linked by a common aim of reducing heterogeneity to an underlying scheme, but neither was able to prevent awkward details from eluding the system. The universal claims of structuralism, like the unifying ideal of serialism, already house the knowledge that will undermine them; deconstruction is at once a continuous transformation of the premises of structuralism and a violent rupture which blows them apart. Something similar might be said of the transition from serialism to post-serialism and indeterminacy, the spatial plan of Boulez's Third Piano Sonata standing on the borderline between the static ordering of structuralism and the temporal deferral of deconstruction. Deconstruction is situated on the cusp between modernity and postmodernity, working within the framework of modernity but challenging its institutions and categories; like the music of Ligeti, it is both inside and outside modernism's institutions.

An interest in Heidegger is shared by both Adorno and Derrida, but it is a more active force in Derrida's work. Adorno argues that there is a sleight of hand concealed in Heidegger's metaphysics of Being and presence, since the system is held together by an idea outside of its own frame of reference; by what Derrida would designate as a transcendental signified. Indeed, Derrida regards the problem of ontology in Heidegger as a manifestation of a suppression symptomatic of the whole of Western metaphysics, hence his texts are shot through with Heideggerian references to Being and presence. As well as owing a debt to phenomenology, Derrida's intellectual position is rooted in the disciplines of semiology and structuralism, which have their own traditions. One of his main lines of attack on logocentrism is derived from Saussure's observation that signifiers and signifieds exist in a relational system governed by arbitrary difference. Derrida's insight is that the gap between signifier and signified can only be closed to make a sign by imposing stability on a system of difference, and he finds just such a contrived simultaneity in attempts to valorize the spoken word over the alleged artificiality of writing.

Derrida's broad, and frequently alluded to, understanding of writing emerges from a detailed examination of the work of Jean-Jacques Rousseau, in particular the *Essay on the Origin of Languages* (Derrida 1974). Through a rigorous reading of the text, Derrida argues that, although Rousseau purportedly claims to emphasize the naturalness of speech over the secondary abstractness of writing, in fact he cannot exclude the supplementary role of writing from pure speech: 'he [Rousseau] says or *describes* that which he *does not wish to say*: articulation and therefore the space of writing operates at the origin of language' (Derrida 1974: 229). Rousseau contends that articulation is the defining feature of language in its pure state, in which it functions as a means of enunciating expression, but this contention is problematic: articulation already supposes the spaces between units of meaning that are characteristic of written language; any dependence on articulation implies a lack in language's original purity which has to be filled. Articulation is not, therefore, a manifestation of sensibility but an intrinsic aspect of it, constituting a structure of deferral that is a function of writing, and thus antithetical to a conception of language as natural, direct expression. The supplementary role of writing can, however, become so advanced that it assumes its own self-presence, as is sometimes the case with notational systems (and this tendency has been noted in high modernism), thereby rearticulating the lack that it is trying to fill at the origin. On the other hand, Derrida's discussion of music within the context of writing provides a timely reminder that even improvisation contains the articulatory features characteristic of musical notation.

In Derrida's text, the notion of writing, or *arche* writing, overlaps with his usage of the terms *trace* and *différance*, amongst others, which are intended to convey the unthinkable lack of an origin at the origin, or the ultimate instability of a system of signification. *Différance* is a variant spelling of *différence*, designed to draw attention to the contingency of the sign and to indicate the dual function of both differing and deferring. The non-simultaneity of *différance* is considered, by Derrida, to be at work within all thought: every attempt to fold discourse back in order to reveal an origin, or to step outside a text to establish some transcendental vantage point, will reveal yet another process of supplementation. Thus the complementary lack that Derrida detects in speech and writing proves to be widespread and not susceptible to being effaced by prioritizing nature over culture, the inside over the outside, or presence over absence, since none of these terms can exclude its other. Metaphysics lives on but has become unnameable and unthinkable – it is placed under erasure.

Derrida's critique of Rousseau finds that his attempt to portray harmony as a polluting influence on the purity of melody runs into the same difficulties as the attempt to valorize the immediacy of speech over the abstraction of writing – he cannot say what he means or mean what he says. By equating music with the voice, rather than with sound as such, Rousseau again opens the whole problem of an articulatory supplement. If song is already 'a kind of modification of the human voice', as Rousseau asserts, then it is difficult to perceive as pure, unmediated expression, since melodic intervals already hint at a technique that is distinguishable from normal vocal articulation (Derrida 1974: 196). Notwithstanding this difficulty, Rousseau claims simultaneously that the 'original and ideal essence of speech is song itself' (quoted, Derrida 1974: 198). He attempts to argue that speech and song suffer a parallel indignity: speech loses its contact with melody, and melody is diminished by the articulatory qualities of harmony. Derrida's point is that there is no origin at which the supplementation Rousseau hopes to avoid is not already inscribed.

Paul de Man's basic point of divergence with Derrida is his contention that the latter's reading of Rousseau is not literal enough: Derrida fails to appreciate that the paradoxes he finds in the standard reading of Rousseau are actually strategies within the texts. Referring to the significant passage from Rousseau's text below, which Derrida omits to mention, de Man draws the radical conclusion that music is pure relationship, signifying, not the full presence of passion, but absence, since it is hollow at the core. Unfortunately, he does not draw attention to the polemic with Rameau at work here.

> For us each sound is a relative entity. No sound by itself possesses absolute attributes that allow us to identify it: it is high or low, loud or soft with respect to another sound only. By itself, it has none of these properties. In a harmonic system, a given sound is nothing by natural right (un son quelconque n'est *rien* non plus *naturellement*). It is neither tonic, nor dominant, harmonic or fundamental. All these properties exist as

relationships only and since the entire system can vary from bass to treble, each sound changes in rank and place as the system changes in degree (de Man 1983: 128).

In keeping with his notion of allegory as temporally deferred meaning, de Man proposes that the musical sign can neither become identical with itself on repetition, nor coincide with another. Instead, it implies the repetition of non-identical units. In this sense, music is the supreme art of non-coincidence, which is why Rousseau emphasizes the relational aspect of melody as opposed to the illusion of unity offered by harmony. The apparent harmony of a single chord is, for de Man, in fact 'the melody of its potential repetition' (de Man 1983: 129). De Man does, however, seem to be driven by the momentum of his own argument when he draws the conclusion that music signifies silence from the following comment by Rousseau: 'sleep, the quiet of night, solitude and even silence can enter into the picture that music paints' (de Man 1983: 130). Because music has this capacity is in itself no reason to posit it as music's ultimate function.

As several writers have pointed out,[1] it is surprising that de Man chooses to take issue with Derrida, given the latter's frequent insistence that many of Rousseau's paradoxes are immanent to the text. For present purposes, the relative merits of Derrida's and de Man's readings of Rousseau are of less importance than both writers' insistence on locating the limits of Rousseau's arguments within his own text. The dispute concerning Rousseau's understanding of music is framed by a larger theme in de Man's *The Rhetoric of Blindness*: that a text prefigures and provides all the tools for its own deconstruction, and is not therefore reducible to a grammar of tropes. For de Man, music appears as the medium *par excellence* of allegory, or as 'the diachronic version of the pattern of non-coincidence within the moment' (de Man 1983: 129). Construed in this way, music gives the lie to Pater's dictum that all art aspires ultimately to the condition of music, since de Man understands music as an unstable system of deferral, not as an absolute essence. This is why considerations of music play such an important role in de Man's deconstruction of that nineteenth-century aesthetic ideology in which the other arts seek the supposed immediacy of music. In the words of Christopher Norris:

> Music is important for de Man because it has served as a source of that potent aesthetic ideology which locates the redemptive capacity of art in its promise of transcending the conflict between sensuous and intellectual realms of experience (Norris 1989: 335).

Art is expected to close the gap between discursive and non-discursive forms of knowlege that Kant had attempted to bridge in *The Critique of Judgement*; and in de Man's view, this false closure is manifest in a preference for symbol, which attempts to fuse objects of perception with nature, over the temporal dislocation of meaning inherent within allegory. Norris puts the argument as follows: 'language in its symbolic mode was treated, like music, as a means of overcoming the insurmountable split between thought and perception, subject and object, concepts and sensuous intuitions' (Norris 1989: 317). An attempt to span the chasm between concept and intuition is made, de Man states, in Nietzsche's *The Birth of Tragedy*, where it is argued that the Apollonian mythical apparatus of Wagnerian music-drama shields us from the absolute *Ding an Sich* of the music. However, Nietzsche's line of reasoning encounters the same paradox that Derrida detects in Rousseau: the originary truth which flows through the Dionysian realm of music can only be articulated through the supplementary medium of the Apollonian.

De Man's wariness of aesthetic thought collapsing into a doctrine of organicism is undoubtedly justified, his later work emphasizing the complicity with political ideology exhibited by this type of perspective, so it is interesting to note that towards the end of his life de Man contemplated some work on Adorno, who shared his deep distrust of idealist aesthetics. Both thinkers employ a concept of allegory as a tool in debunking the symbolism prevalent in German idealism, which reached its apogee in cultural perceptions of music; but there are significant differences between de Man's understanding of allegory as the deferral of meaning embodied in the non-simultaneity of the tropes and figures of language, and Adorno's attempts to break open the 'natural' subjectivity within objects. Though sharing de Man's distrust of organicism, Adorno detects in the notion of artistic self-determinacy an advantageous critical distance. Like de Man, he punctures the alleged union of the concept and the sensuous, yet regards form's sovereignty over the particular as the mark of a damaged subjectivity, not of a constant impossibility. He tries to turn the discursive towards the non-discursive, as well as noting their diremption.

De Man's attentiveness to textual allegory has wide scope to the extent that it underlines distortions of meaning, closed patterns of thought and the gulf between signs and sensuous intuition, but does not facilitate easy access to the historically-moulded subjectivity addressed by Adorno's dialectic. Arguably however, because they focus on particular texts, de Man's readings do allude to specific and historically informed issues. Without the communicative burden of everyday language, music can change stylistically at a great pace; de Man is therefore right to point up what he calls the 'inherent fragility, impermanence and self-destruction of music', though he does not ascribe this quality to a specific objectification of material (de Man 1983: 131). A similar claim is made by Eduard Hanslick, who is able to link historical obsolescence with a formalist argument: 'There is no art', he comments, 'which wears so many forms out so quickly as music' (1986: 35). An historical dynamic is, by association, perhaps implicit in de Man's emphasis on music's temporality; his preoccupation with music as a play of relationships certainly echoes Hanslick's terminology, though the strategy deconstructs Hanslick's claims. One should, however, distinguish between the texts of Derrida and de Man, in which music functions as an organicist metaphor or is used as a deconstructive lever, and Adorno's philosophy of music, which thinks through the materiality of its object.[2] If de Man is able to demonstrate that music cannot be sustained as a 'natural' metaphor, Adorno can locate this insight as a socially-generated field of tension within the medium, as both material and cultural agent. Translated into a materialist aesthetic, Derrida's critique of Rousseau would say that articulation and expression are already mediated in the substance of music.

It is striking that de Man, like Rousseau, should prevail upon music, which cannot speak for itself, at the most extreme moment of his argument, perhaps unwittingly repeating the trope of music as essence.[3] In Derrida's reading of Rousseau music signifies pure presence; for de Man, Rousseau:

> describes music as a pure system of relations that at no point depends on the substantive assertions of a presence, be it as a sensation or as a consciousness. Music is a mere play of relationships. . . . it 'means' the negation of all presence (1983: 128).

But it is only by appealing to an abstract notion of music that de Man can countenance such an extreme form of allegory. Adorno's emphasis on the materiality of the particular in actual music, by contrast, can interrogate unifying impulses without dissolving them by a process of deferral. For him, the crucial turn in late Beethoven is the tendency for the medium itself to react against the hypostatized qualities of tonal unity, diffusing any straightforward correspondence between standardized gesture and its accepted place within a system. The music presents a fractured and discredited totality, but does not jettison an interplay of form and particulars. Contrary to de Man's point, it is evident that it only becomes meaningful for music to signify the negation of all presence in the context of presence. A longing for metaphysical certainty and primal innocence, set against a fragmented existence, is the conflict from which the agonized musical subjectivity of Mahler draws its strength. In discussing Mahler's responses to the problem of the finale, Adorno remarks of *Das Lied von der Erde* and the Ninth Symphony: 'The end here is that no end is any longer possible, that music cannot be hypostatized as a unity of actually present meaning' (1991a: 138). Such absence, however, is only facilitated by the presence in memory of the traditional 'solution' and synthesis offered in a symphonic finale. Contemporary music can replace memories of organic closure with exploration of affinities between discrete objects, but earlier modernist music registers this heritage in three ways: expressionist Schoenberg, to take Adorno's example, allows subjective needs to break through containment by the form, or concept; the excesses of high modernism take closure and containment of the particular to an extreme (and Boulez's Third Piano Sonata attempts to deal with this paradox); the excesses of avant-gardism, whether Dadaist or postmodernist, collapse art into life (with the consequences found, for example, in Cage's *Variations IV*).

Both Derrida and Adorno recognize in the aesthetic a source for a non-subsumptive logic, and both seek to entwine their philosophy with art: Adorno endeavours to open the concept (or form in music) to the object, turning it away from identity-ridden knowledge; Derrida to open the sign-unit, semiology's equivalent to the concept, to what it excludes in the name of closure, or origin.[4] Their efforts are a recognition of modernist art's pull toward reflection, and Adorno's insistence that analysis should not simply describe the work but instead 'become aware of a work as a *force field (Kraftfeld)* organised around a *problem*' advances a mode of insight that, like Derrida's and de Man's rigorous readings, empowers texts to encounter meanings and possibilities within themselves that may be contrary to the main argument (Adorno 1982: 181). A deconstructive reading blurs the distinction between critical response and authorial intent, since it is neither inside nor outside the text, making reading a form of writing and *vice versa*. Likewise, much modern music fuses its compositional technique with what might be called a critical, or aesthetic, concern, inscribing issues that once might have been considered relevant only to the realm of aesthetic reception within the production of the work. If philosophy needs art as a template for an altered notion of the concept, art increasingly veers towards the reflective capacity of critical reading; form almost requiring theory for completion.

At first glance, the fluidity Derrida finds between the inside and the outside of text would seem to undercut artistic autonomy; but deconstruction does not eliminate autonomy because, although the idea of a self-determining frame is questioned, the challenge takes place from within. While Derrida's famous assertion that the outside is the inside may emancipate the reader, it is not a revelation for a philosophy of art that employs a dialectic between the internal configurations of the text (inside) and the social forms (outside) that are sedimented in its material. Derridean *différance* consistently opens the closure of metaphysics, while Adornian determinate irreconcilability is the mark of art's non-identity with the exchange principle imposed by rationalization of modernity. *Différance* is an effective tool for understanding why indeterminacy is produced when a system is imposed upon musical elements, but it is less suited to discerning the ways in which configurations can be formed, from the bottom up, between diverse elements. Derrida's notion of the trace is his equivalent to Adorno's understanding of mimesis, and both refer to the particular;[5] the former invokes the constant impossibility of transcendental philosophy, the latter denotes the scarring left by the subsumption of detail under the general. Because mimesis is a component within a philosophy that seeks to turn the concept towards the object, it refers to the prospect of subjectivity engaging with the intuitive and expressive forms of knowledge, rejected by a dominant history of rationalization. By alluding to a less distorted rationality, the mimetic harnesses greater transgressive and transformative potential than the trace, which registers permanent instability within transcendental closure. Mimesis is what an incomplete form of knowledge must dismiss as irrational.

Deconstruction does not, as sometimes thought, pursue an abrogation of meaning, nor does it posit the vague notion that textual meaning is multiple or even inexhaustible; the analytical rigour with which a text is unravelled is itself evidence that meaning is taken seriously. Yet, although many deconstructive readings are simply more vigorous than other critical approaches, when Derrida, in particular, makes philosophical extrapolations from the practice of rigorous reading, it is questionable whether deconstruction can avoid valorizing non-identity over identity. Derrida is enchanted by the prospect of a philosophy of origin, even as he deconstructs the metaphysics of presence, and he still appears to be fascinated by the philosophical chimera of a standpoint that would lay claim to an essential insight. Herein lies the problem: *différance* cannot be construed as the dialectical opposite of identity, but by the same token, neither can it differ from it in any absolute sense, since *différance* is the determining medium of differences. *Différance* is, then, the unthinkable but defining condition of both identity and non-identity, which are somehow thought to be both the same and different. Derrida states:

> It is evident – and this is the evident itself – that the economical and the non-economical, the same and the entirely other, etc., cannot be thought *together*. If *différance* is unthinkable in this way, perhaps we should not hasten to make it evident, in the philosophical element of evidentiality which would make short work of dissipating the mirage and illogicalness of *différance* . . . (Derrida 1982: 19).

Derrida is aware that *différance* might easily hypostatize into a transcendental term, where non-identity simply replaces identity, so to avoid consolidation he uses other terms such as trace or *arche*-writing. Because, however, Derrida insists on maintaining *différance* as a non-originary origin and emphasizes deferral, he is placed in an impossible situation. David Wood expresses the predicament as follows: 'Derrida either uses transcendental forms of argument in explaining the term *différance*, in which case he undermines his whole project, or he does not, in which case the force of all he says about *différance* (and its intelligibility) evaporates' (Wood 1985: 96). For obvious reasons, Derrida takes the first of these two options and *différance* gravitates towards the transcendental status it is designed to disrupt. Adorno broaches the matter in a discussion of new music, commenting, 'even the postulate of "repetitionlessness", of absolute difference [*Ungleichheit*], demands a moment of "sameness", measured against which difference only becomes difference' (GS 16: 613).[6] Adorno's point is that music can neither generate absolute presence, because – as de Man suggests – repetition introduces deferral, nor absolute absence, because this lack in its turn will be deconstructed by identity.

There is a tendency for poststructuralism to show little interest in alternative post-metaphysical philosophies, presenting itself as if any other mode of discourse is inherently absolutist and shot through with metaphysical assumptions.[7] Adorno's philosophy offers one such differing perspective, better understood as a materialist examination of many issues also tackled by Derrida than as an early manifestation of insights he was to develop, notwithstanding the authors' shared capacity for detecting awkward details submerged beneath generalizations and their sensitivity to the ways in which philosophical oppositions slide into one another. Adorno's utopian hope for a reconciliation of humanity with nature is as elusive as Derrida's idea of trace that would always render this impossible. But when Adorno's utopian aspirations are brought down from an altitude at which instrumental reason appears all-pervasive to the oxygen-rich lifeworld, it becomes obvious that mimesis does break through rigid social forms, facilitating a more modest programme of transformation. Similarly, when employed in critical reading, Derrida's trace generates more urgency than talk of a non-originary origin might suggest. The generalized quality of Adorno's philosophy of history and epistemology is susceptible to critique, and has something of the all-pervasive quality of Derrida's *différance*; but if Adorno's model can be loosened so as to address non-reified subjectivity, this suggests that deconstruction can be employed as a situated tool without collapsing meaning into infinite deferral. Provided that the results of a deconstructive reading are not inflated into a principle, deconstruction functions as a strict mode of analysis which can be powerfully employed to expose the blind spots in thought. Deconstruction suggests that textual instability can be generated by a particular line of critical inquiry, and is not simply encoded by the process of production. When this knowledge is absorbed by a materialist aesthetic, it facilitates a form of reading whereby subjects engage their individual and shared experiences with the subjectivities objectified in cultural products.

Illusion and Space: Ligeti

Space

After fleeing Budapest in 1956, György Ligeti located himself at the heart of modernist musical thought and practice, quickly gaining an intimate knowledge of serialist procedures, as evinced by the analysis of *Structure 1a* that appeared in *Die Reihe* in 1960. Ligeti fully absorbed the central tenets of high modernist musical construction, but never endorsed them uncritically. His oeuvre is located neither inside nor outside the high modernist frame: instead of opposing or replicating serialist and other constructionist techniques, Ligeti assimilated their principles, and to some extent their sound, but transmuted these qualities into something more idiosyncratic. His music is both a critical commentary on the axioms of high modernism and an alternative to them, since Ligeti felt the need to develop the language of music, but was not prepared to replace an old system with a new one. That he chose to embrace the extremes of neither determinacy nor indeterminacy can be attributed to his understanding that the two poles are mutually dependent: one cannot be substituted for the other. Ligeti lets the two forces intersect by establishing structural principles for his works, and, like a deconstructionist, by assuring their stability is constantly questioned by the music. Adorno's observation that 'integration and disintegration are in each other (*ineinander*)' finds sustenance in Ligeti's aesthetic (GS 16: 617);[8] and elsewhere Adorno attributes to Ligeti the insight that 'complete determination – where everything is judged to be of equal importance and where nothing can be left outside the total complex – converges with absolute contingency' (1984a: 224).[9]

Ligeti's feel for the incongruous and his ability to expose one mode of thought to another is apparent at an early stage in his post-Budapest compositions. *Artikulation*, composed on four-track tape, demonstrates a quasi-serialist interest in categorizing sounds and textures and then placing them in various combinations, but the piece itself is somewhat provocative since many of its elements are redolent of a cartoon soundtrack. The electronically-generated speech-like sounds concur with the projects being undertaken at the Cologne studio at this time, and show the influence of Stockhausen's interest in analysing and controlling the components of music. Work in the studio would have encouraged Ligeti to think of sound in a direct textural sense, and this fascination with organizing sonority found an outlet in the early cluster scores, *Apparitions* and *Atmosphères*, which transfer sounds associated with studio techniques into the orchestra, by building cluster sonorities from tiny ingredients.

The serialist integration of horizontal and vertical and the axiom of trying to relate all components to a central scheme rely on a conception of spatial equivalence in music. *Apparitions* and *Atmosphères* use some controls similar to those associated with serialism (there is a quasi-serial scheme for durations in *Apparitions*), but they transform the character of the technique, moving away from complex permutations to a basic, gestural feel of space. A contrapuntal cluster starts in bar 44 of *Atmosphères*, soon increasing to a fifty-six part texture. In this sculpting and transformation of sonic space the instruments weave their canonic, chromatic lines within defined partitions in the overall web of sound. When a line reaches one boundary of its band, it returns to the opposite limit of the partition and resumes its chromatic ascent or descent, but by gradually narrowing these bands Ligeti is able to reduce the texture, in a marked compression, to a dyad of middle C and D♭, giving the overall transformation a very clear, audible shape. The towering sonorities of *Atmosphères*, in which harmonic, rhythmic and motivic interest is reduced to a minimum, suggest that the composer has taken as a starting point the indifference of the material that threatens to undermine serialism. Unlike Cage, however, Ligeti reinvents interest and latency instead of following the logic of this indifference. If, as Adorno might have argued, this music opens onto the machine-like space of a second nature, an analytical intelligence strives to perceive and to transform this space. The coordinates of *Atmosphères* deal with formalized relations of sonorities in space, even thwarting the temporal quality of the medium, but Ligeti's sounds possess an inner life which stands in contrast to the empty space of mechanized exchange.

In a conversation with Burde, Ligeti relates that he had listened to Adorno explaining his ideas about a *musique informelle* to Boulez before the paper 'Vers une musique informelle' was written. At this stage Ligeti felt unable to say that he had already, in *Atmosphères*, composed the music envisaged by Adorno (Burde 1993: 140), but later, having heard *Atmosphères*, Adorno confirmed what Ligeti already knew. The qualities of Ligeti's music likely to have impressed Adorno include the way in which *Atmosphères* dissolves form as something imposed from above in preference for a form that emerges from below – from the nominalism of the particular – and moves to the general, but resists closure. In the paper 'Form in der neuen Musik' of 1966, Adorno observes that 'because there are no more forms, everything must become form' (GS 16: 624).[10] Though such a comment is also applicable to certain works by Schoenberg, in the micro-polyphonic music of Ligeti, where little is pre-established, the interaction between details and larger constructions is felt strongly. The composer certainly planned and carefully notated the fluctuating sound blocks of *Atmosphères*, but was unlikely to have heard from the score exactly what the dense canonic lines would produce in performance, so it is reasonable to claim that this music evinces 'a tension [or, at least, a gap] between what is imagined and what cannot be foreseen', as Adorno once envisaged (Adorno 1992b: 303).[11] Like other modernist works, *Atmosphères* also abandons something Adorno describes as 'the subjectivity which is mirrored in expression and hence is always affirmative, a form of subjectivity which Expressionism inherited directly from neo-Romanticism' (1992b: 280). Indeed, Ligeti has spoken of a deep-frozen expressionism in his music, and declares himself to be averse to obvious displays of emotion in art. This neutrality is more characteristic of his work from the late 1950s and early 1960s – though the music is not without dramatic excitement – than of later compositions, and, like Adorno, Ligeti seems to have felt at this stage that direct expression in modern music was false, though he did not espouse the same theory of mediation. The concept of a deep-frozen expression suggests that subjectivity is encoded at a deep level in the objective demands of the material, where it finds a refuge. Even at this peak of modernism there is, however, a direct immediacy in the sonorities of the music, and this becomes more prevalent later in Ligeti's career.

Ligeti's development as a composer since his arrival in the West follows a trajectory in which the expelled components of his earlier drastically reduced scores are reclaimed. The virtual annihilation of separately identifiable lines that marks much of *Atmosphères* leads to the situation in *Lontano* where the slightest deviation from the sound-mass focuses attention on itself. It is as if having eliminated harmonic and rhythmic functions, Ligeti can start to reintroduce these factors within the organizational possibilities gleaned from his experiments in privation. The strata that function as foreground temporization in *Lontano* become thinned out and glimpsed as melodic shapes amidst the jostling mass of melodies which constitute *Melodien*, the composer asking for every part to be played with an 'inner vitality and a dynamic agogic shape of its own' (score, 1971). This instruction affirms the identity of each line, which must, nevertheless, coexist with other similarly independent lines, all moving out of phase with one another, allowing various gradations of transformation to operate simultaneously. The sustained notes (described by Ligeti as the 'background' level) ensure a continuous sonority against sometimes fragmented textures, and perform the traditional role of static pedals by exhibiting the most defined harmonic motion in the score. The composer also draws attention to an ostinato level ('middleground'), characterized by winding shapes and fast repetition, and a 'foreground' comprising melodies and short melodic patterns, though distinctions between these three levels are not always clear since they are refracted through one another. *Melodien* also exhibits a sensitivity towards rhythmic differentiation: the individual configurations remain fairly imperceptible, but the interaction of levels generates combinatorial rhythms and these surface and sink like the melodic content. Burde (1993: 146–7), again drawing on 'Form in der neuen Musik', refers to Adorno's contention that even after the death of tonality, lines and successions of lines (*Linienzüge*) still have the capacity to expand time beyond the moment (GS 16: 619); and suggests this thought achieves concrete realization in the lines and successions of lines, together with harmonic crystallizations, used to elucidate interrelations between sections of form in the micropolyphonic scores of Ligeti. The perception constitutes more than a trivial observation of a correspondence because the connection of sections is often difficult to achieve for serial and chance-derived music.

Melodien falls into two basic spatial shapes: after the initial ascent, the first half of the work is distinguished by a stable A^{VI} pedal and a gradual unfolding of the lower register, with a quasi-symmetrical extension to registral extremes finishing at bar 72; in the second half of the music a more homogeneous middle register also expands quasi-symmetrically at the end. Three focal points, or windows, occur at the beginning, middle and end of *Melodien*, formed around the pitches A, C and E. The opening bars can be seen as a gradual filtering from the abundant activity of the initial asynchronous runs, within the range G^{IV}–$F\sharp^{VI}$, to a single point: the sustained A^{VI} pedal that emerges in bars 11 and 12 as a moment of repose. The whole opening statement is a play of sameness and difference: the flourishes are almost chromatic but include tones and minor 3rds, they closely resemble one another but are distinguished by small deviations, and the overall identity is blurred by polyrhythmic layering. It is interesting that the unisons in the piano, which a note in the score assures us are not mistakes, are on the pitches A and E, but the chances of them being heard in any structural sense are remote. After all deviations have been reduced to the pure tone of A^{VI} in bar 11, dissolution again sets in, initially taking the form of rhythmic differences on the same pitch, sliding into ostinato patterns which, though including the A, gradually introduce other pitches. At first this process of deflection serves to strengthen the identity of the A, rather as dissonance reinforces harmony, until it is eventually lost in the chromatic expansion. The ostinati figures here function like small pitch sets in which the constituents can be permutated (see Example 4.1), generating an interplay of identity and difference; these shapes open out to form the melodies, which unfurl at bar 25 generating the 'creeper-like, ornamental aspect' of this piece, of which Ligeti speaks (quoted in Griffiths 1983: 84).

The spatial shapes, symmetries, expansions and contractions of *Melodien* are clearly audible; and within these formal shapes the shimmering webs and interlocking lines provide differentiated and sensual articulations of space, offering an ephemeral beauty that constantly renews and transforms itself through a logic of disintegration. Within the work can be heard something akin to the fields of breakthrough and disintegration that appear, Adorno argues, as characters in their own right in the music of Mahler. The windows in *Melodien* (where the sonority narrows to a single pitch) are immanently derived, but have their own quality of fulfilment, and the following fields in which they decay also possess a characteristic that is not wholly determined by the piece (though they are not experienced as catastrophic in the sense portrayed by Adorno's depiction of the phenomenon in Mahler).

celesta p; piccolo pp; xylophone pp, violin B pp. All four instruments at exactly the same volume

Example 4.1: Ostinati shapes in bars 16–17 of *Melodien* (pedals omitted)

© Schott & Co. Ltd. Reprinted by permission.

Repetition and Illusion

Upon his arrival in Cologne, Ligeti quickly utilized the resources of the electronic studio, even translating studio techniques into orchestral compositions. The early experiments in the studio remain Ligeti's only venture in the electro-acoustic medium, subsequent encounters with technology being limited to instrumental portrayals of manic little machines. The use of an antiquated machine like the harpsichord rejects modern technology, but the repetitive quality of the music puts the instrument's mechanics at the forefront of the music. According to Adorno's aesthetics, social categories and methods of organization crystallize in musical material; and through this mediation they become susceptible to the internal dynamics of artistic form, showing allegedly immutable formations to be malleable.[12] The strength of Ligeti's 'mechanical' compositions is that they turn the repetitive principle of fungibility and exchange into something else, taking the mechanism of repetition to an extreme.

The textural transformations of Ligeti's earlier works exhibit a quasi-serialist proscription on repetition because recurring events place a perceptual emphasis on themselves, thereby imparting a certain lumpiness to the texture. Ligeti's ostinato figures would at first blush seem to be diametrically opposed to any principles of non-repetition, yet they too illuminate the contradictory notion of a unique sound event: each repeated event, simply because it takes place in its own moment of time, is in a sense unique, as if Ligeti seeks to eliminate repetition through repetition. Like de Man, Ligeti focuses on the iterative dimension of music, but also shows how a valorizing of non-simultaneity collapses into its opposite: complete simultaneity. Adorno's observation that 'repetition, stasis and 'the Utopia of the unrepeatable virtually penetrate each other through the articulation of time' illuminates the exploration of difference and repetition in this music (GS 16, 622),[13] where elements cross through their opposite. Ligeti uses minimalist-like techniques – including phase shifts – which, while presenting an easily-digested surface 'high' of hyper-activity, at the same time offer a genuine new sense of layered rhythmic complexity – at least to Western music.

A process takes place in the metric plane of *Continuum*, for solo harpsichord, analogous to events in the harmonic plane of *Lontano*: surface phenomena – in this case repetitive patterns – intrude across the synchronic plane, raising a cumulative *gestalt* rhythm which moves temporally against the static background. The shifts themselves are not notated in the score and are difficult to predict accurately in reading; phantom-like, and relying on the immediacy of performance, they float above the surface and appear to come from nowhere. Such illusions explore illusion as illusion: that is, they do not, like traditional organic art, appear to make the artefact a self-contained natural object, nor are they phantasmagoric, since they illustrate that the illusory in art is synthetic. In his celebrated essay 'The Work of Art in the Age of Mechanical Reproduction' Benjamin argues that techniques of mechanical reproduction enable the masses to partake in the camera-view 'orientation of the expert' (Benjamin 1969: 234); similarly, Ligeti's machine-like pieces invite the audience to peer into the internal, clattering, technology of art. Nevertheless, this strategy does not amount to the full-scale rejection of artistic distance envisaged by Benjamin, because the art work is presented as an artefact but produces phantom-like phase shifts: illusion is simultaneously unmasked and invented. How to cope with the end of illusion is a significant question for Adorno, who maintains: 'the question as to the future of art is not simply sterile and indicative of technocratic leanings, it might boil down to whether or not art is able to outlive illusion' (1984a: 150). The question is not answered by Ligeti but instead suspended, since he provides illusion with an afterlife.

In the later polymetric music, such as the piano *Etudes* and the Piano Concerto, Ligeti acknowledges the influence of Nancarrow's music for mechanical piano, the 'additive pulsation principle' of sub-Saharan African music and extends the 'meter-dependent hemiola' principle used by Schumann and Chopin (1988: 4). The diversity of these currents recognizes the limits of Western conceptions of musical material and expands them, but the aesthetic impulse, if eclectic, is not simply plural because it seeks to integrate all these strands into an organizational logic. Ligeti had already anticipated the idea of a metric interplay unrestricted by the bar line, and to this he adds the possibility of 'a *single* interpreter being able to produce the illusion of *several* simultaneous layers of different tempi. The result', he continues, 'is a musical phenomenon which would not be possible within the limits of either traditional European or African polyrhythmic hemiola technique' (1988: 5). The imagination behind this activity is still a spatial one; speaking of the Concerto, Ligeti says that when the music is properly performed 'it will "lift off" like an aircraft: the rhythmic events, too complex to be perceived in detail, hang in a suspended state. This blossoming of isolated structural details into transforming global structure', he adds, 'is one of my basic compositional assumptions' (1988:9). But this suspended state constitutes an inflected space in which Ligeti is able to filter traditional aspects of Western music, such as melodic and harmonic processes, tonal procedures and octaves, back into the mix. These elements do not hypostatize in the music because they are continually reconfigured by Ligeti's kaleidoscopic technique, his sense of 'the "always different yet similar"', which in the Piano Concerto he relates to 'the impression of a huge interconnected network' (1988: 12).

Aura and Tradition

Benjamin outlined his notion of aura as the presence and authority of the traditional art object: like a natural object, the auratic art work exudes 'the unique phenomenon of a distance, however close it may be' (1969: 222). Mechanical reproduction of the art work into multiple copies of the original causes this aura of uniqueness to wither away; with the context of tradition drained off, Benjamin argues that the art object is perceived by the viewer in a more direct way and it becomes imbued with political potential. Though he acknowledges that a bad aura can return with the cult of the film star, Benjamin's optimistic analysis is blind to the capacity of the culture industry to generate a uniform perception instead of facilitating an engaged response, and Adorno was quick to point out that, notwithstanding Benjamin's nostalgia for auratic art, his undialectical view of it misses the potential for critical dissent within autonomous art. As a composer of new music, Ligeti fits the framework of Adorno's critique better than the context of Benjamin's essay; nevertheless Ligeti's ability to include aspects of traditional music within his own highly-constructed creations is usefully explored through the concept of aura. Like illusion in Adorno's aesthetics, aura is unmasked by modernist art yet still exerts a fascination for Ligeti. He evokes a sense of near and far in music and shows how distance can be dissolved, but, contrary to Benjamin, he is anxious to preserve the autonomy and aura of art: 'I don't want that fence between the piece and the audience to be abolished . . . It's the feeling of distance' (Jack 1974: 30).

Ligeti describes lucidly the way in which tradition, as well as aspects of the everyday world, is absorbed in his music. He speaks of:

> A huge reservoir of existing models relating to the historic as well as ethnic, technical as well as melodic and harmonic . . . One also finds in this conglomerate other things from everyday life, from the fine arts, from politics – a highly held example would be *Ulysses* by Joyce, where everything from different spheres is included and is present (Dibelius 1984: 59).[14]

This statement can be partially reconciled with Adorno's understanding of the way in which social conditions are inscribed in music: for him, the tensions and forces within the musical material are considered to be historically sedimented, but the art work is at the same time autonomous and purposeless. Nevertheless, Ligeti suggests that various aspects of the external world are incorporated by music in a more *ad hoc* and jumbled way than Adorno's argument indicates, in a process that has an affinity with the poststructuralist idea of intertextuality. But Ligeti's music absorbs influences into an autonomous logic in a way that finds a balance between assimilation and the irreconcilable pluralism characteristic of some postmodernist culture. Similarly, his response to Joyce constitutes a middle path between Boulez's extraction of formal procedures and Cage's plundering of random objects. Ligeti is influenced both by Joyce's technique and by his capacity for bringing the everyday into art.

One of the main structural features of the Horn Trio is a fascination with the relative distancing of tradition, evoked by the dedication, '*Hommage à Brahms*', together with the sound aura of the horn and its network of associations. Ulrich Dibelius points out that the 'horn fifths' of classical two-part horn writing (which became a standardized motive in their own right) are used as a structural resource and reference point for this work, most obviously in the opening violin double stops (1984: 47). Further, the horn sound evokes for Ligeti distant Romantic sonorities, particularly those of Bruckner and Mahler, and the effect of a warm tone emerging from a huge orchestral sonority is conveyed by the frequent use of muting and of sustained pedals. This sense of aura does not always remain filtered: the raucous horn fanfares which invade the reprise of the 'Scherzo' retain their bucolic hunting flavour, thereby imparting a rough immediacy. Klaus Kropfinger notes that Adorno's exchanges with Benjamin led him on one occasion to describe aura as a dialectical coupling of 'dissolution and restoration' (*Auflösung und Wiederherstellung*) (Kropfinger 1973: 134n). In the Horn Trio dissolution is found in the pull towards the amorphous, and restoration evoked by allusions to tradition. The sense of aura applies not only to the appearances of traditional components, but also to the layering of the music itself, which both reclaims and dismantles events. In *Melodien* elements are pushed up from the background fabric of lines and subjected to the kind of scrutiny that enables them to dominate the texture before collapsing back into the fabric, in a continuous process of restoration and dissolution.

The influence of tradition extends further in Ligeti's music than the Horn Trio's debt to Brahms. The influence of Chopin (presumably the presto from the B♭ minor Sonata) is acknowledged in the second movement of *Monument, Selbstporträt, Bewegung* and Ligeti informs us that the 'meter-dependent hemiola as used by Schumann and Chopin' is influential on his later polymetric works, such as the piano *Etudes* and the Piano Concerto (1988: 4). The absorption of traditional components suggests that the icy grip of high modernist construction has released its hold for this composer, though Ligeti's response to tradition is very different to the postmodernist acceptance of it as an available resource; for him, it is something to be filtered and transformed by a methodological matrix. There is a sense in which past and present are simultaneous possibilities within the space of Ligeti's music, but the past is alluded to more as an idea than an actuality, and diversity is immanent to the music instead of being encountered in the choice of styles available to the artist. The elision of past and present that Ligeti encodes, both with regard to tradition and by means of techniques such as transference between foreground and background, is for some postmodernists inscribed within the coexisting resources provided by a museum without walls. Ligeti's music, on the other hand, draws succour from the evocation of aura, even in disintegration, not its neutralization.

Boundaries

Despite Ligeti's attachment to the idea of autonomous art, he is aware of its boundaries and limitations, some of the most powerful moments in his music suggesting a frustrated pacing around the cage of possibility. The Requiem outlines a trajectory from the extraordinary deep pulsating clusters with which the Introitus opens, to the more transparent high (celestial) textures into which the Lacrimosa dissolves, and the Horn Trio (bars 80–81, first movement) takes the violin up to such high harmonics that the tone disappears into 'a noise like a breath', whilst the final horn pedal G (fourth movement) makes formidable demands on the player's breathing capacity. These musical extremes, which include virtuosic demands, are matched by the sheer physicality of involvement in performance. Ligeti's music also explores often stark oppositions: surface/depth; loud/soft; dense/transparent; empty/full; near/distant (Sabbe 1987: 84 gives others). Though these oppositions are sometimes stated with structuralist-like bareness, like deconstruction the music shows an awareness that one extreme is inscribed in its other; but by stating them so strongly, the composer draws attention to the physical and material limitations of music, indeed to those of human experience. Ligeti's almost mystical desire to peer behind music, to comprehend what is beyond it, becomes apparent in his fascination with a major framing device: silence. This is an almost mandatory requirement at the end of compositions (often notated by blank bars), but also occurs elsewhere: the first five bars of *Monument*, for example, are silent and the cut-off is a frequent feature of Ligeti's ostinati-based music, where the incessant babble of repetition is suddenly juxtaposed with emptiness. There is a sense in which, just as a sculpture can be considered to be found in the stone by its sculptor, so Ligeti discovers forms in the silence of the space that surrounds them.

A sense of the ridiculous and the satirical pervades Ligeti's music, but there is a body of works in which what might be called a Dadaist impulse is particularly prevalent. The most prominent of these were composed in the first two years of the 1960s: *Fragment* for ten instruments, *Trois bagatelles* for pianist, *Die Zukunft der Musik* for lecturer and audience, and *Poème symphonique* for 100 metronomes. But this influence is also marked in *Aventures*, *Nouvelles aventures* and *Le grand macabre*. The germinal aspects of these pieces for the composer's later development have often been pointed out: the use of silence in *Trois bagatelles* and the layering of rhythmic strata in *Poème symphonique*. For Ligeti, these experiments provided insights into possibilities for stacking and reconfiguring elements within art by translating a radical aesthetic of reception, influenced by Cage, into the production method. But in place of the political assault on the institution of autonomous art that runs through Dadaism and Surrealism, there is a sense of hopelessness and humorous acceptance.

Ligeti saw well the potential for chance procedures to destroy the autonomy of art, yet he was sensitive to the antinomy of construction and aleatoricism that was being played out in new music during the 1950s and 1960s. Instead of shattering the art work as an entity or constructing open forms, Ligeti sought a continual decentring within his music, and he comments as follows: 'an open form for me is not that I can change the music, or form, but I have to create with the music the illusion of openness' (Jack 1974: 26). The statement is astute about the need to find a passage for artistic expression between subsumptive form and indifferent openness. Martin Zenck argues that the influence of Adorno's 'Vers une musique informelle' can be seen in *Aventures* and *Nouvelles aventures*. He writes: 'The result is a form which is determined by its global character of movement but free in detail as far as succession and stratification are concerned: a form of indeterminate determination' (Zenck 1979: 164). Indeterminate determination is not, however, the same as Adornian determinate irreconcilability, because if detail is endlessly exchangeable it is not experienced as other to the form, or concept. The challenge is for form to take the non-conceptual into itself, not simply to render it fluid.

Ligeti's frustration with limited systems and stable meanings becomes explicit in the absurd libretto to *Le grand macabre*, which deals in its half-mocking, half-serious way with questions of temporality and death, though scorning anything resembling an insight. If the Day of Judgement does not take place, which is one interpretation of the opera, it is death itself that dies on the fictitious Day of Judgement, hence the unknowable other to life fails to become a stable sign that would confer metaphysical significance on the opera. The Day of Judgement collapses into the duplicity of difference: in the Epilogue two lovers emerge from the tomb, in which they have spent the remainder of the opera in erotic oblivion – indifferent to the end of the world – unsure whether they are still awaiting judgement, or whether they have died yet nothing has changed. In Ghelderode's original play Nekrotzar is explicitly revealed as a charlatan,[15] but Ligeti's distillation of the drama introduces an element of doubt: this pathetic parody of a monster, though ridiculing the machinations of dictatorship, might just be real. The meaning of the meaningless drama is that the administered world of a rationality preoccupied with means instead of ends is meaningless.

An opera in which death is deprived of meaning suggests a deliberate and contrived artificiality, or hollowness, in Ligeti's music. This feeling is reinforced by a radio interview in which the composer remarks that 'you really find meaninglessness in my music on a deep level, which is not deep at all, because I hate deepness' (1993). Ligeti's hatred for deepness might be more formally described as a distrust of the illusion of meaning associated with metaphysical wholeness and this causes him to question continually systematic strategies in his own work, hence the music operates on a level where artistic illusion is transparent, and fixed configurations which generate stable meanings are avoided. Nevertheless, an interrogation of metaphysical meaning itself has historical aesthetic meaning, as the work of Beckett indicates. Indeed Ligeti's aversion to overt expression and his credo of constructive rigour associate him obliquely with the high modernism of the 1950s. Though mathematical and scientific ideas exert a strong hold on his imagination, such models are not imposed on musical organization; instead, Ligeti invents musical analogies to their principles.

Just as deconstruction threatens the values of modernism yet works with them, so Ligeti's musical discourse maintains contact with the principles of new music; but instead of adhering to them, it mutates the techniques from within. While his sensitivity to the in-built historical redundancy of musical material is borne out by his avoidance of stable musical systems and by his placing of traditional elements in an alien environment, this historical awareness has not led to an extensive search for an advanced material. Ligeti's clouds and textures do modify musical material and he exhibits an unswerving allegiance to the principle of inventing something new, but his technique and thought are more suited to reconfiguring existing materials and ideas than to radical innovation. The great strength of Ligeti's music is that it is permitted an exuberance that does not become bogged down in the morass of excessive construction, but the other side of the equation is that the play of materials takes place around a void constituted by the absence of an alternative. Like Derrida, Ligeti works with transcendental ideas but continually dissolves them: both figures trace a non-originary origin.

Part of Ligeti's aesthetic concurs with Adorno's depiction of modern subjectivity as catastrophic, and his ability to let the inner life of the sounds lead the music is thoroughly Adornian; but another aspect of the composer shows an awareness, beyond anything contemplated by Adorno, of the possibilities to be found within a spatial mode of existence. Ligeti is remarkable for the clarity with which he understands his own aesthetic position, the significance of his compositional approaches and for the way in which he is able to convey this knowledge:

> Now with the Piano Concerto I offer my aesthetic credo: my independence both from the criteria of the traditional avant garde and from those of fashionable postmodernism. The musical illusions so important to me are nevertheless not pursued as an end in themselves, but rather form the foundation of my aesthetic considerations. I favour musical forms that are less process-like and more object-like. Music as frozen time, as an object in imaginary space that is evoked in our imagination through music itself. Music as a structure that, despite it unfolding in the flux of time, is still synchronically conceivable, simultaneously present in all its moments. To hold on to time, to suspend its disappearance, to confine it in the present moment, this is my primary goal in composition (1988: 13).

By developing an imaginary space, Ligeti provides a creative response to surroundings in which apparently unrelated events are simultaneously linked together, and, perhaps, helps us to develop strategies for perceiving our environment.

Notes

1. Norris 1982: 104; 1988: 155; Jonathan Culler, 'Frontiers of Criticism' (review of de Man's *Blindness and Insight*), *The Yale Reviewer*, Winter, 1972.
2. Kramer (1995: chapter 2) makes a distinction between music as 'cultural trope' and music as 'disciplinary object'. If this terminology is applied to my argument, de Man is seen to concentrate on deconstructing the ideology of music as cultural trope; and Adorno is able to analyse the illusory dimension of music as it appears in the interlocked realms of both cultural trope and disciplinary object. For an application of de Man's ideas to music as disciplinary object see Street 1989.
3. A similar point is made by Abbate 1991: 18.
4. Bernstein points out the equivalence of concept and sign-unit (1992: 227).
5. I am indebted to Bernstein's comparison of the Derridean re-mark with Adornian mimesis (1992: 238).
6. This passage is quoted in translation by Paddison 1993: 179.
7. Habermas's project is an attempt to construct a post-metaphysical philosophy of society; the question of the limitations of transcendental consciousness occurs in the work of Schelling and Fichte. For an account of this topic in relation to Derrida, see Dews 1987: 19–31.
8. My translation.
9. My translation.
10. My translation.
11. My brackets.
12. See Zuidervaart 1991: 129 for an account of this topic.
13. My translation. Also quoted in translation by Paddison 1993: 179.
14. My translation, Dibelius's brackets.
15. Michel de Ghelderode, *La Balade du Grand Macabre*.

Part III Consequences of Modernism

5 Separate Ways

A Dialectical Circus on *Roaratorio*

Cage observes that

> the Happening business came about through circumstances of being at Black Mountain where there were a number of people present – Merce was there, David Tudor was there, there was an audience. . . . The Happening resulted from the fact that there were many people and many possibilities and we could do it quickly (Kostelanetz 1988: 103–4).

Cage's notion of the happening obviously has much in common with the environment of simultaneous but non-synchronous sounds found in *Variations IV*. Contrary to popular perception, Cage was anxious to emphasize that the happening is an exercise in self-discipline and not simply an opportunity to do as one wishes; it should not, he argues, be an expression of an individual's idea or of a feeling, since this leads to a careless approach. The cessation of these desires facilitates the possibility of 'increasing one's awareness and curiosity' because, by reacting to the complexity of the situation in a neutral way, something may happen one did not have in mind (Kostelanetz 1988: 113).

Cage's multi-media events subjected other media to compositional processes he had conceived primarily with reference to music. In a happening the reading of a poem might be dissected by the specific and separate durations allocated to its presentation, and some, or all, of it might also be obliterated by simultaneous events. A non-semantic approach to language is continued in other Cage texts outside the realm of happenings; indeed, this tendency is evident in some of the earliest writings and lectures published in *Silence*, and in the 1970s this linguistic practice started to manifest itself in re-writings of authors whom Cage acknowledged to be influential on himself. Writings through Joyce's *Finnegans Wake* form the basis of *Roaratorio. An Irish Circus on 'Finnegans Wake'*. Cage's oeuvre resists the idea of a central, or focal, work but *Roaratorio* comes close to occupying such a position: it combines aspects of the multi-media pieces and writings, and has been produced in both radio and concert versions.

Roaratorio was conceived over the period 1977–79 and was shaped largely by a number of commissions. The frame of the work is commensurate with Cage's espoused ideas of indeterminacy and non-subjectivity, but its construction was quite complex and involved the high-technology facilities of IRCAM (Institut de Recherche et de Coordination Acoustique/Musique, Paris): in particular, the use of four sixteen-track tape recorders. *Roaratorio*'s starting point was *Writing for the Second Time through 'Finnegans Wake'*, which was constructed by subjecting the whole of *Finnegans Wake* to 'mesostic' writing. The aim was to produce a rewriting of the text with the name 'JAMES JOYCE' running as a column straight down the middle of the page, words adjacent to the middle one containing the capital being chosen at Cage's discretion, but in obeisance to the rule that a capitalized letter should not be anticipated in the passage between itself and the previous capital. An extract from the text of *Roaratorio* is shown below: the numbers indicate page references to Joyce's text (but punctuation, which Cage takes from the original and scatters by chance procedures, is not included).

```
        Jist                                           11
         Apppear
 toonigh Militopucos and toomourn
         wE
         wiSh for a muddy

        muJical                                        13
         chOcolat box
    i saY
        inCabus
        usEd we
```

When commissioned to write some music to place alongside *Writing for the Second Time through 'Finnegans Wake'* as a radio play, Cage decided to recreate Joyce's text in a different medium. The initial idea was to collect the sounds mentioned in *Finnegans Wake* and to make recordings at places named in the novel; the immensity of this task was, however, diminished by using chance methods to reduce the number of locations and sounds. The samples were put into fourteen categories, thus making them manageable, but Cage regretted the procedure because it diminishes the 'complexity which is characteristic of life itself' (Schöning 1982: 107). Many of the sounds were recorded on a trip made by Cage to places in Ireland mentioned by Joyce.

The montage of these sounds, together with recordings of Irish traditional music, was superimposed on a recording of Cage reading his 'Second Writing'. The text and the recording of it together functioned as a ruler, which enabled sources to be inserted so as to correspond with the line numbers of Joyce's original text, and chance decisions determined stereo position, relative duration, attack, loudness and decay for the objects. The whole assemblage was then mixed down from the multi-track tapes to a stereo tape for radio broadcast, resulting in a heterogeneous combination of sounds that becomes thicker and less definable in the second half of the work. For concert performance, a single multi-track tape is used, and a live reading of the text and a circus of traditional

Irish music can be substituted for the pre-recorded versions. The voice, fiddle, flute, uillean pipes and bodhran, though comprising the instruments of a traditional ensemble, are instructed to play in chance-determined places, performing separately and without regard to whatever else is going on. The Merce Cunningham dance company has also been used in performance.

Roaratorio was understood by Cage to be a specific realization of a score that comprises a set of instructions for transcribing any book into a different performance medium. The general score is entitled:

—————————— ——— ——— CIRCUS ON ————————
(title of composition   (article)   (adjective)   (title of book)

Cage views the word 'circus' in a way commensurate with a buddhist outlook: 'it means that there is not one center but that life itself is a plurality of centers' (Schöning 1982: 107). The word 'roaratorio' occurs in *Finnegans Wake*, Cage interpreting it in the following rather pleasing way:

> An oratorio is like a church-opera, in which people don't act, they simply stand there and sing. And so a 'roaratorio' is – well, you don't roar in church but you roar in life, or roars take place in life and among animals and nature and that's what this is. It's out in the world. It's not in the church (Schöning 1982: 89).

The central aesthetic, then, is one that tries to capture the plurality and chaos of life, and this is reflected at all stages in the conception of the work.

Influenced by Thoreau's claim 'that when he heard a sentence, he heard feet marching' (Schöning 1982: 85), Cage's readings through *Finnegans Wake* seek to demilitarize language, the random scattering of Joyce's punctuation contributing to this end. If Joyce explores the materiality of language by entering inside a word or phrase and revealing the myriad directions in which it could lead, Cage pushes further, nearly reducing language to non-semantic material. He is more interested in individual moments of *Finnegans Wake* than in its overall meaning, so instead of attempting anything like a critical interpretation, he brings the book to life in other configurations. Cage's writings through *Finnegans Wake* cannot be understood as a sequence of ideas, though there are comprehensible passages; they demand a response such as running the eye over the page or listening to the sounds generated in a reading – a form of scanning. Gregory Ulmer views Cage as a primary practitioner of what he calls post-criticism: for him, Cage explores the materiality, or concrete particularity, of language without trying to saddle it with meaning; he is preoccupied with the signifier rather than the signified. Cage writes through the text, not about it, and thus breaks down the distinction between author and reader, text and critic: there is neither primary medium nor message (Ulmer 1983: 101).

In Ulmer's opinion, text and response assume a saprophytic relationship, similar to that which exists between a fungus and its organic host (a suggestion that confers some significance on Cage's interest in mushrooms) (Ulmer 1983: 103). Attractive though this metaphor is, it attributes to the interplay between source and reaction a reciprocity that is hard to detect in Cage's work, since, unlike deconstructionist readings, Cage's rewrites do not loosen contrived closure through the immanent power of the text; instead, they expose the object to indifference. Deconstructive analysis reveals the fluidity between text and response, but Cage's approach is more extreme: instead of destabilizing the sign-unit, he veers close to abandoning it. An interest in *Finnegans Wake* seems, initially, to have been aroused by the multiplicity of meanings in Joyce's treatment of language, but this playful flexibility is neutralized by Cage's operations – concrete poetry would have provided a text closer to his own medium. Meaningless as Cage's mesostic technique is, its rule-based formula does, nevertheless, hark back to the formalist procedures of high modernism and their debt to Joyce. The Boulez of the Third Piano Sonata finds in Joyce something anonymous, self-reflective and open-ended: the puns and cyclical forms of *Finnegans Wake* are understood as formal strategies, which Boulez tries to embed within a post-serial syntax, but he misses the degree of irony and resonance that Joyce's linguistic virtuosity generates. If Boulez abstracts principles from Joyce's writing, attempting to limit them to a contained openness, Cage works with the text of *Finnegans Wake* and draws from it such diversity that diversity as a technique loses meaning.

Cage applies the principles used to write through *Finnegans Wake* to the musical dimension of *Roaratorio*, which is not surprising, given that he seems to view music as a nascent form of mesostic text; he comments: Joyce 'didn't mean *Finnegans Wake* to be understood. He meant it as a kind of piece of music' (Schöning 1982: 103). Cage's approach to the book is commensurate with his view that music is to be experienced rather than understood, saying of *Roaratorio*:

> I wanted it not to be music in the sense of music, but I wanted it to be music in the sense of *Finnegans Wake*. But not a theory about music. I wanted the music to turn itself towards *Finnegans Wake* (Schöning 1982: 89).

In much the same way that Cage concentrates on the physicality of words, so he focuses on the particularity of sounds, though it is debatable whether the sonorities are divorced from pre-established meanings, as many of them, especially the water recordings, are evocative. But by emphasizing the individuality of sound objects, Cage perhaps ventured beyond his espoused aim of making art replicate life, and instead used art as a direct model for life as it should be: sounds are released from groups and categories to be heard for what they are. The following statement provides support for this hypothesis: 'Progress may be the idea of *dominating* nature. But in the arts, it may be *listening* to nature' (Kostelanetz 1988: 230); nevertheless, Cage has little to say about the social conditioning of what appears to be 'natural', and a compositional process with no understanding of the mediation of nature and history is likely to reproduce the indifference of objects to one another, instead of illuminating their socio-historical configurations. Illusion, in Adorno's aesthetics, is the illusion of art appearing to be natural, and it resists the counter-tension for art to collapse into its individual components. Cage's music renders illusion fully transparent, since it breaks down any sense of auratic distance from the receiver or the rest of the world; but by abandoning an ideology of nature, it reduces art to the heterogeneity of an actual second nature. The question is whether the work simply emphasizes the isolation of these objects, or whether it can evoke affinities between them.

The nature we listen to in *Roaratorio* teems and surges: particular sounds are often submerged beneath the rush of multi-tracking, and there is a two-way traffic between the individual parts and the general environment of the music – sounds taking on new connotations in the changing context – but any configuration formed is little more than accidental amidst the jostling mass of material. A montage of objects rammed against one another in an unfamiliar context is suggestive of Adorno's and Benjamin's concept of constellation; nevertheless, despite the aim, shared by Cage and Adorno, of releasing the particularity of objects, there are crucial differences: constellation, for Adorno and Benjamin, holds open the tension between object and concept (in music, between form and content), while Cage's constructions tend to collapse this dialectic and capitulate to the object, as if it were unmediated. The idea of a cluster of concepts that illuminate the interior of an object, thereby revealing its strangeness and social mediation, is far removed from *Roaratorio*'s sea of co-existing objects. But whatever the theoretical limitations of Cage's claims, at places in *Roaratorio* sonorities do dislocate one another and produce new configurations, even if the result falls short of determinate irreconcilability.

Cage seems to have been touched by the history of Ireland: he admits that the tolling of the church bell he recorded and the voice of Joe Heaney contain an element of suffering:

> The whole place [Ireland] is a graveyard of architecture and they leave it that way to remind themselves that they suffered. It's almost Hebraic.
> SCHÖNING Some of this in the voice of Joe Heaney, I think.
> CAGE – and in that bell you hear in the piece, that sounds so cracked and so sad. It's both sad and joyful: laughtears (Schöning 1982: 107).

Indeed, the music of the Irish traditional musicians contains a whole history of subjectivity that is not erased by the randomized context. By using these sounds Cage invokes a history not entirely synchronous with the subsumptive logic of modernity, and, probably inadvertently, challenges consciousness with the density of individual experience, seeming to hear an expression of suffering in the voice of Heaney. The other side of this coin is that the sense of Irishness that pervades this work becomes a screen on which to project an unspecific sense of origin, which has little to do with the actuality of Ireland.

Joyce's language is ironic and self-aware, but, like a chain of signifiers in which everything is different yet the same, the texture of *Finnegans Wake* shares an affinity with the fickleness of commodity exchange.[1] Cage is sensitive to this fluidity but fails to understand that the celebration of difference and plurality can itself become a dogmatic generalization, as unyielding as a rigid adherence to order and stability. He does, however, perceive that experiences of contingency and diffuseness are linked to global commerce.

Nations belong to the past. They merely fight one another. We must study carefully the ways of large industry, so that we can implement the fact that there is no limit to the place in which we live (Cage 1987: Foreword).

A dialectical understanding of modernism shows that there is another side to this naive optimism: modernism, Raymond Williams has argued, 'is among other things a running battle between a new mode of rootless, cosmopolitan consciousness and the older, more parochial traditions from which this consciousness has defiantly broken loose' (paraphrased in Eagleton 1990: 320). Despite elsewhere espousing the cause of the particular, Cage's comment suggests the battle is over, that industrial production has irrevocably severed the link between place and identity. Such internationalism may, as Cage indicates, break down the nation state and traditional divisions, but it also renders the individual a faceless creature bobbing on the tide of commerce. Something of this transitory state is captured by Cage's use of indeterminate procedures, which access a realm he admits to not fully understanding:

> In the case of chance operations, one knows more or less the elements of the universe with which one is dealing, whereas in indeterminacy, I like to think (and perhaps I fool myself and pull the wool over my eyes) that I'm outside the circle of a known universe, and dealing with things that I literally don't know anything about (Kostelanetz 1988: 218).

The mysterious universe that indeterminacy enters for Cage bears a striking resemblance to the inscrutable world of commodity exchange, and his procedures for generating indeterminate music are not so different from the repetitive tasks that are carried out in offices throughout the world every day. The self-discipline required to deny subjectivity and to accept a situation veers dangerously close to the self-effacement demanded of the individual by an anonymous system. At its worst, the traditional aspect of the music evokes a film or advertisement sound track designed to evoke 'atmosphere', and the whole edifice simulates the confusion of television channel hopping: a welter of sounds is ripped out of context and dumped into a rush of fragments.

Mesostics may constitute a neutral method of reconstructing *Finnegans Wake*, without the impediment of interpretation and analysis, but the use of Irish music suggests a sensitivity to the duality mentioned by Williams. The conundrum posed is whether *Roaratorio* draws attention to the void nature of uprooted sounds by foregrounding the chaos of a multi-media event, and reasserts the individuality of sonorities by focusing on their commodified status, or whether it celebrates indifference and equivalence. Does the music reproduce capital's formal non-identity with itself, or does it assert the opaqueness of its objects? The two strands are not easily separated: a combination of rural sounds with traditional music is not far removed from the ambience of a butter advertisement, yet sometimes these ingredients generate a resonance and poignancy that touches older strata of history, and the surface flux of activity occasionally activates deeper modes of consciousness. These mythological folds contain both the second nature of advanced industrialism and the nimbus of an older type of knowledge: 'naturalized' historical meanings are imposed but members of the audience are also challenged to engage their own associations and experiences with the text. Because the work is non-auratic and invites the audience into its sound stream, it provides a good model for the form of intersubjective aesthetic response envisaged by Habermas and Wellmer. The question is whether anything in this text is likely to offset the audience's pre-established patterns of subjectivity, or to illuminate the social content of the sounds. That *Roaratorio* is inscrutable is, in part, an accolade to Cage, but without some provisional configuration of its components, whatever emancipatory potential lies in the work must remain dormant. Adorno's point is that the determinate irreconcilability of modernist art empowers disparate impulses to pursue a logic of their own and to find affinities that would be marginalized by a discursive medium. It is by miming the internal configurations of the music that a listener is able to engage with a non-discursive form of rationality and to understand that social formations are not immutable.[2] Meanings brought to the work should be susceptible to transformation by the work.

If one compares *Roaratorio* with an earlier score, such as *Variations IV* (in which Cage first made the association between sound and space), the later text has a stronger sense of identity. There is no mention of *Roaratorio* becoming part of another performance nor of separate events intruding upon it, and however diverse the materials that went into the piece, there is a finished version that uses a defined set of sounds. Urban noises – traffic, industry and rock music – are in general avoided in preference for natural and unprocessed human sounds; this absence lends a deliberate quality to the sound field, which is enriched by the incantatory style of Cage's reading. The traditional musicians strengthen the sound aura of the work and contribute to it a coherent musical style and skilled performance: we hear sections of folk music sufficiently long to appreciate both what the musicians are playing and their technical ability, but because this traditional musical style is based upon principles of melodic embellishment, its vitality is not extinguished by hearing the instruments separately. This pre-established musical tradition adds a syntactical component to the sea of randomness, injecting order and identity straight into the fabric; in places, however, the traditional music functions more like the other sound objects, becoming an indistinguishable part of the acoustic environment. Obviously the dancers, when used, add a further dimension, since they operate within a more improvisatory matrix than the musicians, but, as an audience will appreciate, they are both trained and skilled. In the past, Cage had undercut his own creativity by composing determinate music using indeterminate means and by creating situations for indeterminate performance. *Roaratorio* and the encompassing genre of music circus partly extricate the composer from this situation – and tacitly confirm its limitations – by organizing codes or units of meaning, instead of notes, in an indeterminate way. Such 'meta-music' – and this category includes the *Europeras* 1 and 2 – relies on pre-established connotations and connections to a greater extent than Cage's writings and theories suggest: it is composition with semantic codes, some of which have become transparent. Cage has registered a transition from working with musical material to composition as an all-inclusive semiotic code.

Further Particulars

In 'Mapping the Postmodern', Andreas Huyssen contends that 1960s postmodernism tried 'to revitalize the heritage of the European avantgarde and to give it an American form along what one could call in short-hand the Duchamp-Cage-Warhol axis' (1986: 188). Cage's music complies with at least three of the four characteristics ascribed by Huyssen to 1960s postmodernism; in fact it meets them over a wider time span. Firstly, there is the sense of rupture and discontinuity with the past that is reminiscent of Dada, and which was given a personal link by Cage's friendship with Duchamp. Secondly, in a tenet derived from Bürger's *Theory of the Avant Garde*, there was the attack on autonomous art as an institution with a dominant set of aesthetic values, and this came at a time when American institutions were rapidly assimilating modernist art. The historical avant garde's attempt to sublate art into life (to use Bürger's Hegelian terminology) finds a strong advocate in Cage's activity: 'What is happening in this century,' he says, 'whether you accept it or not, is that more and more there is no gap between art and life' (Kostelanetz 1988: 211). Cage also shared in the sense of technological optimism and exhilaration associated with the idea of a post-industrial society, the third of Huyssen's tenets for 1960s postmodernism; but this strand was tempered by a sense of the potential meaninglessness of modern urban existence. Despite his links with the pop avant garde, it is doubtful whether Cage does meet Huyssen's fourth crierion: an interest in popular culture. Had Cage paid more attention to this arena, concrete lifeworld experiences might have played a greater role in his output.

Huyssen argues that American 1960s postmodernism was a genuine avant-garde movement, with its own impetus; it was not simply a commodified repeat of the 1920s European avant garde that eluded America the first time around. This contention is historically problematic in the case of music because Charles Ives fits the model of the historical avant garde, and from him can be traced an iconoclastic lineage passing through Charles Seeger and Ruth Crawford to Cage; furthermore, Cage himself was in touch with Duchamp in the 1930s, thereby representing a continuous link between historical avant-gardism and postmodernism. Nevertheless, Huyssen's analysis is instructive in so far as Cage's ideas blossomed in the 1960s, and to some extent remained there. The crucial issue is this: does Cage's escape from high modernism simply recycle the project of the historical avant garde in a cynical, or naive, manner that commodified avant gardism, or does his work really have a genuine critical edge? Huyssen's dialectical view of the larger situation as simultaneously 'an American avant garde *and* the endgame of international avantgardism' is perceptive (1986: 195).

Both moments are there in Cage, the happening being either anti-establishment or a 'daring' society event, depending on circumstances; but collapsing art into life is always, in a sense, an endgame, ultimately reducing art to gesture. Cage reached that endpoint in the 1960s, though, in the case of *Roaratorio* and other later works, he moved beyond the posture of an empty gesture by working with semantic codes. But by clinging dogmatically to a schematic indeterminacy, he attributed wider significance to a particular historical circumstance than it deserved.

Cage's philosophy of 'purposive purposelessness' inverts Kant's formulation of aesthetic contemplation: for the latter, a beautiful thing is perceived purposively, as if a concept were to be formed, but this criterion is not met because a concept is not formed, hence the purpose is unfulfilled. Adorno reformulates this mode of purposeless purposiveness, beyond the context of Kant's model of reception, into the internal dialectics of organic art: art works are deemed purposeless in relation to instrumental rationality – they are functionally useless – but are purposive in so far as they integrate parts into a whole. The purposeful relationship between the part and whole becomes an area of tension in modernist art unless, as happens in the work of Cage, it is diffused, and Adorno's reworking of Kant's formulation is reversed. Now the work itself is internally purposeless but, at least according to some of Cage's statements, has the purpose of consciousness raising; it is a purposeless collection of parts, on a continuum with reality, with the purpose of changing people's outlook. But purposive purposelessness is precisely the condition that Adorno ascribes to the in-strumental rationality that he hopes the non-discursive medium of art can challenge. Cage's formula simply describes a world in which reification moulds consciousness, instead of consciousness transforming reification. The pervasion of reification is not, however, as extreme as this code, and indeed Adorno at his most pessimistic, suggests: mimetic impulses do emerge from Cage's work. Cage both reproduces the indifference of an exchange network and alludes to experiences that elude it; indeed, on occasion Cage does succeed in drawing attention away from the realm of music to larger issues. He rightly contends that 'what can be analyzed in my work or criticized are the questions that I ask' (Kostelanetz 1988: 85). Nevertheless, it is the wider aesthetic sphere Cage opened up that frequently undermines the principles of his work. By abandoning illusion and autonomy to indifference, Cage also sacrifices critical distance.

Cage's attack on the autonomy of art, his use of indeterminacy and pluralism, all align him with a postmodernist sensibility; but he never lost touch with the high modernist idea of constructing art by means of a strategy or plan. Though his schemes are anti-schematic, and allow their own momentum to blow themselves apart, they can be related to the issues that Boulez explores in a more formal manner. Cage also anticipated later forms of postmodernism: *Roaratorio* and the *Europeras* 1 and 2 work with coherent segments of music, the latter applying indeterminacy to the system of the arts and its history. It is at this stage that the radicalism of indeterminacy encounters tradition.

The Persistence of Modernism: *Répons*

Spatial Configurations

Like much of Boulez's music, *Répons* is a work in progress. Since its initial composition in 1981, two further and extended versions have appeared: *Répons* 3 (1984) is the latest of these, lasting approximately forty-five minutes. The title of the composition is derived from a medieval term for a specific type of responsorial choral music between soloist and choir, and, according to Gerzso (1984: 24), Boulez views the distant historical derivation of the response idea as analogous to the medieval origin of the title *Trope*, used in the Third Piano Sonata. *Répons* is scored for chamber orchestra, computer sound-processing equipment and an ensemble of soloists. In the past, Boulez had been frustrated by the division between the inherently hierarchical organization of acoustic music – even when not based on pitch structure – and the non-hierarchical tendencies of electro-acoustic music. He also found the timbral break from one medium to the other to be problematic: as early as 1958, in *Poésie pour pouvoir*, he had tried to establish a timbral continuum across the gap by the use of percussion. The computer technology used in *Répons* enabled Boulez to draw the acoustic and electro-acoustic dimensions of the work into a single organizational logic, evincing an advance in the control of music material, but the music is not held in the grip of a quasi-scientific mode of exploration that expects aesthetic considerations to take care of themselves. Boulez rejects a strand in post-war music in which 'the connection between certain aspects of musical thought and the sciences is exaggerated in order to conceal the difficulties of aesthetic choice' (quoted in Jameux 1991: 171).

Répons is intimately tied to the research objectives of IRCAM and therefore shoulders the burden of legitimating the musical activities of the institution; in particular it is linked to the development of the 4X computer and embodies the institution's commitment to a live interface between performers and electronics. The score thus represents the dominant research interests of IRCAM and occupies a complex nexus of technological, aesthetic, political and ideological interests exceptional for one composition. The intention of the present study is not, however, to discuss these specific influences – important though they are – but to show how the immanent processes of the music work in themselves and how they open onto more general social and cultural concerns.[3]

Notwithstanding Adorno's portrayal of space as reified time (at least with regard to Stravinsky), the experience of time-space compression is too strong in an age of global communication and travel for the spatial not to exert a hold on our imaginations. The intensified cycle of time-space compression experienced today, as a result of moves away from central production to diversified techniques of flexible accumulation, also grips the internal and external organization of music. The earlier serialist intersection of horizontal and vertical, which often operates alongside a bonding of surface non-repetition with an underlying repetition of the series, suggests a sense of time-space compression but fails to generate significant spatial interplay within the music. *Répons* takes on spatial organization as a creative issue: its constructional procedures continue to show an interest in the formal properties of spatial articulation, but the music also projects a sensitivity to the feel of space, more sophisticated than a miming of the prevalent mode of production. *Répons'* array of sound trajectories and the intricate, shifting mirages of its surfaces demand an aesthetic response as much as they suggest exploration of the techniques of chord transformation underlying this profusion of sound.

Répons and its associated theoretical statements have remained consistent with Boulez's frequently stated objective that the organization of music should be immanent and perceptible in musical terms, rather than imposed externally. This belief has been a decisive factor in the composer's attempt to integrate the electronic and instrumental aspects of this work under the same scheme. The dramatic entry of the soloists and the 4X computer at rehearsal figure 21 (see Table 5.1), and the spiralling electronic echoes which follow it, are all based on transpositions and transformations of a chord – the fifth chord of Example 5.1. – dubbed by Deliège the '*Répons* chord'. The soloists' opening sonority is derived from three versions of the *Répons* chord: that is, transposed up a semitone, down a semitone and placed in different octave transpositions. Within the initial sound mass, the vibraphone plays the basic chord, while the rest of the instruments perform aggregates constructed from sections of the three modified chords. The soloists' extended responses are built from further multiplications of the *Répons* chord.[4]

Boulez regards the computer as a tool for extending his preoccupation with the multiplication, superimposition and accumulation of material, announced as early as 1952 in 'Possibly . . .' (Boulez 1991). His notion of a three-dimensional arpeggio moving across from the soloists' responses to the electronic echoes, all derived from transformations of the same chord, displays a concern with isomorphism and difference – with obtaining something syntactically related yet distinct – that goes back to the problems he tried to solve with the serial proliferation of the Third Piano Sonata. The underlying logic remains abstract, but it is not prey to the assumption that a pre-compositional scheme is itself a repository of musical meaning. Whatever Boulez's intention, however, the gap between the abstract pitch derivation and the immediacy of the computer transformations hinders a smooth continuum, and the echo is the most salient point of perceptual organization, aiding the less clear sense of pitch derivation. The frequency-shifted echoes of the 4X can be scarcely related to the *Répons* chord in a direct way, but they constitute the most obvious transformation in perceptual terms and, despite the electronic medium and its timbral alteration, are commensurate with traditional notions of transposition. Placing the soloists on separate rostra, to facilitate various trajectories of sound around the auditorium, provides a visual dimension to *Répons'* spatial procedures; and it is indicative of Boulez's desire to derive the physical qualities of the music from the properties of the material that the speed at which responses rotate around the performance hall is determined by the loudness of the sounds. The technological manipulation of source material dominates the soloists' first entry, but this type of response across space is also built into much of the acoustical writing in the work.

Boulez has acknowledged that 'much of the harmonic material in *Répons* can be traced to five chords which are played in the first bar of the piece' (see Example 5.1) (1988: 31).

Example 5.1: the five primary chords

This background derivation is also partly an abstraction, since the speed at which the opening statement passes makes perception of the chords as anything other than timbre – with perhaps the exception of the fifth, the *Répons* chord – well-nigh impossible. Characteristics of these chords are, nevertheless, enlarged in the subsequent music: as other writers have pointed out,[5] the string of upturned pedals that anchors much of the music from rehearsal figures 1 to 9 can be related to the opening collection of chords, outlining a retrograde of the top line of this sequence. These pedals also provide expanded responses to the melodic gestures of the opening, but the strongest sense in which the introduction fulfils its role is by providing a palette of the techniques and textures to be used and dilated later in the course of the music.

Initiated by the entry of the soloists, the real exposition of these chords occurs in the passage between rehearsal figures 21 and 27, which is characterized by the idea of a tutti sonority followed by episodes for the soloists, and is based harmonically on a retrograde statement of the five chords. After the episode derived from chord V, chord IV is announced by the orchestra in a block of aggressive counterpoint characteristic of this piece whilst the soloists play transformations of the same material; this process is repeated with varying types of counterpoint through to chord I, and the whole passage is rounded off by a statement of chord V from the soloists. These chords provide a constancy against the diversity of the whole section and, in addition to offering a harmonic framework, constitute a timbral resource. Indeed, the sheer excitement of sonority commands this segment.

The huge amount of information in *Répons* makes it complex, but the gestures used are simple. From aural perception, it is evident that the work continually refers to the same ideas and that surface diversity and background structure trigger associations with each other. Furthermore, it is apparent that the work is structurally conceived, yet the composer has felt free to add splashes of colour for their own sake. Through its extensive tropes and elaborations, *Répons* exudes an awareness of itself as text and of its own non-identity with itself; it invites a response whereby technical analysis constitutes a dimension within a larger critical theory that can address the boundary between itself and the text to which it refers, enabling the latter's procedures to find a theoretical outlet. A discussion of the techniques of chord multiplication can explain why there is a consistency to the sound of the score, but is remote from the experience of the music, which demands a form of cognitive mapping. There will always be a gap between any linguistic or graphic description of music and its object, but if technical knowledge can be embedded within a theoretical response capable both of emulating and distancing itself from the music, then the work is opened out to wider aesthetic consideration. Because *Répons* itself deals with the whole issue of the general and the particular, it initiates a form of commentary that shuttles back and forth between these poles.

System and Idea

The arena of problems and possibilities addressed by Boulez in an article contemporary with *Répons*, 'Le système et l'idée' (1986b), is redolent of the discourses addressing the claims and potential of art that inform contemporary cultural theory. The dialectic of system and idea, which reappraises the complex interaction between structure and chance, is conceived in terms commensurate with the Adornian dialectic of concept and object. Boulez's inclination is weighted more towards the whole than the part, but his solution is an Adornian one in so far as it pays homage to both the universal and the particular by loosening the hold of the former over the latter, thereby engaging the pull towards the particular detected by Adorno in modernist art. Boulez envisages a musical material in which the system manifests itself in the structural properties of the music, but relinquishes its grip sufficiently to allow local and contingent configurations generated by the material to have an intrinsic role in the musical discourse: the system organizes the musical object, but recognizes its concreteness and its ability to generate local configurations. This concern with musical objects can be traced back to Boulez's fascination in the 1950s with Cage's aggregates, but in 'Le système et l'idée' and *Répons* it is recognized that such particulars create their own forcefields and cannot therefore be tamely organized as neutral components within a system.

The enhanced notion of a sound object expounded by Boulez suggests further comparison with Adorno's object-centred philosophy. Boulez outlines in 'Le système et l'idée' and uses in *Répons* a variety of techniques for elaborating simple and complex sound objects, and explores the configurations needed within a syntax to organize blocks from the inside or the outside. Adorno's practice of constellation, as a rethinking of part and whole beyond the idea of organic unity, has affinities with Boulez's intentions. Constellation seeks to illuminate the historical crystallisation of phenomena, so as to reveal the social tensions contained within, and to allude to a reconfiguration of the internal components within a transformed society. An object is understood in the context of its constellation; it is liberated into its own space without being effaced by some higher totality.

An aura of adjacent phenomena is formed in two basic ways in *Répons*: as an extended anacrusis-type figure before a complex sonority or as a cloud of auxiliary notes attracted to a sustained, often trilled, sonority (usually found in the soloists' writing). Boulez argues that these adjacent phenomena graft themselves onto the principal sound object without actually becoming part of it. While they do give the centre a focus it would not normally have, the embellishments possess a life of their own which enables them to form vertical aggregates with one another. The embellishing notes are not literally the system (concept) nor is the focal pitch or collection literally the idea (phenomenon), but the constellation frames its centre and illuminates the 'object's' mediation by the system along with its potential for transformation. Constellation is also pertinent to the construction of sound blocks that have an overall envelope but are made up of an array of interacting sound objects. Finally, the sense of unfolding and transformation associated with constellation is relevant to the configurations formed by blocks, to the way in which blocks can interpenetrate, and to the transformation of blocks from within by elements from the outside.

Instead of trying to legislate for unpredictability, as Boulez did in the Third Piano Sonata, in *Répons* he takes a less dogmatic approach: it is acknowledged that the exact configurations of adjacent phenomena cannot be foreseen, yet the fluidity of surface events need not upset the syntax of more stable units. Thus there is a certain immediacy on the surface of the music constituted by these adjacent phenomena, or 'free particulars', which are at liberty to make provisional connections. In the language of semiology, *Répons* allows a limited play of signifiers without the burden of fixed signification.

Table 5.1

rehearsal fig.		21	27	32
section	A	B	C	D
	introduction	soloists' entry		'Bali' ostinati
tempo	*vif, lent, vif*	*varié*	*rapide*	*vif*

rehearsal fig.	42	47	53	69/71	102
section	E	F	G	H	I
	'slow movement'		'scherzo'	'new section' (*Répons 3*)	'coda'
tempo	*lent, mais de plus en plus chargé*	*lent*	*rapide*	*rapide*	*lent*

The interaction of trills and their associated auras of adjacent notes is most extensively explored in the 'slow movement', which provided the conclusion for *Répons* 1 (section E in Table 5.1).[6] The overall effect of this movement is a gradual crescendo in volume and intensity which disintegrates towards the end, the soloists closing the section with a statement of the *Répons* chord. Although there is a beaten pulse throughout, the slow tempo, quaver = 80, and long bars render it distant against the sustained harmonies of the orchestra and the embroidery of the soloists.

The backbone of this slow section, which lasts just over five minutes, is the chord transformation shown in Example 5.2. None of these chords is obviously related to the primary chords, but they do have the predominant tone/third grouping characteristic of the *Répons* chord and the fixed E in the top could be related to chord I.[7] D, E♭ and E remain registrally fixed throughout this transformation. It is a different matter in the soloists' parts; here the main pedals – B, C, F, G and B♭ – constitute five notes of the *Répons* chord and are rotated in the soloists' parts, amidst the thick ornamentation, throughout the section (see Example 5.3). Two notes of the *Répons* chord are missing (D and A), but D operates as a pedal in the orchestra for the duration of this passage.

This chain of pitches becomes the basis for a succession of elaborate tropes. As a compositional principle this can be traced back to the tropes and grafts of the Third Piano Sonata, but in *Répons* there is not the same emphasis on deriving ornamentation and elaboration from predetermined properties of the underlying material.

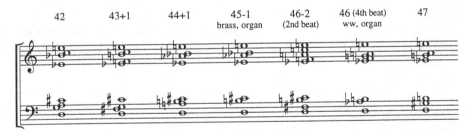

Example 5.2: principal chord changes (in orchestra) between rehearsal figures 42 and 47

© Universal Edition Ltd. Reprinted by permission.

A second set of pedals, also in the soloists' ensemble, function as 'dirty' notes, at least initially, as they cloud the line of the chord V pitches; and this secondary succession of pedals can be traced to a version of chord III, the two chords (I and III) having B♭, B and C in common. Initially the lines of pedals are quite clear, but as the ornamentation becomes more profuse the pedal notes become increasingly buried in their auxiliaries: the music takes a turn towards non-identity, or – to use Derridean terminology – the margins encroach on the centre. Through its extensive tropes and elaborations, *Répons* exudes what might be considered to be an awareness of its own textual strategies and of its own internal diversity. The ornamentation becomes thickest around rehearsal figure 46 (see Example 5.4), which is also the climax of the section in general.

Example 5.3: Principal pedals in piano 1 and vibraphone between rehearsal figures 42 and 43 (texture rhythmically simplified)

© Universal Edition Ltd. Reprinted by permission.

It is worth looking at this point in more detail. In the soloists' parts, the auxiliary notes have become a web of motion perceived more as contour than as constituent lines, and this block (or space), as a whole, permeates the three complex blocks in the orchestra. Of the orchestral blocks, the strings and woodwind respond to each other with similar material whilst the brass interject with their punctuating figures. The composite woodwind line moves in homophonic flourishes – although the deviations in the texture create a heterophony – using adjacent phenomena in a manner linked more closely to anacrusis than to the embroidered lines of the soloists, and the responding collective line in the strings utilizes the same features. The clearly contoured flourishes are obviously derived from the soloists' embellishments, but here serve to mark beats instead of to efface them; they are like slices removed from a Ligetian cluster and used as independent sound objects.

The two composite strands of woodwind and strings are distinguished by timbre but respond and interact with each other across the orchestra to form a continuous texture, into which the brass interject with rather more limited flourishes. The staccato marking, the *ff* dynamic and the metallic tone ensure that the latter cut through the texture as temporal markers instead of becoming part of the interwoven fabric; the brass also play groups of fast repeated notes – the 'morse' patterns that occur throughout the score – often as rhythmic counterpoint within a block. The staccato flourishes have the precision of the repeated note figures but are also readily related to earlier string and woodwind

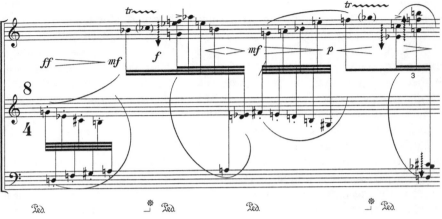

Example 5.4: *Répons*, rehearsal figure 46, from second beat, piano 1

© Universal Edition Ltd. Reprinted by permission.

figurations. Indeed, staccato flourishes are distributed throughout the two/three strands of the orchestral chain of responses, but it is the brass that dominate. Finally, although it is the brass that really distinguish beats, the whole orchestra functions as a single, complex block in the sense that everything is contained within a beat, unlike the lines of the solo ensemble which weave around the beats. The cumulative result is one of heterogeneity within a contained space. It is a swelling and extension of this web formed with the soloists that results in the tropical growth of section G, where adjacent phenomena become the texture itself: melodic material is swamped by its own aura of auxiliaries, non-identity becomes stronger than identity.

One starts to see what Boulez means by a flexible hierarchy of events and an interaction of detail and structure: individual occurrences – such as a trill, flourish or heterophonic fragment – constitute both an ingredient of a block contributing towards its overall identity and at the same time denote that block, so that a larger texture is prefigured by the local detail. Thus the interplay of figures, as discussed above, triggers larger associations. At the other pole, dense and potentially chaotic sections of the work achieve some coherence because the blocks of sound initiate connections reliant on the listener's awareness of the figures constituting events from earlier sections – even though the actual details may not be audible in the immense proliferation. Thus there is a fluidity between small-scale and larger-scale events whereby each denotes the other. The blocks are also elastic: they can be stretched out in a developmental framework, as in the slow movement, or a variety of configurations can participate in a dialogue. In his technique of constellation Boulez has managed to achieve relative weighting between sound objects and a fluid hierarchical organization, thereby side-stepping the hazard associated with Adornian constellation of levelling out the components.

Boulez outlines a syntax for composing with sound objects. Blocks can be organized from the inside or the outside; but though the criteria for one type of morphology may influence the other, they are not interchangeable. Complex external structuring, on the one hand, develops material, requiring fairly simple or neutral objects that can modify their characteristics so as to relate to other events; complex internal configurations of a block, on the other hand, require a simple, external organizational logic because 'a complex object possesses a centrifugal force', Boulez maintains, 'making it capable of entering into a conflict with the context since it retains its identity' (1987: 166–7). The constellation of components within a complex block attracts other objects to it, while the components within a simple block interact more strongly with other blocks. Form in the music is, then, generated neither exclusively from a system working down, nor from diverse elements working up, since a shape that dominates its components encounters non-identity with other blocks, and a shape that cannot stamp an identity on its components experiences stronger identity in the organization between blocks.

Not surprisingly, Boulez locates the origins of a technique of block construction in Wagner and especially late Debussy, notably in the Debussyian coagulation of complex timbres and incorporation of slight divergence within a uniform sound block (1987: 169). Célestin Deliège argues that Boulez has realized something that was only on the horizon for Debussy:

> We are then – at least if we seek to situate ourselves through some reference to heritage – closer to the clarity Webern maintained in a project of variation. More than that, Debussy's dream finds an expression he could only glimpse, unable to realize it. However, whether it is Webern, Debussy or Stravinsky in his prospective phase, the shackles of an old outline had never been suppressed (even of an indelible ABA). This time the break with the outline is consummate: the form develops through the generation and regeneration of its fundamental moments without having to define a framework agreed in advance (1988: 201–2).[8]

Debussyian intricacy is apparent in the minute gradations within blocks and the delicate mixing of timbres, but there is also the presence of Stravinskyian blocks and cells – evinced in the cellular counterpoint and heterophony within blocks and in the juxtaposition and superimposition of aggregate sounds. The relationship of Boulez's technique to that of Stravinsky is complex: the cell technique, whereby lines weave around a pitch and close adjacent notes function more as colouring of the central pitch than as harmonic entities, is clearly Stravinskyian; but it is moderated by a Debussyian concern with minute deviation within the same sonic block, to some extent sacrificing the raw energy of Stravinsky. Given that Boulez conceives of construction within the sound object as organized timbre and the manipulation of sound blocks from the outside as raw timbre, it is to the external organization of blocks that one should look for the atavism of Stravinsky. Despite the sonic excitement of *Répons* and its emphasis on timbre, the overall impression is that the influence of Stravinsky's Russian period is dissipated by Boulez's fascination with language in itself. The modification of Stravinsky's technique does, however, allow Boulez a greater degree of flexibility and sophistication in a morphology of blocks than was facilitated by Stravinsky's juxtapositions and superimpositions.

Clearly the use of block techniques in *Répons*, particularly when the influence of Stravinsky is implied, calls attention to the, in Adorno's opinion, potentially regressive qualities of static music. Boulez too is well aware of the drawbacks, and his notion of structuring blocks from the inside and the outside creates an environment in which no single type of temporal organization will prevail: the primarily static forms of construction found within blocks are placed in a temporal dynamic by the configurations of blocks utilized by the composer. There is, therefore, what might be termed a narrative, or temporal, flow throughout the piece, and some of the more chaotic sections occurring later in the work would not be comprehensible without the setting out of material earlier. Nevertheless, the temporal organization amounts to far more than a simple unfolding. In perhaps a radical conception of developing variation, one in which timbre is a significant organizational factor, the basic sound objects of the piece are always there in a form that constantly renews its instants, but rather than dominating the texture they are thrown into different configurations. *Répons* thus utilizes a degree of repetition, but because this is inlaid with constant divergence the music is not domineering. Instead of Adorno's notion of a static form in which events are equidistant from the centre, Boulez has created a spatial form whereby each configuration changes through time, but refers to the same idea (Adorno GS 18: 68). It is actually closer to Adorno's own perception of aesthetic theory as a collection of incomplete complexes arranged concentrically around an undefined centre of gravity, understood more as an overall constellation than as a succession of events. *Répons*' cross-fertilization of individual moments with a non-coercive whole is embedded within Boulez's recognition of and response to the issues of identity and non-identity, mimesis and construction. The way in which objects constituting a block retain their identity, whilst interacting within the block and within the constellation of blocks, is inseparable from their spatial framework, while the timbral dimension of the work ensures that such objects, or moments, contribute to the larger events. The overall vision does indeed suggest an idea of form that lies beyond the boundaries of an impaired mode of discursive rationality.

Phantasmagoria

In 'Timbre and Composition – Timbre and Language', Boulez comments as follows:

> The small ensemble primarily uses the analysis of discourse by means of timbre, creating interest by refinement and division, while the large ensemble primarily uses multiplication, superimposition, accumulation, creating an illusion, what Adorno called (in another context) phantasmagoria. The large ensemble, the orchestra, is the model, even, of the instrument of illusion, of phantasm, while the small ensemble represents the world of immediate reality and analysis. The small ensemble is

preferably the world of articulation, while the large ensemble is essentially the world of fusion. Articulation and fusion, these are the opposite poles of the use of timbre in the instrumental world (1987: 167).

That *Répons* is the background for these remarks seems likely, but it offers interactions of ensemble and orchestra, articulation and fusion more complex than the clear distinctions of Boulez's statement would suggest. The soloists might, at a basic level, be the ensemble of articulation, but their rich elaboration frequently reaches a level of complexity that passes into fusion; equally, although the orchestra often does function on a level of fusion, the blocks it fuses are internally articulated, and the orchestral writing is at times more defined than that of the ensemble. This kind of role reversal is seen in section B: the orchestra articulates the basic chord in blocks while the soloists play a conglomerate of the same chord.

Boulez's reference to Adorno's musical conception of phantasmagoria is extremely suggestive. The context in which Adorno uses the word – to which Boulez alludes but does not cite – is the Wagner monograph, in which there is a chapter entitled 'Phantasmagoria'.[9] Wagner generates phantasmagoric textures when the drama has recourse to a magical or mystical realm, as a way of escaping reality or as the image of a superior order; and these moments are, in Adorno's judgement, precisely those in which the music converges most directly with reality in the shape of a commodity form that effaces its means of production. Thus, although Wagner's phantasmagoria exert a fascination on Adorno, his analysis depicts such passages as insidious deception, as an intensification of illusion.

It is surprising, then, that Boulez should use the designation in such close proximity to his own ideas; although it does prove to be provocative in relation to *Répons*, he leaves as a residue the original context of the idea. That remainder is the aesthetic and ideological field to which the term refers in Adorno's analysis, and this cannot be simply filtered from a compositional adaptation of the phenomenon. When Boulez implements the idea, however, he intends to make phantasmagoria an integral part of the compositional fabric instead of using it primarily as a tool for the masking of constructional procedure, though it is questionable whether the latter procedure is prevalent in Wagner.

Phantasmagoria relates to the outward manifestation of the music – its aesthetic appearance or illusion (*Schein*) – and to the object's capacity for hiding its artifice. In a sense, the outer shell of *Répons* does conceal its methods of fabrication: the sheer sonorities and intricate surface textures achieve a certain independence and tantalizingly deflect the ear away from their construction. But a counter-process is usually at work: just as the motivic shapes that constitute the Wagnerian illusion of endless melody are not always as rigid as Adorno suggests, so the often seamless flood of sound in *Répons* does not always absorb its minutely differing sound objects. Boulez has achieved a dialectic of articulation and fusion, although it is conveyed more by means of a dialogue between the inside and outside of blocks than by configurations of ensemble and orchestra. What Boulez refers to as the organization of large ensemble writing does pertain to phantasmagoria, but the negative Adornian implications are weakened by the articulation as well as fusion between blocks. Picking up the correlation that Boulez draws between articulation versus fusion and reality versus phantasmagoria, it is almost as if the composer has created a language of composition as a distillation of construction and illusion in which the border between the one and the other is blurred. In other words, the music has taken on as an inner dynamic the dialectic of illusion and the amorphous moment. Illusion is knowingly used as illusion to create distance, but it cannot stamp a rigid identity on particular moments.

The dimension of *Répons* closest to the outward appearance of a commodity is obviously the computer sound transformation, and here the criss-crossing of aesthetic currents is complex. The resonance of magic and distance, which in Adorno's analysis of Wagner merely reaffirm the historical conditions of the time, reappears in *Répons*: the vast pulsing sound masses of the soloists' entry and coda have a magic dimension, and impressions of distance are intensified by the echoes, spiralling around the system so that various areas of the audience hear different aspects of the sound. All of this suggests a short circuit, in which the 'other' world of Wagner becomes the super-modernism of information technology – 'phantasmagoria as the point at which aesthetic appearance becomes a function of the character of the commodity' (Adorno 1981: 90). On this level, and to the extent that these techniques permeate further aspects of the composition, the complexity of the score mirrors the impenetrable web of information exchange; indeed, the techniques of *Répons* are powerful methods for organizing large amounts of data and emulate the contemporary shift in modernity.

Boulez is, however, at great pains to point out that he is not a servant of technology, and that the crossover between the instrumental and computer domains of this work is reflective of a compositional logic rather than technological supremacy. The music seems to work on two levels: on one level the impact of the soloists chords (rehearsal figure 21) does appear to hold out the impossible and illusory promise of computer technology; on another it elicits an excitement in sound for its own sake which, like passages in Stravinsky and Debussy, breakthrough reified subjectivity. The flow of information in *Répons* does not share the rigid identity of much technical information manipulation. It offers ways of opening difference within a flow of repetition: the differing and deferring inscribed in Derrida's notion of *différance* are evident in the interplay of particulars, but interact with other processes in the music, thereby not haemorrhaging formations of identity.

In Wagner's phantasmagoria, according to Adorno, the 'music pauses and is made spatial' (Adorno 1981a: 86). Certainly, in the fire music that engulfs the end of *Die Walküre* the constituent parts are very much components of the whole, but Adorno is insensitive to the degree of internal articulation within this sonority. Despite his intolerance of the spatial in Wagner, Adorno's own notion of constellation is a spatially-derived metaphor and invokes an understanding of statics and dynamics more sophisticated than he brings to bear on Wagner. In the case of *Répons*, the enclosed internal construction of some blocks is frequently offset by the constellations in which they are set, and one is aware that the particular processes contributing to even those blocks possessing a strong overall identity retain a certain individuality of their own. To draw a social analogy: within a defined social space people are able to construct their own spaces, which are not totally identical with the perceived social surface. In other words, reification can be resisted on a more local and provisional basis than Adorno often indicates. Similarly, spaces within music can resist the dead time of reification, and Adorno does seem to envisage something like this in a passage that draws attention to the inability of constructivist art to suppress all heterogeneity:

> Those tiny spaces between single elements in constructivist art betray the cleavages that exist in an otherwise homogeneous work, just as they exist in a society in the age of total administration (1984a: 224).

Boulez attempted to manage the cleavages that find their way into constructivist art in the Third Piano Sonata, but in *Répons* individual details are given a certain independence from the underlying system. On a slightly larger scale, much of *Répons* evokes the feel of objects reacting to one another in space, but without a sense of emptiness or of events happening despite the compositional logic. *Répons*, together with Boulez's associated ideas of construction in music, moves beyond a traditional conception of successive events unfolding in time, but does not transform development into 'the space of simultaneous possibilities' which, David Roberts maintains, is the 'other' of Adorno's own paradoxical modern paradigm (1991: 219).[10] Simultaneous possibilities with a degree of contingency do occur within the spaces of *Répons*, but they operate within the latency of an organizing material that is not exhausted by contingency.

What then of the utopian potential in art which informs so much Frankfurt critical theory? Boulez asks a similar question:

> So then, what can be done to ensure that variance and coherence, global vision and accident of the instant, the abolition of chance and the preservation of free will, primacy of order and transgression of the law, exist simultaneously? (1986b: 95).[11]

Though perhaps overstressing the need for control, this statement alludes not only to a utopian vision of music but also to a radical politics, and Boulez seeks to combine the best aspirations of both modernism and postmodernism without either cancelling the other. The objective remains an ideal, but Boulez has succeeded in creating a musical style with sufficient flexibility to achieve a crossover between the universal and the particular without one crushing the other. Momentous as this achievement is, its heavy reliance on a conscious advancement of musical material weakens the mediation through the subject which lies at the heart of Adorno's fascination with Schoenberg. Though at times achieving the directness of sonority associated with Wagner and Stravinsky, *Répons'* blocks fail to convey the rawness of experience that projects through those composers, and which at its best cuts through the circle of regression circumscribed by Adorno. This lack of bite is reflected in the homogeneous saccharine tendencies of the choice of instrumentation for the soloists' ensemble. The inner consistency of the music and the absence of hard dissonance dissipate a sense of tension and release, encouraging a certain disinterested contemplation of the music. Boulez's network of shifting configurations extends beyond anything concretely envisaged by Adorno, but the interplay of system and idea is better conveyed as 'determinate difference' than 'determinate irreconcilability'.

And what of the Adornian dream of a second mimesis emerging on the other side of rigorous construction as envisaged in *Doctor Faustus*? The loosening of structural rigour in *Répons* reveals this as a forlorn hope, since it binds construction with a primary instead of a secondary sensuality; with the immediacies of individual moments and of the surface aura, which, because they cross through larger configurations, are not atrophied tokens of spontaneity. The mimetic qualities of the music, to use Adorno's term, can be perceived here less as a recalcitrance in the material than as a freedom in those moments that intersect the constructional technique without being completely controlled by it. That this mimesis fails to permeate all levels of the work is not indicative of the inadequacy of the material but, again, of the investment placed in the efficacy of the substance: form and content establish a fluid dialogue, but it is not put under strain. Boulez has found a way of working within the language-in-itself sphere of Mallarmé, which does not collapse the whole edifice, but the result lacks the potential critical force afforded by expressive tension. As befits a work composed in the era of poststructuralism, *Répons* progresses through an elaborate series of tropes and grafts, with a self-awareness of its own textual strategies, but does not collapse coherence into unbridled difference. Through his dogged attachment to the Adornian precept of historically advanced musical material, Boulez has forged a mode of musical thought that, even if it does not achieve its full expressive and critical potential, is capable of embracing the diversity and contradictions of advanced industrial society on a level that invites theoretical reflection. This late-twentieth-century work cannot bypass completely the aporias detected by Adorno in modern art, but it offers resources and possibilities that both vindicate and expand the hopes locked in his convoluted aesthetics.

Notes

1. This point is made by Eagleton 1990: 318.
2. See Zuidervaart 1991: 142–3 for an account of this topic.
3. See Born 1995 for an ethnographic investigation of IRCAM as an institution.
4. Boulez and Gerzso have published details of this transposition process (1988: 183).
5. See Bradshaw 1986, and Nattiez 1989.
6. The diagram of *Répons* 3 given in Table 5.1 is based upon the plan of *Répons* 2 given by Dominique Jameaux (1991: 368). Jameaux also provides details of the instrumentation, sound-processing equipment and seating arrangements for *Répons*.

7. It seems likely that this chord progression, and indeed much more of this music is based on a transformation of the primary chords, but without information from the composer the derivation is abstract. In technical discussion I have sought to identify features in which there is a clear sense of basic ideas being constantly present.

8. My translation.

9. See Chapter 2 for further discussion of phantasmagoria in Wagner. For more extended discussion of phantasmagoria in Wagner, see Alastair Williams: 1997.

10. See Chapter 6 for more on Roberts' critique of Adorno.

11. My translation.

6 Discourses of Modernity

Aesthetics Reclaimed

The problem with Adorno's social theory, according to Habermas, is that his understanding of instrumental rationality takes on the all-pervasive tendency of the phenomenon he is describing: he simply fails to recognize the existence of non-reified rationality in any sphere except an agonized thought process which is itself implicated. It was argued in Chapter 1 that this diagnosis is too extreme but, though Habermas's interventions have their own problems, the distinction he makes between system and lifeworld is useful. Accepting Habermas's critique of Adorno's theory of instrumental reason, Albrecht Wellmer has attempted to translate Adornian aesthetics into the framework of a theory of communicative action receptive to Benjamin's sanguine appraisal of modernism. The argument is based on the claim that if Adorno's concept of rationality is expanded communicatively, 'then his truth aesthetics may also be expanded "pragmatically"' (Wellmer 1985c: 65). The utopian dimension is shifted away from Adorno's dialectical constructs towards a multidimensional perspective of unblocked communication, whereby individuals communicate both with themselves and with one another. By emphasizing art as a dialogical *medium* rather than a *model* of such communicative relationships, Wellmer intends to redirect the emphasis placed by Adorno on the power of art to point beyond itself, towards

> the social life-process itself as it can be affected by aesthetic experience. Understood in this way, aesthetic experience, by illuminating our life praxis and our self-understanding, by pushing back the boundaries of muteness and inarticulate silence, and by making accessible the hidden depths of our lives to ourselves, is, as Adorno thought, the presence of a utopian perspective (1985c: 65).

Wellmer's 'stereoscopic' reading of Adorno claims that the mimetic only functions as the other for Adorno because it is excluded by a philosophy of consciousness that cannot encompass the mimetic in conceptual thought; but, he contends, when one shifts to a philosophy of intersubjectivity, the mimetic becomes a communicative moment of mind, grounded in language. In the course of his argument, however, Wellmer comes close to claiming that, for Adorno, mimesis functions as the other of reason; a stance that is skewed, since it is only the other of a reason governed by a fetish of identity. An emancipated rationality, in Adorno's opinion, would be able to function without subsuming or marginalizing the particularity voiced by aesthetic-expressive considerations.

When Wellmer redirects the utopian dimension of Adorno's aesthetics, art works are no longer understood to be windowless monads, which are partly accessible to philosophical knowledge; instead, cultural artefacts are considered to affect, in Wellmer's words 'subjects' relationships to themselves and to the world, where art-works intervene in a complex interrelationship of attitudes, feelings, interpretations, and value judgements . . . "knowledge" here denotes a result which stands closer to a knowing-how than a knowing-that' (1985a: 105). How this model would function is not immediately clear, but Benhabib provides some help: she (and to some extent Habermas in his recognition of the world-disclosing potential of art) views aesthetic forms of expression as a means of rendering inner nature communicatively fluid and transparent, to the extent that unarticulated needs can be released from their paleosymbolic prelinguisticality (Benhabib 1986: 333). Art thus seems to be given the function of making internal experience available to linguistic formulation, of making possibly unconscious needs accessible to rational discourse, though art, of course, expresses a wider range of experience than the prelinguistic. So the interaction of intersubjective communication with the art work 'is both interpretation (commentary) and actualization (confrontation, immediate emotion), and becomes criticism by combining these two aspects' (Rochlitz 1989: 26); but the model risks eliminating the specificity of the object.

Adorno's aesthetics may benefit from an emphasis on dialogically negotiated meaning, but the following passage demonstrates that his dogged tracking of the object is not inimical to a communicative dimension in art:

> Listening as becoming through the many (*Das Vernommenwerden durch viele*) lies at the basis of musical objectification itself, and when it is excluded, it is necessarily degraded almost to a fiction – to the arrogance of the aesthetic subject, which says We while in reality it is still only I – and this I can say nothing at all without positing the We (Adorno 1973a: 18–19).[1]

Adorno's idea of collectivity is locked into the material of artistic production – which already contains a sedimented layer of subjectivity – and prefigures an emancipated collectivity. Wellmer's plurality of voices (which is sympathetic to some tenets of poststructuralism), by contrast, foregrounds a receptive frame-work whereby art feeds into a potential communicative network. He suggests, with justification, that different lifeworld experiences will impact on aesthetic reception, and these interactions can be discussed in an intersubjective discursive practice where art's embodiments of, and effects on, subjectivities are contest-able. Such a model of active reception need not be incompatible with Adorno's aesthetics, though his emphasis on artistic production provides a corrective to the excessive attention paid to the reader in some modern theory, providing the art work is understood as a multitextual intersection fed by formations ranging from the institutions of art to personal experience. In other words, musical material already contains a confluence of system and lifeworld practices, and this will interact with whatever is brought to bear upon its reception. Mahler's music, to take an example, draws on the composer's childhood and the institution of bourgeois autonomous art, while engaging in a dialogue with symphonic form.

Wellmer suggests that the full truth potential of art can only be released through an aesthetic discourse in which the participants' life experiences in all three validity spheres are brought to bear upon the issue of aesthetic rightness. Following Habermas, and in contradiction with Derrida's strenuous efforts to show that philosophical truth claims cannot be divorced from literary language, he tries to insulate cognitive truth claims from the rhetorical devices of artistic practice, claiming that artistic truth can only be metaphorical, but through the medium of aesthetic discourse has access to functional and moral-practical, as well as aesthetic-expressive validity claims. Wellmer frames the argument as follows:

> Neither truth nor truthfulness may be attributed unmetaphorically to works of art, if one understands 'truth' and 'truthfulness' in the sense of a pragmatically differentiated everyday concept of truth. That truth and truthfulness – and even normative rightness – are instead *metaphorically* bound up with each other in the work of art may only be explained by the fact that the work of art, as a symbolic construct with an aesthetic validity claim, is at the same time an object of life-world experience in which the three validity domains are *unmetaphorically* intermeshed (1985a: 109).[2]

This statement has been enthusiastically quoted by Habermas, in an attempt to indicate what a communicative aesthetics might look like (1985: 203). Adorno's argues, on the contrary, that all three validity spheres are mediated in art, and it makes contestable, not absolute, truth claims by exposing a prevalent rationality to elements normally excluded from its domain. But, while one can agree with Wellmer that a dialogical exchange takes places between artistic truth claims and the lifeworld experience of its audience, Adorno is surely right to insist that artistic material, because it sediments prevalent modes of rationality, is not entirely metaphorical. Artistic truth must, for Wellmer, be metaphorical because he limits truth claims to statements made in discursive logic.[3] Nevertheless, alongside this view, Wellmer's attempt to bring out a latent voice in Adorno's aesthetics, one that addresses aesthetic validity or rightness (knowing-how), alongside the more obvious attention to cognitive truth (knowing-that), is important. It brings to the fore music's capacity to be an interventive medium, connecting with lifeworld experience, the particular and sensual, instead of merely registering a subjectivity damaged by instrumental reason. Intersubjectively negotiated aesthetic validity thus becomes a possible political force. Little is gained, however, by suggesting that artistic insight should be grounded in a quasi-transcendental philosophy of language.

Wellmer considers that happenings, which sometimes have an improvisatory component, might be a fruitful area for communicative aesthetics; and these events certainly create a forum in which the exchange of lifeworld experiences becomes feasible, but they also embody a tendency, not mentioned by Wellmer, for standard modes of discourse to be simply confirmed, without engaging anything other than themselves. The earlier discussion of *Roaratorio* demonstrated that the associations conventionally attached to objects are not easily estranged. The model of artistic reception theorized by Wellmer does nevertheless provide a good image for production of music with an improvisatory component: skilled improvisers generate a collective identity through the material or score and their historical location, they can respond to contingent situations, and yet are able to maintain individual identities by way of their personal contributions. The constant danger that haunts this type of practice, however, is that performers will lapse into predictable patterns because placing an emphasis on open groupings does not eliminate problems of technique, form and musical content.

Wellmer seeks to continue the project of modernity, but his communicative aesthetics – and it shares this quality with many postmodernist theories – places more emphasis on the reception of art than on its production, tending to leave issues of material, construction and form to take care of themselves. His argument overemphasizes the sensuous moment of world-disclosure at the expense of the rational, constructive pole of art, and he fails to grapple with the whole modernist problematizing of immediacy. However, the stress on reception seeks to highlight an imbalance in Adorno's work where a two-tier system operates: autonomous art is judged according to criteria of production and popular culture according to standards of reception. Actually, in the latter case production and reception merge; and, because Adorno locates artistic truth in material production, he concludes that production and reception of popular culture are locked in a vicious circle of regression. To put the matter more formally, Adorno argues that the forces of production (composition and performance) are dominated by the relations of production (economic circumstances and the mentality of reception) in the case of popular music; autonomous music he suggests, on the other hand, can resist or even partially transform the prevalent relations of production.[4]

It is more fruitful to envisage a dialectic of production and reception traversing the cultural spectrum: if Adorno's torn halves of autonomous and mass art cannot be reconciled, they can at least interact with each other (1977a: 123). Such a reconstructed aesthetic framework need not dissolve into an uncritical absence of differentiation; instead, it allows one to analyse dialectically the interaction between manipulative and emancipatory aspects of artistic practice. Adorno's own dialectic of identity and non-identity, geared to demonstrating how individual elements evade the system, provides the tools for a less dogmatic approach to popular culture and offers a way of recognizing the possibility for individual popular songs and associated lifeworld practices to be non-identical with the system of production, hence opening space for manoeuvre within the monolith. As Ernst Bloch recognized, most popular and, indeed, mass art contains a mimetic impulse, whatever the extent of its distortion, and Adorno himself finds an 'indelible mimetic element in all cognition and all human practice' (1973b: 150).

Once it is recognized that contemporary culture is simply too diverse to be adequately embodied by a single stock of historically-sedimented material, then it becomes necessary to examine the dialectic of reified and responsive subjectivity within various artistic practices and to judge each case on its merits. An expanded aesthetic apparatus will recognize that subjectivities are negotiated within intersecting cultural fields, and that, though the process is more obvious in popular music, it is no less true of austere music, whatever the sedimentation of its codes and its apparent distance from the lifeworld. One artefact might strive to envisage new formations of the whole and the part, another might associate itself with accessible forms of subjective expression. A popular music, for example, that elicits a sense of non-administered pleasure or bodily freedom possesses more than an affinity with such feeling, and suggests behaviour close to the actual forms of non-instrumental subjectivity. Whether popular music embodies non-coercive social configurations or, conversely, manipulated desires, has much to do with whether its social forms are imposed from above or emerge from the lifeworld. Popular music depends less on the subjectivity encoded in the material for its validity than on the subjectivity encountered in performance and reception, and it is just conceivable that emancipated conditions of production and reception might illuminate and transform the social content of material acted upon. If the challenge for popular art is to defy the culture industry; the task for autonomous art is to avoid becoming a celebration of its own techniques and institutions. It is crucial for both areas that conditions of reception are not completely determined by the systems of production and distribution.

In the case of art music, intersubjectivity is encountered in socially-sedimented materials and to a lesser extent in performance. This distillation, it should be remembered, embraces a multitextual ensemble of practices and influences, components of which will appear in different weightings according to the receptive framework. Readers may choose to emphasize particular features, or even generate innovative ones, by asking new questions of familiar art works or practices. Autonomous art is called upon to absorb into its construction and reception the diversity of available cultural experiences (at risk to its own survival), though not necessarily to absorb their content or particular features. Diversity, experienced as an immanent dynamic, is far more compelling than an array of manifold contents, and it may well be this self-reflective ability that distinguishes art music from other practices. Autonomous art cannot claim to be the only authentic mode of subjective creation, but its seriousness and mimetic dimension will be attested to by its ability to contemplate diversity and coherence within the same arena.

Postmodernism

The various logics of disintegration pursued by Boulez and Cage can be related to both Adornian critical theory and deconstructive practice, but all these streams of thought also pertain to the larger body of ideas and practices encapsulated by the term 'postmodernism'. Just as Adorno is often portrayed by poststructuralists either as a precursor of deconstruction or as a dogged dialectician, so he is frequently interpreted by proponents of postmodernism as a prototype postmodernist or a hard-baked advocate of an outmoded modernism.[5] The designations 'postmodernism' and 'poststructuralism' are sometimes loosely used synonymously – or, at least, poststructuralism is understood as a way of thinking commensurate with the epochal shift to postmodernity – but there are differences between them: poststructuralism's textual explorations of metaphysics, artistic autonomy, narrative and history challenge but do not jettison the discourses of modernity; many forms of postmodernism, in distinction, claim to be beyond this framework.[6] Indeed, the tools of deconstruction can be used to challenge effectively some of the essentialist claims made by postmodernists.

The work of Jean-François Lyotard bridges the two tendencies, by challenging the philosophical systems – which he refers to as grand narratives – of Enlightenment thought. He argues that the great socio-historical narratives of modernity collapse into a heterogeneity of self-regulating little narratives, maintaining that no master narrative can govern the narratives of social exchange and daily life. In Lyotard's view, modernist art, for which Proust and Joyce serve as examples, 'allows the unpresentable to be put forward only as the missing contents; but the form, because of its recognizable consistency, continues to offer to the reader or viewer matter for solace or pleasure' (Lyotard 1984: 81). The postmodern in art, by contrast,

> would be that which, in the modern, puts forward the unpresentable in presentation itself; that which denies itself the solace of good forms, the consensus of a taste which would make it possible to share collectively the nostalgia for the unattainable; that which searches for new presentations, not in order to enjoy them but in order to impart a stronger sense of the unpresentable (1984: 81).

There is, then, a clear distinction between modernist and postmodernist art, but Lyotard also argues that the two are inextricably linked moments of each other. Although postmodernism takes art to its limit, it functions less as an historical condition than as a continual possibility, and is thus interpreted not as the successor to modernism but as the latter in its nascent state, the stage of disintegration that precedes a period of artistic consolidation. Lyotard suggests that postmodernist art should extend beyond existing rules to something which can be thought but not presented, that is, brought under the concept. Art and theory meet in postmodernism: theory becomes the continuation of art.

Comparing Adorno's and Lyotard's theories of art, Wellmer notes that 'for Adorno, the work of art is the sensuous appearance and the appearing presence of what may neither be thought nor represented – reality in the state of reconciliation; for Lyotard art becomes the allusive reference to what may be thought but cannot be represented' (1985b: 345). A similar symmetry was observed in Chapter Four between, again, Adorno's utopian perspective and Derrida's elusive notion of the trace, and it was suggested that both could be brought down from their elevated positions. Lyotard's vision of postmodernist art is less transposable: though, like Derrida's trace, it is described as an instability associated with modernism, Lyotard champions heterogeneity, associating a reconciliation of the concept with the sensible as a desire for terror (1984: 82). Now Adorno's strong utopian dimension may be extreme and his exaggeration of instrumental reason excessive but, because he abandons neither identity nor non-identity, his tools are sensitive to non-reified subjectivity. Lyotard, on the other hand, finds an exact fit between the concept and totality, so is forced to celebrate heterogeneity, without envisaging an intersubjective interplay of affinity and non-identity. Instead, then, of contemplating how art might be rooted in the specialized languages of the lifeworld, Lyotard confers on it the paradoxical aim of presenting the unpresentable. Cage's *Variations IV* can be examined from this perspective: its form is unpresentable and, apparently, cannot be brought under a concept, but this type of experiment tends to reproduce the homogeneity of the administered world which, so to speak, comes with a prepacked concept. The result has little transformative potential because, without subjectivities interacting with the estranged objects, altered perception is unlikely. Lyotard, like Cage, identifies a fragmentation which is more a product of system pervasion than a lifeworld antidote.

Postmodernism is frequently assumed to have superseded a flawed modernism, but the perception of modernism that accompanies this claim is often stereotyped because it views modernism as little more than a correlate of industrial and technical modernization, with its concomitant insistence on progress. There are two streams of postmodern response to this limited understanding: one registers the shift from heavy industrial production to service industries, information technology, advertisement-generated demand and the increased compulsion towards innovation; the other, related to new social movements, attempts to break out of production-oriented parameters. Many of the art forms that arose during the 1960s, such as chance music and pop art, are frequently understood as reactions against the determinist, technological modernism of the 1950s and the serious, modernist art at this time being canonized by institutions such as the New York Museum of Modern Art. The situation is, however, more complex than this interpretation indicates: the pop avant garde and experimental art may challenge the divide between elitist and mass art, but they are still very much at one with the notion of the new and of technical advancement, pop art, in particular, using the symbols of a society bent on technical advancement and registering the penetration of the lifeworld by system functions. By contrast, the postmodernism of the 1970s and 80s, with its reclamation of traditional techniques through pastiche and quotation – both in their conservative and radical vein – reacts strongly against that core of high modernism which rejects the past in favour of a technological future.

Huyssen is right to contend that postmodernism should be understood less as a reaction against modernism *per se* than as a rejection of a particularly determinist brand of high modernism prevalent in the 1950s, characterized by integral serialism, abstract expressionism and Le Corbusier's style of architecture (Huyssen: 1986). It was undoubtedly important to assert that spontaneity could survive the grip of high modernism, but neither the artistic activities nor the conceptual framework of the pop avant garde advanced beyond the frontiers of Adorno's rich aesthetic understanding of modernism. Adorno, too, was well aware of the problems posed by an over-determinist modernism, but remained wary of erasing the distinction between art and life; and if Adorno was sceptical about the projects of Dada and Surrealism, then his aesthetic remains a salutary warning to the optimism of a pop avant garde.

The blurring of high- and low-art distinctions characteristic of much postmodernist culture in the 1960s bears resemblances to the project of the historical avant garde, as interpreted by Bürger (1984). Certainly, pop art initially registers as an attack on the institution of autonomous art: by flooding the art world with images from everyday life and openly acknowledging mechanical reproduction, notably in the silkscreen technique of Andy Warhol, it attempts to break through the aura of the art work. Nevertheless, if the initial avant-garde movement was a disappointment, pop art merely repeats the same scenario with an important difference: it accepts the primacy of commodity fetishism and thereby surrenders its critical function, becoming an affirmation of art as exchange-value;[7] after all, it is Warhol's reproductions of Campbell soup cans that are in the art gallery, not the actual goods.[8] Even if one agrees with Huyssen's contention that the experimental art of the 1960s in the United States functioned as something close to a genuine avant garde, owing to the European location of the historical avant garde (Huyssen 1986: 188–95), this impulse was quickly absorbed into an affirmative culture.

Minimalist music, with its hedonistic feel, tonal shapes and derivations from African rhythmic patterns, constitutes a striking rejection of high modernism as an institution, and emphasizes the semiotic – understood in Kristeva's sense of the term as articulation of desires prior to language or formation of the subject – in contrast to the high modernist fetish of symbolic articulation (see Kristeva 1986: chapter 4). In Adornian terminology, the area of experience Kristeva dubs 'semiotic' is addressed by his theory of mimesis, but Adorno is insistent that the mimetic can only be brought out through a crossover with construction – indeed Kristeva is clear that the semiotic is accessed through symbolic forms. The problem is that if the constructive element of music is reduced to repetitive cycles, then the mimetic dimension is likely to mime the prevailing systemic logic of equivalence instead of rechannelling it. Indeed, minimalism does bear striking parallels with the image-dominated aspects of contemporary life: the ceaseless activity of self-referential ostinati suggests a surface with no depth, an endless circulation of signifiers, and Reich's and Glass's techniques resemble information banks that disgorge huge quantities of repetitive data, criss-crossing to form new permutations within the identity of a self-contained system. The constant busy patterns are like an auditory analogue to the repetitive flow of information technology, and, in common with much advertising, the music has a monistic, safe feel to it, though its phase shifts are innovative.

The attack on institutionalized high modernism by minimalism and the pop avant garde is more damaging to the high modernism of the 1950s, which widened the distinction between art and mass culture, than to an Adornian conception of modernist art. Many of the art forms of the 1960s, together with the more recent cultural practices associated with new social movements, emphasize the sociality of art against the remote abstraction that had prevailed, and indicate rightly that there is more social spontaneity to be tapped than Adorno envisaged. However, Adorno too argues that 1950s abstraction often mimes an instrumental rationality instead of approaching it through the density of experience, but his fear is that, without a degree of autonomy, art will simply mime the ways in which system integration bears down on the lifeworld, to use Habermas's terminology. Warhol's most significant achievement was to expose and to flaunt the mechanisms of the art market by openly substituting exchange value for use value; but by drawing attention to art as a commodity with exchange value, Warhol merely made explicit a condition that runs right through Adorno's ruminations about culture, whilst sacrificing art's internal ability to resist such commodification. While it is true that the role attributed to instrumental rationality by Adorno is over pervasive, and he fails to recognize areas of immediacy that are not commodified or administered, his insistence that art's significance lies in its resistance to standardized practices remains salient. The pop avant garde may draw attention to mechanized shallowness, but its mapping onto the commodity form fails to subvert this condition.

The penetration of everyday experience and the art world by the image forms of the commodity, as registered by Warhol, is recognized, but vastly inflated beyond its actual sphere of influence by Jean Baudrillard, perhaps the most extreme theorist of the postmodern. For him, the pervasion of the image is such that it totally absorbs reality into the simulacrum, leaving no remainder: because the simulacrum shortcircuits reality, it can be neither true nor false, since one does not have access to the real as a vantage point from which to criticize it, and there can be no talk of ideology because this concept is predicated on the ability to analyse distortions of reality. The world is perceived as a surface with no depth: one cannot peep behind it because 'it is always a false problem to want to restore the truth behind the simulacrum' (1988: 182). This viewpoint takes the Adornian fear of an administered world, which is in itself too generalized, to a nihilistic extreme; but, while Baudrillard's outlook is politically bleak, it is obvious that he provides very little evidence to suggest that truth is squeezed out by the hyperreal, or that people are held in thrall to simulacra – after all, suffering remains real enough. Baudrillard's theory provides a description of certain areas of advanced industrial society, such as the communications industry, advertising and credit finance, but makes the mistake of applying these observations to other phenomena in an indiscriminate manner.

Harvey argues that the kind of hyperreality described by Baudrillard can be traced to an intense phase of time-space compression, this experience being the latest in a succession of time-space compression waves generated by the dynamics of capital accumulation. Allied to this current phase, Harvey argues, is a move from the economics of Fordist modernity to the finances of flexible accumulation, meeting every demand by rapid production and fast transportation in preference to holding large warehouse stocks. Under these conditions employment becomes unstable – it is characterized by the short-term contract – and production processes become more geographically dispersed; typically to exploit cheap labour in advantageous locations. This situation is matched by increased advertising, greater variation in consumption, entrepreneurialism and neo-conservatism. Capital becomes more globally differentiated but creates substantial homogenization: the same chain stores and fast food outlets are found in most of the world's major cities. Money itself becomes a self-serving system: unhooked from active production and from a material monetary base, it calls into question the mechanisms by which value is represented. Harvey's analysis, in effect, provides confirmation of Adorno's depiction of capitalist exchange value as an intensification of the instrumental rationality that dominates modernity; it demonstrates the momentum within economics to make phenomena measurable and hence comparable. Postmodernist theories that are not grounded in an analysis of modernity tend to duplicate the logic of capital, so that non-identity becomes a marker of capital's non-identity with itself; contrary to such orientations, Adorno's ability to provide a history of the subject in modernity enables him to invoke expressive resistance to the mutations of capital.[8]

The web of simulacra referred to by Baudrillard – images of fashion, travel and identity – includes a sometimes vicarious interest in world musics, as an area of consumption that can be fed into internal image banks. A simultaneous return to traditional values, a desire for stability and a resurgence of cultural forms from the past oppose this flux of information, but, ironically, do so within the latter's own system. This contradiction lies at the heart of the recent conservative politics favoured in the UK and USA: a voracious market economy, which serves little but its own needs, is yoked to a politics of traditional values, and the cultural dimension of this tendency manifests itself in nostalgia, pastiche and kitsch. Quinlan Terry's Richmond Riverside Panorama, a copy of eighteenth-century classicism virtually indistinguishable from restoration of original architecture in this style, provides imitation without a hint of parody or irony.[9] Exact mimicry does not take place in music, since this would amount simply to writing out an existing work, but evocations of the past do occur, as both non-ironic imitation and schizophrenic pluralism. Schnittke's Concerto Grosso No. 1 juxtaposes and distorts a variety of styles, ranging from music for prepared piano to Baroque techniques, in the manner of a confused image bank, blending irreverence and nostalgia as it rifles through music's warehouse. It is akin to a form of surrealism without the unconscious – to borrow Jameson's term – reducing historical depth structure to surface configurations of the present.[10] Penderecki, exemplifying non-ironic pastiche, has turned away from his texture compositions of the 1960s to direct and unselfconscious imitation of Romantic style in his Second Symphony (the *Christmas* Symphony), a work with strong resonances of Bruckner's monumental symphonic aesthetic. Harvey's theme of space-time compression says much about a situation in which the time of history is discounted in the present space of different styles; but, given that Penderecki and Schnittke were both Eastern bloc composers at the time of these compositions, it would seem that an evocation of the past is more closely linked to currents within the process of modernization than to specific Western economic configurations. The search for tradition exhibits both a heartfelt resistance to the fragmentation of contemporary life and a conservative striving for gentrification. Acknowledging the identity of a particular place or space can resist the process of homogenization, but such behaviour might also invoke an essentialist mode of being or generate yet another image for marketing.

Two predominant streams of thought are evident in music's attempts to engage a sense of tradition: one is marked by an aversion to modernity and the Enlightenment, the other is distinguished by a less drastic turn away from high modernism towards the *fin de siècle* and the nineteenth century. The former strand is illuminated by a meditative quality and, in some cases, by a religious rootedness, these qualities being particularly evident in the so-called 'trinity of godly minimalists': Arvo Pärt, Henryk Górecki and John Tavener (Mellers 1993: 714). The music from recent years of all three composers is imbued with religious reverence, cyclical, repetitive, spatial and static structures, and has met with outstanding popular success. Tavener and Pärt in particular are linked by having embraced, respectively, the orthodox Greek and Russian churches and by their shared interest in pre-Renaissance musical techniques.

The music of Pärt invokes a sense of Being that stands apart from the material world: the ideal, pursued by modernism, of an emancipated and self-reflective subjectivity is replaced by an ontological world order in which the subject fits into a natural system.[11] In its expressive simplicity, it is easy to see how this music fulfils a need unaddressed by high modernism and appears to push past the veil of simulacra that informs much contemporary experience, but such music can only be historically located and it forms part of the search for tradition that has accompanied the crisis of modernization. In the absence of a clear sense of what constitutes modern subjectivity, Pärt evokes a form of ur-subjectivity that seeks ritualistic grounding; the solace this repertoire induces raises questions, however, given that most listeners do not share the orthodox spiritual outlook of its composer. Pärt's music does not generate the hum of minimalism, but its essentialist, slow-moving repetitive cycles suggest a closed world in which huge amounts of activity change nothing: a music of libidinal intensity – a sonic representation of Baudrillardian simulacra – and a music of spiritual contemplation – which seeks firm ground beneath the surface of simulacra – both present subjectivity with something immutable. At best such experiences unlock inner nature, at worst they warm up and spiritualize reified social relations. In endeavouring, partly by recognizing the non-conceptual and mimetic, to find an alternative to a pervasive rationality and to overcome the limitations of aesthetic autonomy, the music attempts to combat fragmentation of the lifeworld with an ontological worldview.

A meditative quality and a desire to move music away from the institutions of autonomous art are also found in the work of Pauline Oliveros, though her ideas are linked to Cage's activity and to the American experimental lineage. Cage's later works invite audiences to bring their own meanings to events, thereby invoking some form of subjectivity (although it lies mainly outside the material); Oliveros takes this dimension further by relying on the interaction of performers and audience, often without a formalized chance component, to generate musical events. The *Sonic Meditations*, like much of Cage's music, depend on strict instructions and self discipline, but usually emphasize untutored or intuitive sound making: *Teach Yourself to Fly*, for example, asks performers to allow their vocal chords to sound through deep breathing. This piece is neither improvisational nor consciously constructed: the performers are instructed not to imitate or to respond to one another in the hope that sound can function as a conduit towards a meditative state, that it can take the rationalization of material back to a physical origin. But by emphasizing bodily-produced sounds and intuitions over trained production and construction such texts draw a distinction between a natural state and an artificial one, recalling Rousseau's championing of speech over writing and of melody over harmony, and are therefore susceptible to the kind of deconstructive unravelling to which Derrida subjects Rousseau. Nevertheless, *Teach Yourself to Fly* does reassert the physical dimension of music sacrificed by much modernist abstraction.

Jann Pasler argues that 'in her recent work, *DreamHorseSpiel* (1990), she [Oliveros] intends to "cue listeners into their own experience" in a much broader and more socially defined sense than in the meditation pieces' (1993: 23). This objective is achieved in the mentioned work and in the planned *Nzinga* by performers interacting with one another by means of sounds that have a cultural trace. The central point made by Pasler is that

> it is no longer the pseudo-scientific search for the fundamentals of the medium that interests many explorers, but inquiry into what makes people connect to and through music. The composer's orientation toward the listener's experience is critical in this inquiry, as are the expectations a composer may have of listeners' interactive participation, the positive value of memory and contemplation of the past, as well as the celebration of personal and cultural diversity (1993: 25).

The model outlined by Pasler resembles Wellmer's Habermasian account of intersubjective aesthetics, except that in this case the intersubjective dimension is situated in the internal configurations of the music instead of being located in a quasi-transcendental idea of communication. *Nzinga*, as envisaged, is certainly an attempt to reclaim lifeworld experiences as a compositional resource in a more intersubjective manner than Cage's music facilitates: Oliveros explores the differences inherent within life histories instead of subjecting events to arbitrary decisions. Such an approach once more veers towards the avant-garde project of sublating art and life and is not immune from the same difficulties, despite its intersubjective dimension. Using sound objects as a medium of intersubjectivity tends to detract from their specificity, their internal resistance to standard modes of rationality; and sounds that invoke memories may well do so in a standardized manner because, unless the objects are dislocated, their mediated, or even ideological, content, which may be locked into the memory pattern, will not be recognized. It is, however, possible that in good performances the intersubjective interaction will succeed in reorienting existing associations and memories. Pasler's reading of Oliveros displaces the modernist paradigm of abstraction and foregrounds the role played by institutions and discourses in negotiating music's meaning, a strategy congruent with musicology's current predilection for opening formalist understandings of the canon to intertextual readings. The recognition that compositional and analytical procedures are not sealed from other discourses associated with music is significant; but neither this musicological comprehension nor its compositional equivalent invalidates perception of material as a distillation of social experiences.

Composers who have re-engaged romantic and expressionist idioms also wish to inscribe an emotional inner life to their music, but do so from a different stance to the music discussed so far in this chapter. Instead of invoking a presubjective, ontological source or an intersubjectivity within their music, these composers often refer to the bourgeois idea of individual subjectivity that was suppressed, or rechannelled, by highly rationalized techniques of composition. George Rochberg has drawn a parallel between the trajectory of his career as a composer and the creative life of the artist Philip Guston: both careers map a line from the concrete (figurative/tonal) to the abstract (non-figurative/dodecaphonic) and back to the concrete (figurative/tonal). Rochberg understands this process as part of a *Zeitgeist* which ran deep '. . . and it clamored for and demanded concreteness again, i.e. concreteness in human expression, warmth and passion of feeling, working from an emotional, living core in the making, projection and response to art' (1992: 7). The need Rochberg discerns is conveyed in his Third String Quartet, which extends beyond the quotation techniques employed in some of his previous works to composition in the style of Mahler and late Beethoven.

Robin Holloway contends that we can only approach the past through our immediate heritage of modernism (1989: 66); nevertheless, he experiences a need to translate modernist fervour into nostalgia, understood as an alternative to disaster instead of an expression of it. For him, there is a strong sense that the fragmentation of tradition, which was created by the impact of modernism, should be redressed. Nostalgia, Holloway argues, enables composers to express the types of emotions that music has always expressed in the kinds of ways in which it has always done so. Because it is possible to feel some compositional empathy with earlier European music through the veil of modernism, the break with the past, when things were better – Holloway implicitly argues – cannot be total. Indeed, it is unlikely that links with the past are completely severed, but when overemphasized they promote nineteenth-century bourgeois subjectivity and aesthetic transcendence to an ahistorical universal. Were the rupture with previous music complete, then we would be inhabiting the world museum diagnosed by extreme postmodernists, who surmise that, because organic lineage is redundant, any culture is a readily accessible resource for anyone. A less extravagant variant on this theme is put forward by Robert P. Morgan who suggests, metaphorically speaking, that the modern composer occupies a house with many rooms; each one containing components from the past that can be drawn upon at leisure (1991: 488). Such eclecticism enables a composer to try on various costumes, but it is hard to see why one might be any more convincing to composer, performer or listener than another or what could replenish the options available. Unless some framing or distancing device is embedded, capable of inducing a tension between the material and its form, or unless diversity is experienced as an immanent idea, the composer who occupies assorted styles will simply produce an atrophied subjectivity.

André Malraux's notion of a museum without walls envisages a universal intertextuality and, according to David Roberts (1991), this development can be traced to the exhaustion of latency within musical material, as described by Adorno's *Philosophy of New Music*. Roberts takes as his starting point the contradiction within Adorno's text at its most bleak: if the total rationalization of material leads to an impasse whereby it becomes indifferent to subjectivity and the traditional, organic art work is perceived as mere illusion, then why continue with the discourse of autonomous art when it can only ponder the end of a lineage? To elaborate, Schoenberg and Stravinsky bring music to full rationalization: material is no longer a blind object because its latency is completely manifest and thus exhausted; consequently, the approach taken by the two composers represents 'the search for new languages on the one hand and the search for new latencies on the other' (1991: 175). In Roberts' opinion, both paths register the indifference of material and are replaced by contingency (following Luhmann, Roberts defines contingency – somewhat opaquely – as that 'which is neither necessary nor impossible: which can be seen as it is (was, will be) but which is possibly other') (1991: 173). He argues that Adorno's categories are cancelled: progress becomes stasis, essence becomes virtuality and necessity becomes contingency (1991: 157).

If Schoenberg's quest for new languages leads to the determinate, formalist contingency of serialism and Stravinsky's search for new latencies preludes the indeterminate contingency of aleatoricism, Cage's transformation from chance methods for determinate composition to chance methods for indeterminate composition, to extend Roberts' argument, depicts a movement of contingency from idea to system. Cage arrived at, but did not fully contemplate, a situation that responds to the end of tradition brought about by the 'convergence of progress and historicism' (1991: 212). The past becomes one of our own invention and creativity turns into 'a species of problem solving for which any style or combination of styles can constitute the basis of construction' (1991: 221); philosophical aesthetics completes the history of art and takes it towards an open-ended dialectic: the conclusions of theory constitute the 'critical identity' of artistic practice. In contrast to Baudrillard's diagnosis, Roberts argues that the image is not the replacement of reality; instead, it registers that the latency, which has drained away from material, is regenerated by the self-reflection of art as a sphere of activity. The system is totally transparent to itself.

In this account of contingent art, the expression of subjectivity is reduced to the task of managing a world museum or of problem solving with pre-given materials, making it difficult, therefore, to see how the possible worlds prefigured by art can be anything other than reconfigurations of the same one, or what would make one alternative more desirable than another.[12] The condition of postmodernism becomes a universal for world art, and is even applied to cultures with intact, continuous traditions which have not experienced an exhaustion of latency. The argument accurately describes certain aspects of contemporary cultural practice, but applies its premisses too widely. It is certainly true, to take a particular case, that parts of the popular music industry function as a system in which the internal transformations of the mechanism are of more interest than the results it generates, but this scheme does not embrace all cultural production. In general, a move towards an idea of art that seems to require theory for its completion is certainly apparent in much recent practice, but since it is thoroughly anticipated by Adornian aesthetics, there is not a compelling reason to abandon these categories. Roberts considers the break with tradition to be absolute because he understands the dialectic of enlightenment as a fatal embrace: instead of looking at ways in which Adorno's negative dialectic might be thawed, Roberts accepts as a premiss Adorno's worst prognosis of the reification of rationality.

Adorno's notion of advanced musical material can be modified to become a theory capable of contemplating different materials, representing historically and geographically variant subjectivities; indeed, Adorno's comments on Janáček, Bartók and Schreker indicate the existence of non-synchronous historical paths. Further, the components of music have a capacity to advance at different speeds within a single style, and it is this facet that allows Schoenberg to use the rhythmic techniques and phraseology associated with tonality long after the break with tonality itself. The indifference of the material is not as absolute as Roberts suggests since, whatever the perils of serialism, Schoenberg's resistance to his own system ensured that expression was not annihilated by construction; and the crisis of hierarchical pitch organization represented by Schoenberg did not, *pace* Roberts, exhaust the latency of other musical dimensions or of tonal procedures in different contexts. Neither does the extremity of Adorno's Stravinsky critique prevent us from searching for unrealized latencies in this repertoire. Procedures that have been rationalized fully in one art form may acquire new latencies in different lifeworld contexts, given felicitous conditions of production and reception. On the other hand, the idea of advanced material is not redundant, though the notion of it being represented by a single strand is no longer tenable, and it remains possible to produce innovative material and fresh latencies in a post-tonal idiom: *Répons* generates original methods of organization that embrace the concept of simultaneous possibilities in space as an internal logic, as an interaction between system and idea. The style and idea dialectic, which Roberts posits as central to the modernism versus postmodernism debate, need not, therefore, be collapsed into style in order to accommodate contingency and reflexivity.

A re-engagement with tradition does draw attention to the narrowness of a high modernist aesthetic, but often prefers to reject modernist techniques instead of rendering them more inclusive. It is hard not to agree with Harvey's contention that some of the more extreme forms of nostalgia and pastiche answer a need on the part of consumers in search of a cultural identity: the homogenizing flow of the markets undercuts bourgeois individualism, but also generates a need for the stability and traditionalism evoked by nostalgia. The process of gentrification actually recreates the institutions of high art that other currents in postmodernism try to undermine, but the renewed forms are linked, ultimately, to the turbulence of the markets and to the condition of modernity from which their consumers seek respite.

This point is not lost on Habermas, for whom the eclecticism of postmodernist architecture constitutes an attempt to find a stylistic solution to a problem whose solution lies in the social forms of the lifeworld (1989: 19). Neo-conservative attempts to compensate for a depleted lifeworld by inappropriate means can be found in music, but it is not grounded by architecture's obvious functional purpose. Stylistic innovation in music is not, therefore, pitched at the wrong level, even though, like contemporary architecture, it should be capable of distilling subjectivity in a manner that does not simply reflect administered society. The current fascination with the *fin de siècle* suggests a desire to find a creative outlet that, although influenced by the achievements of later modernism, will develop the interaction of material and subjectivity instead of attempting to advance material as a self-referential language. The prevailing historical experience to be encoded into music is an understanding of diversity that can recognize difference but also find affinities.

Postmodernism, whether represented by the pop avant garde or by traditionalism, reveals that the historical advancement of material is not the only authentic method of artistic expression, though it is still a viable path if not pursued with the tunnel vision of certain high modernist practices. Tradition is not exhausted, but for art to generate new latencies from it a distancing from organic art of the past must, to some extent, be immanently encoded within its material. Whether the compositional practices of the nineteenth century are recreated in a contingent sense or in quotation marks, the forces that originally led to their dissolution are still embedded within the material. If this point is not recognized, music will repeat the idealist mystification that modernism rightly criticized.

Notes

1. Translation modified.
2. Translation modified.
3. Zuidervaart 1991: 296–8, puts this argument.
4. See Zuidervaart 1991: 106 for an account of this topic.
5. Wellmer 1985b and Hodge 1989 both emphasize the overlap between Adorno's ideas and postmodernism. Jameson 1984: 65 and Huyssen 1988: 194, 197 & 187 associate Adorno with an outmoded modernism.
6. Huyssen also makes this point (1988: 207).
7. This point is also made by Eagleton 1985.
8. This point is also made by C. Bürger 1986.

9. Bernstein makes a distinction between the formal non-identity of capital with itself and non-identity proper (1992: 266).
10. Harvey makes this point (1989: 84).
11. 'Surrealism without the unconscious' forms a heading for the chapter on video in Jameson 1991. He also uses this description to 'characterize the newer painting' (1991: 174).
12. See Clarke 1993 for another discussion of subjectivity in Pärt.

7   Engaging Tradition

Wolfgang Rihm

The touchstone of Rihm's aesthetic is an ideal of freedom, unrestricted by a system or by rules; a perspective that departs significantly from the constructionist aesthetic of high modernism, but not necessarily from its achievements. Rihm's compositional outlook is an inclusive one capable of embracing whatever style or sound fits his needs. His willingness to handle large forces and big sonorities in, for example, the early orchestral works *Dis Kontur* and *Sub Kontur* can be attributed both to the Mahler revival that took place in the 1970s and to the feel for proportion and texture gained from his one-time teacher, Stockhausen.[1]

An interior subjectivity lies at the centre of Rihm's compositional practice, and his music has been described under the headings of 'neo-expressionism', 'neo-romanticism' and the 'new simplicity', none of which is entirely appropriate. Rihm himself provides a very direct statement on his relation to the musical heritage, commenting: 'tradition can always be only MY TRADITION' (1985: 67). In one sense this standpoint is naive since it appears not to understand the social mediation of material, but Rihm is trying to convey the way that, as an individual, he engages with a history of compositional freedom: he belongs to a tradition in the sense that art is understood as freedom, as growing out of freedom and being committed to freedom. Composers who correspond to this conception of tradition include Debussy, Schoenberg – as represented by the works dating from around 1910 – the Beethoven of the late quartets and, to some extent, Varèse. Schumann, however, provides the great example of a free composer unwilling to strangle inner or outer impulses, but Rihm's reference to him suggests a conception of musical freedom more grounded in social circumstance than Rihm indicates. Schumann's bourgeois individualism and his estimation of music as a medium that communicates states of the soul, his genius notwithstanding, are very much facets of the age in which he lived; they are not directly transferable to the late twentieth century, at least not in a non-ideological form. But Schumann seems to signify something that was threatened by high modernism: Barthes detects in his music a pulsing and beating body (Barthes 1985: 300), and Rihm also finds a physical quality in his music, though neither he nor Schumann are defined by an individualist hedonism of sensations.

Following Schumann's lead, Rihm's own ruminations on contemporary music start from the direct experience of working with the material: musical freedom is almost a mystical process for him and the work is a search for the place of imagination, the work seeks itself (1985: 74). Music is near nature and therefore intolerant of anything false, for Rihm, and free musical thought draws upon a muffled knowing and a deep, learnt premonition; he wishes to convey the essential and subversive nature of music – 'music without a shell' – so as to create less a piece of music than a condition of music (1985: 16). In accordance with this primary understanding of musical imagination, the composer postulates that understanding of a work should extend beyond its individual moments: the macro form as well as its components must be in place from the start, and – as in the heroic phase of free atonality – the form must be found anew for each piece. It is to the energy of association obtained in Debussy's sound objects that Rihm turns for renewed possibilities in modern music, arguing that Debussy discovered the idea of the whole form as an individual moment; extending the idea, he proposes a type of music in which unconnected events would cross over with a logic of unity and development. It is, however, notable that, despite his interest in Debussy, Rihm has not explored the technical potential of Debussyian sound objects to anything like the extent undertaken by Boulez.

Rihm's acknowledgement of Debussy is indicative of his view of the past: 'Knowledge of the past' he claims, 'is only threatening for the unimaginative; concern about the future of art runs parallel to the general anxiety about survival' (1985: 81). In his music there is a tension between present and past, a struggle between breaking and bending; Rihm's allusions to romanticism constitute less an attempt to recapture bourgeois transcendence than a wish to address the subjectivity submerged by high modernism. Nevertheless, initial encounters with Rihm's early scores, at least, suggest he is overly indebted to the romantic idea of the creative individual who writes from the heart, and this conception of music is more grounded in social circumstance than he indicates. In contrast to Adorno's notion of an alienated modernist art, for Rihm the task of art in unfavourable conditions is not to function as a refuge, but as an energy store; though at times his aesthetic goes so far as to suggest that music is a medium of primeval intensity that has no truck with the rational forms of society.

It is with music from the mid-1970s, when the composer was in his early- to mid-twenties, that Rihm achieved major recognition. Works from this time such as *Dis Kontur* (1974) and *Sub Kontur* (1975), the Third String Quartet (1976) and *Klavierstück 5* (1975) established him as a composer who engages tradition through a predilection for late-romantic style. Both the orchestra pieces involve huge forces and open with large percussion textures, *Dis Kontur* including a Mahlerian march and utilizing hammer blows, with obvious allusions to Mahler's Sixth Symphony. Like Mahler, Rihm has a talent for finding new latencies in used material; instead of offering a negative imprint of a rationalized society, he wants to oppose standardization with the intensity and immediacy of sound. There is also a feel for Mahler's depiction of a symphonic afterlife:

Jungheinrich talks of Rihm's symphonies as symphonies after the end of the symphony, since they indicate that the form no longer exists (1987: 59). Certainly, the metaphysical wholeness of symphonic forms is only a memory, but Rihm's engagement with the past does more than emphasize the absurdity of the present: it evokes a yearning for directness within the fragmented space of the modern.

Drum strokes open and close *Sub Kontur*, where they establish a frame and also mark what might be called a recapitulation. Wolf Frobenius draws attention to the sonata form shape to be found in *Sub Kontur* (1981: 55), suggesting the following plan of the work:

I.   Introduction (bars 1–68)
II.   Exposition (bars 69–108)
III. Development (bars 109–250)
IV.   Recapitulation (bars 251–290/306)
V.   Stretto (bars 291–306)

The central tonality of the music is C major, and, as Frobenius observes, this is the key of the introduction and stretto; it also occurs in the middle of the work (bars 187–191), overlaid by heavy drum rolls. What Frobenius names 'Theme II' (see Example 7.1) is heard in F major, both in the exposition and in the recapitulation (though in both cases it is succeeded by another key), and he also discusses the proportional tempo scheme used in the music, which shows the influence of Stockhausen's interest in proportion and duration. The primary tempo scheme of *Sub Kontur* is an increase from crotchet = 40 to crotchet = 160, the main interruptions to this scheme being the extreme tempo fluctuations between bars 152–213 – crotchet = 40 → 152 – and the drop to crotchet = 72 and 60 for Theme II in the recapitulation. The projection through time in *Sub Kontur* is more attributable to the increasing tempo and thickness of texture – though the recapitulation is marked by a tempo reduction – than to the sense of departure and return that embodies sonata form. But the temporal dimension is not sufficient to overturn the feel of co-existing, irreconcilable objects.

Sub Kontur dispenses with a conventional woodwind section, instead using three contrabassoons, which add to the reservoir of inchoate sounds in the music and emphasize the 'crushing, squeezing preponderance of the bass' (Riethmüller 1983: 32).[2] Such sonorities are, of course, not without attached associations, but they do suggest a mimetic invocation of raw nature, and in one instance Adorno suggests that individual elements or, at least, their configurations, can elude mediation:

> No doubt, a certain immediacy is undeniable in such elements [the individual note], as is the fact of a spontaneous, specifically musical experience. Of undoubted significance for music theory is Hegel's insight that although all immediacy is mediated and dependent on its opposite, the concept of an unmediated thing – that is, of something which has become or has been set free – is not wholly engulfed by mediation. Reduced

to an element of music the unmediated is not the individual note, but the internal configuration [*Gestalt*] (Adorno 1992b: 299).

The larger-scale configurations in *Sub Kontur*, with their late-romantic derivations from the symphonic adagio, certainly are mediated, but these conventional associations are skewed by the brutal and direct sounds that frame them. Discussing Mahler's Ninth Symphony, Adorno mentions the indefinite pitch of the bass drum, 'which is closer to mere noise, to something un-domesticated and alien to the realm of musical culture' (1992b: 108); in Rihm's piece the both audibly and visually direct strokes of the percussion suggest blows to the physical body, while hammering into shape the subjectivity and transcendence of the adagio pulsing effects. The evocation of primeval sounds is also close to the phenomenon that Adorno describes in the first movement of Mahler's Third Symphony, where 'form itself becomes something both fearful and monstrous, the objectification of chaos' (1992a: 78). The drum blows, together with the very low passages for contrabassoons and brass, help to articulate the overall form and are objectified by it, but also associate it with something inchoate. Nevertheless, these basic elements retain their identity too strongly to facilitate the crossover between mimesis and construction that Adorno locates in art: at their extremes, the two poles impinge on each other but remain apart.

Riethmüller suggests that *Sub Kontur*

> illuminates those dimensions of sublimity which still retain their ties to suffering and terror, and in whose overpowering effect the element of violence can still be discerned (1983: 32).

The sublime, which in Kant registers the inability of a concept to subsume an object, becomes for Adorno the mark of the particular breaking through form in modernist art. Rihm tries to capture both senses of the sublime: the object is both monstrous and immeasurable, its physical excess fracturing form. It is not, *pace* Lyotard, the form of the work that is unpresentable, however, but what it indicates to the listener: within the same space it articulates a subjectivity that stands in thrall to nature, a subjectivity that appears to have a direct expressive outlet and a subjectivity that cannot ground itself in the heterogeneity of the modern environment. The clearly tonal, Bruckner-like, melodic passages (at bars 81 – see Example 7.1 – and 268) constitute less a form of nostalgia than an attempt to place this association alongside the alienated subjectivity of modern-ism. These moments are closer to what Adorno identifies as the category of breakthrough in early Mahler symphonies, which seeks to suspend the immanent context, than to the type of fulfilment, which emerges from an immanent context, found in later Mahler. Like the Mahler-type adagio that the pulsing effects of this music resemble, Rihm wants to invoke a whole world in itself: *Sub Kontur*, he says, 'is a music that does not stop before mud, it leads you into it' (quoted in Osswald 1985: 143), and it is infused by a full range of emotional states.

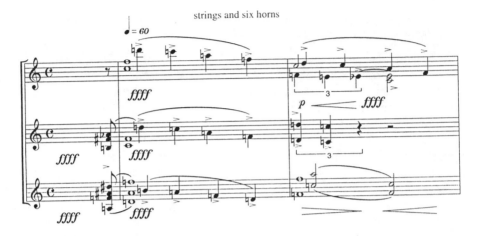

Example 7.1: Theme II, bar 81, *Sub Kontur*

© Universal Edition Ltd. Reprinted by permission.

An analogy can be drawn between the various impulses contained in *Sub Kontur* and the faint utopian possibility glimpsed by Jameson in his discussion of an 'untitled installation' by Robert Gober.[3] The installation comprises a room, with a door leading off, containing a representational picture of the Hudson river – 'the ideology of a particular kind of landscape' – and a mound (1991: 169). Unlike Gober's installation, *Sub Kontur* is not a multi-media work but, like Jameson's reading of the room, it does offer constellations of nature and culture, tradition and the modern in ways suggestive of an unthinkable synthesis. Gober's project 'can be seen', Jameson argues, 'not so much as the production of some form of Utopian space but rather as the production of the *concept* of such space' (1991: 165). Jameson carries on to discuss the sense in which 'mixed media' works are 'the contemporary equivalent of the *Gesamtkunstwerk* but with all the differences already enumerated': that is, 'the "mix" comes first and redefines the media involved by implication a posteriori' (1991: 172). Similarly, *Sub Kontur* presents a conglomerate of music, emotions and spaces, the various components of which are redefined retrospectively: it is an attempt to think a whole range of emotional intensities at once, but the constituents are not fixed in one constellation. The music alludes to the idea of the *Gesamtkunstwerk*, or perhaps the complete experience work, but in a way that fails to form a single configuration. *Sub Kontur* refuses to mould its components into a definitive shape, but it is more than simply a pluralist composition because it possesses a logic of expressive associations.

In 'Vers une musique informelle' Adorno argues that 'informal music had been a real possibility once before, around 1910' (1992b: 273); he carries on to say that 'A *musique informelle* would have to take up the challenge posed by the idea of an unrevised, unrestricted freedom. But not a repeat of the style of 1910' (275). The date Adorno mentions is significant because it is the expressionist

Mahler and Schoenberg who have provided Rihm with some of his richest seams of inspiration. Certainly, Rihm has not returned to the music of this period, but, as Adorno implies, he has sought to re-open a way of thinking for which the form of a work must be reinvented in each composition and where the material is close to a psychological, interior monologue. It is no coincidence that figures close to insanity, such as Lenz and Artaud, have proved to be inspirational for Rihm's work: the attempt to convey states of mind is partly carried out by writing extreme music, as found, for example, in the intensities of loudness, density and bass textures encountered in *Sub Kontur*. Peter Andrasche mentions the paradoxical, if not impossible, instructions in the Third Quartet, such as '*morendo in ffff*' at the end of the fourth movement; elsewhere in this work there are fast transitions between extreme dynamics within short durations.

Andrasche also notes that this quartet, *Im Innersten*, contains resonances and allusions to the historical genre of the quartet: there is the presence of Beethoven's late quartets, Janàček (not least in the title of his Second Quartet, *Intimate Letters*), Bartók and Second Viennese School chamber music (Andrasche 1978: 138). The work is characterized by meditative, tonal passages and by the inclusion of unison and octave sections amidst fragmented outbursts. The question is whether these sections function in an entirely traditional sense or whether they are framed by modernist thought? The role performed by the octave and unison passages, and occasional tonal chords, is more straightforward than that of the extended tonal passages. The C major chord in the last moments of the piece is, as Andrasche mentions, diffused by the scratch tone (*Kratzton*), which virtually converts it into noise, and the final G♭–E♭ oscillation in the viola: the chord is used as a symbol of stability which is undermined. Tonal chords are scattered elsewhere in the work, frequently functioning as points of transparency in the midst of volcanic eruptions. Tonal centres are also used: A♭, for example, functions as a core around which the first movement is constructed; it is heard as a unison in the sustained sonority of the opening bar and of bars 13 and 14; it also appears in pizzicato octaves in bars 35 and 36; at times A♭ emerges as an anchor, because of its preponderance in the individual parts, or as a sustained pitch in the background of other events; in other places its presence fades or is masked, quite frequently by an A. The octave A♭s at bar 35 of the first movement emphasize the movement's focal pitch, but the interval is alienated from its own stability by the mechanical repetition and intensity (the composer's instruction reads *vom Griffbrett zum Steg*) and by being finally unsettled for the last beat of the movement by a B♭, after some disruption by cello triplets (see Example 7.2).

The adagio idea seen in *Sub Kontur* returns in *Im Innersten* in the guise of a melodic line, heavy with appogiaturas, moving over sustained chords to generate a perception of inner tranquillity: it occurs in movements II and IV, and is the dominant mood in movement VI. When the music occurs in the sixth movement Rihm makes explicit instructions about using neither crescendos or diminuendos, nor dynamic crossing between parts, even in places where the harmonic context seems to support a standard expressive vocabulary: the traditional material is placed in a vacuum where its expressive content is more alluded to than stated. The turbulent second movement gradually funnels down to the calm adagio concluding it which, though approached by transition, is experienced as a separate section offering repose (see Example 7.3); because the mood is not sustained, it offers little more than a moment of sanctuary. The transitory quality of this refuge is apparent in its elusive ending on what sounds like a passing chord, though the third movement opens with related material. The section is permeated by a basic motivic shape: this occurs either as a stepwise descending pattern of 3 notes, (a); inverted as a 3-note rising figure, (b); or truncated as a 2-note descending figure, (c). These cells are marked in Example 7.3. Textual analysis does not however tell us how such music functions in a work composed in 1976 or within the quartet in general; such matters demand theoretical reflection beyond the confines of this instance.

Example 7.2: The closing bars of the 1st movement of *Im Innersten*

© Universal Edition Ltd. Reprinted by permission.

Jameson's comments on the technique of wrapping used in architecture are here of some relevance. He discusses a frame, entitled 'The Russian house inside

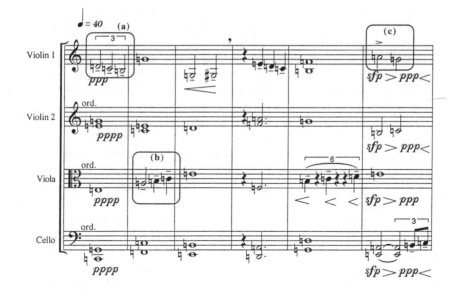

Example 7.3: The opening of the last section of the 2nd movement of *Im Innersten*
© Universal Edition Ltd. Reprinted by permission.

the Italian cathedral', from Tarkovsky's film *Nostalgia*: a hut – which appears to be a place of refuge – is wrapped by an imposing and misty ruin. In Rihm's quartet there is a corresponding sense in which the adagio passages in movements II and IV are wrapped by the fragmented eruptions elsewhere in the quartet, but Jameson is careful not to make a brisk distinction between inside and outside: 'What is wrapped' he writes, 'can also be used as the wrapper; the wrapper can also be wrapped in its turn' (1991: 102). This second sense can be heard in movement VI where the predominantly still music wraps corrosive outbursts. Such passages achieve a certain autonomy in their own right but are contained by their surroundings. Jameson argues that a stronger manifestation of this procedure happens in contemporary theory where 'one text is simply being wrapped in another, with the paradoxical effect that the first – a mere writing sample, a paragraph or illustrative sentence, a segment or moment torn out of its context – becomes affirmed as autonomous and as a kind of unity in its own right' (1991: 103). The wrapped passages in *Im Innersten* are not generally quotations from other works but they do achieve a certain independence, suggesting that the emotional world of late romanticism can be drawn upon as a secondary 'mode of representation': islands alluding to traditional artistic illusion are presented alongside the forces that undercut them. Tonality provides a culturally established system for distilling experience into music, and Rihm's tonal references allude to the possibility of a music that draws sustenance from social participation, more than they evoke nostalgia.

These sections enhance the notion of sound object pioneered by Cage and Boulez, but they clearly are not the neutral entities that Boulez once envisaged would function in a quasi-serial system. *Répons'* complex objects interact within the music – even though the dialectic of system and idea has relevance beyond the boundaries of the piece; Rihm's allusions participate in a richer intertextual network of associations, but have to work hard to generate specific associations within a piece. In Rihm's work tonal sections are wrapped – as levels of expression – in sequences of intensities that are not tonally derived. Wrapping registers a form of affinity between potentially very different objects: they take the shape of each other without surrendering their internal differences, in a version of what Adorno identifies as pseudomorphic transformation in Mahler. More than that, the procedure is an attempt to work consciously with something that Adorno regards as an inherent capacity of art: the ability to preserve or to find affinities between sensibilities that are not apparent to discursive rationality. The future of art may well lie in its ability to discover such similarities and associations.

An altered quotation from the Cavatina of Beethoven's Quartet Opus 130 is found in bar 6 (second violin) of the Fourth movement.[4] This 'quotation' is certainly well wrapped but it nevertheless fits into the mode of extreme stretching (*aüsserst gedehnt*) Rihm asks for, and alludes intertextually to the internal dialogue suggested by the quartet's title. But the idea of interiority conveys, for him, much more than a sense of internal calm: it involves a full range of psychological feelings that extend from extreme turbulence to tranquillity; engaging with tradition provides a way of articulating this battery of feelings, though the music does not seek to be above the material world. Rihm muddies both the bourgeois category of transfigured inwardness and the modernist principles of construction that Adorno, at an early stage, had hoped would replace it.

The discontinuity of late Beethoven, in this case partly filtered through the impact of Nono's quartet *Fragmente-Stille, An Diotima*, is also apparent in Rihm's Eighth Quartet: both Nono and Rihm use fragments of sound isolated from one another by silence, and Rihm's quartet is heard as a sequence of gestures which concentrate the inner life of the sounds. A dialectic of pre-rational and rationalized sound is again invoked, this time by the inclusion of non-conventional musical sounds, such as the rhythmically notated crumpling of paper. At the last general pause the players are asked to 'write' *con amore* on the parts with the tips of their bows; a direction suggestive of the influence of Nono's quartet, which employs the marking '*mit innigster Empfindung*', taken from the Adagio of Beethoven's Quartet Opus 132, together with quotations from Hölderlin which the players are asked to contemplate silently. As Danuser suggests, such markings can perhaps instil an intersubjective sense of inwardness that is communicated between the players and externalized for the audience in performance (1990: 25). The influence of Nono's late style is evident in many of Rihm's works from the 1980s and early 1990s such as *Kein Firmament* and

Abgewandt 2: music in memoriam Luigi Nono, in which, at their most successful, a hard-edged discontinuity is offset by islands of sound establishing affinities with one another across space without a linking 'narrative'.

The idea of a stream of intensities is reworked into the spun melody that threads its way through *Gesungene Zeit*, composed in 1992, for solo violin and chamber orchestra. By writing in a consistently high register – with Anne-Sophie Mutter in mind – Rihm imparts a transparent intensity to a feeling of remoteness; as if it is at the outer edges that life is found. The delicate high register gives a radiance to the sounds that is hard to capture in the normal violin register with its standard range of associations. Rihm is lucid about his intentions in this work:

> In a 'chanted time' I find the unalterable forward movement of time and the absurd commentary of one who, while living in time, wants to make it stand still, enclose it within the moment, lock it in the moment as if in the living rock – but as movement, energy, breathless but not rigid in death. . . . This calls for a medium with the virtuosic skill to make nerves and strands of thought audible, make them stand out from the immaterial configuration as palpable, sensual shapes (Rihm 1992: 2).

The composer does not say as much, but he appears to be pursuing the fullness of a moment in time – Benjamin's *Jetztzeit* – in opposition to the empty, repetitive time of reification. Rihm comments that this music is almost monophonic and suggests that the orchestra plays the role of *Doppelgänger*: 'The violin speaks its nerve-line out into the resounding space – inscribes it there' (1992: 2). The orchestra does indeed fulfil a doubling role, differing from the central pitch and deferring to it, well described by the concept of *différance*: accompanying instruments frequently double or play in close proximity to the soloist, the violin line emerging as a chain of brightness and cloud.

Rihm himself is again insightful on the strange configurations of part and whole that take place in his work:

> The line, is it a whole? Its all is only a part, a segment, a fragment; it is delivered up to our observation without beginning and without ending – and as we listen we draft the outline of a whole that isn't there. But it must be there . . .' (1992: 2).

The enigma of Rihm's music is that it possesses immediacy but invokes the idea of an organic wholeness that cannot be completely grasped. Individual moments are released into a logic of expression but they suggest something larger: the space of simultaneous possibilities and contingencies is infused with vitality instead of empty choice, and the idea of art after the end of illusion is evoked. Reference to the past generates the remembrance of illusion but not its actuality; the whole to which the music alludes but cannot capture is the shaping force of modernity. Having rebelled against the most abstract and narrow features of modernism, and made it a more inclusive artistic language, Rihm now seems to be pursuing a more obviously modernist language, but one that, at its best, is illuminated from within and pursues the inner life of the sounds.

In Search of Subjectivity

Looking to the past is double edged: on the one hand it reflects a desire by an unstable political and economic culture to find reassurance and identity in history, to assimilate and to tame in the present the revolutionizing impulses of modernism; on the other, the interest in the *fin de siècle* pertains to the most turbulent phase of modernism before its impetus became weakened by systems of construction. In a striking irony, modern culture looks to a time of rapid historical change from the alleged simultaneity and homogeneity of the present. The past can be approached either as a heritage severed from its layered subjectivity, or, as Rihm demonstrates, as a source of latency and historical depth.

There was a sense at the end of the nineteenth century in which subjectivity did find a correlate for itself in the social forms of the time, but in the present the gap between what Jameson calls 'the phenomenological description of the life of an individual and a more properly structural model of the conditions of existence of that experience' has widened (1991: 410). Adorno, of course, was acutely aware of the way in which political and economic systems of social production and reproduction penetrate individual consciousness as ideology, but the two halves – designated by Habermas as system and lifeworld – have become harder to understand in terms of each other. Place and particularity can be opposed to the increasingly opaque space of global capital with varying results: the most alarming of these manifestations reinvent a sense of being that can feed into fascism and militant nationalism, but the specific qualities of communities and individual structures of feeling – to use Raymond Williams' term – do offer an alternative to the empty space of capital exchange. It is important, however, that a sense of the vernacular does not become atrophied so as to obscure the extent to which it too is shaped by larger forces. Jameson speaks of the discontinuities within the present as follows:

> I take such spatial peculiarities of postmodernism as symptoms and expressions of a new and historically original dilemma, one that involves our insertion as individual subjects into a multidimensional set of radically discontinuous realities, whose frames range from the still surviving spaces of bourgeois private life all the way to the unimaginable decentring of global capital itself (1991: 413).

These discontinuous realities exist simultaneously as non-reconcilable qualities of the present, but their non-identity is not absolute.[5] The difficulty is one of perceiving simultaneously non-identity and affinity, within various forms of subjectivity, while not losing sight of the steering forces of advanced modernization. Modern subjectivities frequently occupy two or more such spheres and have to 'translate' between them, which is undoubtedly unsettling for individuals and groups, but the experience may forge links between non-synchronous forms of subjectivity and thereby invest them with transformative potential. Against the experience of heterogeneity stands the prevalence of standardization: that is, domination of subjectivity by an instrumental reason, or systemic dysfunction, that renders the sensuous, the body and desire irreconcilable with rationality and the law.

Adorno's work in sociology, philosophy and music led him to envisage configurations of part and whole beyond the concept of unity. Such constellations can be traced by musical forms that take difference into themselves; but beyond the notion of a single work, differentiation in society is more likely to be reflected by multiple styles than to be grasped within a single configuration. Mimesis, understood as a non-coerceive relation to inner and outer nature, is encountered on a more provisional and localized basis than Adorno countenanced, and the sense of a permeability between subject and object encoded within the concept of mimesis suggests that independent events within music, or even between musics, might form non-subsumptive associations with one another. Future musical practice is likely to involve efforts to articulate affinites and differences between objects with rich textual associations generative of more than mere heterogeneity. The utopian dimension in Adorno's aesthetics of music becomes understood in a more transformative than absolute sense: the social content of music can constitute a form of resistance to dominant and deceptive ideologies, and may anticipate social structures in which individual fulfilment is congruent with the everyday organization of life. This idea is commensurate with an understanding of music in which the multiplicity of historical experiences sedimented in material are re-engaged by the social formations in which music participates.

It is clear that for music advanced material is not the only way of embodying the subject's engagement with intersubjective and objective conditions. It is, however, one way of doing so: a system that does not override surface contingency can be encoded within the unfolding of material, as the interplay of objects in *Répons* evinces. Another way of tackling the same issue is to evoke variant spaces within the lifeworld, by referring to different musics: in an echo of Mahler's practice, the sound objects, effectively, would be second-hand parts invested with a new latency by means of their configurations with one another. There does, however, need to be some syntagmatic continuity between the constituent elements, and it is essential that they refer to something other than themselves. A further possibility, already mentioned, is to introduce an intersubjective component into the actual form of the music; but the difficulty here is that the subjectivity of the performers and the experiences encoded within the material may affirm one another, impoverishing the creativity of at least partial displacement.

If music is to register non-identity in the configurations of its particulars and spatial co-existence in the constellations of its objects, it is vital that the substitution of one type of material or object for another (paradigmatic) is justified by the relations and associative links (syntagmatic) generative of the inner life of the sounds. The recognition of differences between music objects needs to be matched by a search for identities imbued with the capacity to transform one type of object into another, or, at least, to find some affinity between them. The inner life of the sounds demands to be released onto a level that can contemplate more than a rigid autonomy (or its other, functionalism), and more than the heterogeneous array of signifiers in which we are immersed. Cultural events are themselves particulars within an international system, and it is equally important that they can form links and generate associations with transformative potential between themselves. As the outside world and the body are increasingly read as texts, it falls on music to provide ciphers for how discourses might be interpreted or challenged, and on aesthetics to unmask the interests they represent. Configurations of identity and non-identity within music provide incentives for men and women to determine their own lives and to create a responsive social fabric.

Since we are experiencing an intensification of modernization, it is unlikely that modernism is over, though a paradigm shift has certainly taken place. One might call this switch 'postmodernism', were it not for the tendency found in much contemporary theory to celebrate less a critical transformation of modernism than its defeat. An inclusive modernism embraces much hitherto dismissed, without collapsing into an aimless eclecticism. Internal nature, a mute knowledge, and structures of feeling excluded by over-bearing systems are unlikely to register themselves in the same way across the range of lifeworlds eaten into by administrative logic, but aesthetics remains a privileged site for challenging the identity principle with the concrete experience. Art's ability to jolt consciousness is no less needed in the present than it was in the early days of modernism. Adorno identifies this process as follows: 'Traumatized by art, the subject is able to experience itself properly, dissolving its petrified features and waking up to the narrowness of its self-posited standpoint' (1984a: 380). As artistic practice turns towards reflection, theory becomes a continuation of the condition of art and of its capacity for critical distance: because there is no longer a given function or role for art, practice is dependent on theory's ability to envisage what aesthetics might be.

Notes

1. Dibelius 1988: 158 and Hill 1992: 777 both note the influence of Stockhausen.
2. Riethmüller quotes from Rihm's notes on *Sub Kontur* in the *Programmeheft der Donaueschinger Musiktage 1976.*
3. The installation is illustrated in Jameson 1991: 169.
4. Andrasche 1978: 141 points this out.
5. In fact, counter to the general argument put forward in Jameson (1991: 366), this passage implies that the historical non-synchronisms he takes to be characteristic of modernism have not all caught up with one another in the present.

Bibliography

Abbate, Carolyn (1991), *Unsung Voices: Opera and Musical Narrative in the Nineteenth Century* (Princeton: Princeton University Press).

Adorno, Theodor (1967), 'Perennial Fashion – Jazz', *Prisms*, tr. S. Weber and S. Weber (London: Neville Spearman).

—— (1973a), *Philosophy of Modern Music*, tr. A. G. Mitchell and W. V. Bloomster (London: Sheed and Ward). (The translation of the German *Philosophie der neuen Musik* has been modified to *Philosophy of New Music* in references throughout the present volume.)

—— (1973b), *Negative Dialectics*, tr. E.B. Ashton (London: Routledge).

—— (1974), *Minima Moralia*, tr. E.F.N. Jephcott (London: Verso).

—— (1976a), 'Alienated Masterpiece; the Missa Solemnis', tr. D. Smith, *Telos*, 28. Also in Adorno 1993, alongside some other comments on the *Missa*, under the title 'Spätwerk ohne Spätstil'.

—— (1976b), *Introduction to the Sociology of Music*, tr. E.B. Ashton (New York: Seabury Press).

—— (1977a), Letters to W. Benjamin, tr. H. Zohn, in *Aesthetics and Politics*, (London: Verso).

—— (1977b), 'The actuality of philosophy', *Telos*, 31.

—— (1978), 'On the Fetish Character in Music and the Regression of Listening', tr. M. Goldbloom; A. Arato and E. Gebhardt (eds) *The Essential Frankfurt Reader* (New York: Continuum). Also in Adorno (1991c).

—— and Horkheimer, Max (1979), *Dialectic of Enlightenment*, tr. J. Cumming (London: Verso).

—— (1981), *In Search of Wagner*, tr. R. Livingstone (London: Verso).

—— (1982), 'On the Problem of Music Analysis', introduced and translated by M. Paddison, *Music Analysis*, 1/2.

—— (1984a), *Aesthetic Theory*, G. Adorno and R. Tiedemann (eds), tr. C. Lenhardt (London: Routledge).

—— (1984b), 'The idea of natural history', tr. R. Hullot-Kentor, *Telos*, 60, Summer.

—— (1988), 'The Ageing of the New Music', tr. R. Hullot-Kentor, *Telos*, 77, Fall.

—— (1990), 'The Social Significance of Music', tr. W.V. Blomster; R. Katz and C. Dahlhaus (eds) *Musical Aesthetics: A Historical Reader*, III, *The Twentieth Century* (New York: Pendragon). Also in *Telos*, 35, Spring 1978.

—— (1991a), *Alban Berg: Master of the Smallest Link*, tr. C. Hailey and J. Brand (Cambridge: Cambridge University Press).

—— (1991b), 'Trying to Understand *Endgame*', tr. S.W. Nicholsen, *Notes to Literature*, 1, (New York: Columbia University Press).

—— (1991c), Jay Bernstein (ed.) *The Culture Industry: Selected Essays on Mass Culture*, (London: Routledge).

—— (1992a), *Mahler: A Musical Physiognomy*, tr. E. Jephcott (Chicago: Chicago University Press).

—— (1992b), *Quasi una fantasia: Essays on Modern Music*, tr. R. Livingstone (London: Verso).

—— (1993), *Beethoven: Philosophie der Musik* (Frankfurt am Main: Suhrkamp).

—— *Gesammelte Schriften*, (Frankfurt am Main: Suhrkamp). Abbreviated as 'GS' in text.

   14 (1973), 'Dissonanzen. Musik in der verwalteten Welt'.

   16 (1978), 'Form in der neuen Musik'.

   17 (1982), 'Spätstil Beethovens', *Moments musicaux*. Also in Adorno 1993.

   18 (1984), 'Neunzehn Beiträge über neue Musik'.

Anderson, Perry (1983), 'Structure and Subject', *In the Tracks of Historical Materialism* (London: Verso).

Andrasche, Peter (1978), 'Traditionsmomente in Kompositionen von Cristóbal Halffter, Klaus Huber und Wolfgang Rihm', R. Brinkmann (ed.) *Die neue Musik und die Tradition*, (Mainz: Schott).

Attali, Jacques (1985), *Noise: the Political Economy of Music*, tr. B. Massumi (Manchester: Manchester University Press).

Babbitt, Milton (1978), 'The Composer as Specialist', R. Kostelanetz (ed.) *Esthetics Contemporary* (New York: Prometheus Books).

Barthes, Roland (1985), *The Responsibility of Forms*, tr. R. Howard (Oxford: Blackwell).

Baudrillard, Jean (1988), Mark Poster (ed.) *Selected Writings*, (Cambridge: Polity Press).

Benhabib, Seyla (1986), *Critique, Norm, and Utopia: A Study of the Foundations of Critical Theory* (New York: Columbia University Press).

Benjamin, Walter (1969), *Illuminations, Essays and Reflections*, tr. H. Zohn (New York: Schocken).

—— (1977), *The Origin of German Tragic Drama*, tr. J. Osborne (London: Verso).

Bernstein, Jay (1987), 'The politics of fulfillment and transfiguration', *Radical Philosophy*, 47.

—— (1989), 'Art against Enlightenment: Adorno's Critique of Habermas', Andrew Benjamin (ed.) *The Problems of Modernity* (London: Routledge).

—— (1992), *The Fate of Art: Aesthetic Alienation from Kant to Derrida and Adorno* (Cambridge: Polity Press).

Bloch, Ernst (1977), 'Non-Synchronism and the Obligation to its Dialectics', tr. M. Ritter, *New German Critique*, 11, Spring.

—— (1985), *Essays on the Philosophy of Music*, tr. P. Palmer (Cambridge: Cambridge University Press).

Bonnet, Antoine (1987), 'Ecriture and Perception: on Messagesquisse by Pierre Boulez', tr. L. Jones, *Contemporary Music Review (Music and Psychology: a Mutual Regard)*, 2/1.

Born, Georgina (1995), *Rationalizing Culture: IRCAM, Boulez and the Institutionalization of the Avant-Garde* (Berkeley: University of California Press).

Boulez, Pierre (1964), 'Alea', tr. D. Noakes and P. Jacobs, *Perspectives of New Music*, 3/1. Also in Boulez (1991).

—— (1971), *Boulez on Music Today*, tr. S. Bradshaw and R.R. Bennett (London: Faber).

—— (1976), *Conversations with Célestin Deliège* (London: Eulenburg).

—— (1986a) Jean-Jacques Nattiez (ed.) *Orientations: Collected Writings by Pierre Boulez*, tr. M. Cooper (London: Faber).

—— (1986b), 'Le système et l'idée', *InHarmoniques*, 1.

—— (1987), 'Timbre and composition – timbre and language', tr. R. Robertson, *Contemporary Music Review (Music and Psychology: a Mutual Regard)*, 2/1.

—— and Gerzso, Andrew (1988), 'Computers in Music', *Scientific American*, 258/4.

—— (1990), 'From the Domaine Musical to IRCAM: Pierre Boulez in Conversation with Pierre-Michel Menger', tr. J.W. Bernard, *Perspectives of New Music*, 28/1.

—— (1991), *Stocktakings from an Apprenticeship*, tr. Stephen Walsh (Oxford: Clarendon).

Bowie, Malcolm (1978), *Mallarmé and the Art of Being Difficult* (Cambridge: Cambridge University Press).

Bradshaw, Susan (1986), 'The Instrumental and Vocal Music', William Glock (ed.), *Pierre Boulez: a Symposium* (London: Eulenburg).

Buck-Morss, Susan (1977), *The Origin of Negative Dialectics* (Hassocks: Harvester Press).

Burde, Wolfgang (1985), 'Es geht weiter . . .', D. Rexroth (ed.) *Der Komponist Wolfgang Rihm*, (Frankfurt am Main: Schott).

—— (1993), *György Ligeti: Eine Monographie* (Zürich: Atlantis Musikbuch-Verlag).

Bürger, Christa (1986), 'The Disappearance of Art: The Postmodernism Debate in the U.S.', *Telos*, 68, Summer.

—— (1990), 'Expression and Construction: Adorno and Thomas Mann', tr. Ben Morgan; A. Benjamin and P. Osborne (eds) *Thinking Art: Beyond Traditional Aesthetics* (London: Institute of Contemporary Arts).

Bürger, Peter (1984), *Theory of the Avant-Garde*, tr. M. Shaw (Manchester: Manchester University Press).

—— (1985), 'The Decline of the Modern Age', tr. D.J. Parent, *Telos*, 62, Winter.

—— (1988), *Prosa der Moderne* (Frankfurt am Main: Suhrkamp).

Cage, John (1968), *Silence* (London: Calder and Boyars).

—— (1976), *For the Birds* (Belfond: Boyars).

—— (1987), *X Writings '79–'82* (London: Boyars).

Campana, Deborah (1989), 'A Chance Encounter: the Correspondence between John Cage and Pierre Boulez 1949–1954', *Bucknell Review: John Cage at Seventy-Five*, 32/2.

Carroll, David (1987), *Paraesthetics: Foucault, Lyotard, Derrida* (London: Methuen).

Clarke, David (1993), 'Parting Glances: Aesthetic Solace or Act of Complicity', *Musical Times*, December.

Dahlhaus, Carl (1970), 'Soziologische Dechiffrierung von Music: Von Theodor W. Adornos Wagnerkritik', *The International Review of Music Aesthetics and Sociology*, 1/2.

—— (1979a), 'Zu Adornos Beethoven-Kritik', Otto Kolleritsch (ed.) *Adorno und die Musik*, (Graz: Universal Edition).

—— (1979b), *Richard Wagner's Music Dramas*, tr. Mary Whittall (Cambridge: Cambridge University Press).

—— (1982), *Esthetics of Music*, tr. W. Austin (Cambridge: Cambridge University Press).

—— (1983), *Foundations of Music History*, tr. J.B. Robinson (Cambridge: Cambridge University Press).

—— (1987), 'Das Problem der "höheren Kritik": Adornos Polemik gegen Stravinsky', *Neue Zeitschrift für Musik*, 5.

—— (1989), *Nineteenth-Century Music*, tr. J.B. Robinson (Berkeley: University of California Press).

—— (1991), *Ludwig van Beethoven: Approaches to his Music*, tr. M. Whittall (Oxford: Clarendon).

Danuser, Hermann (1990), 'Innerlichkeit und Äußerlichkeit in der Musikästhetik der Gegenwart', Ekkehard Jost (ed.) *Die Musik der achtziger Jahre* (Mainz: Schott).

Deathridge, John (1983), 'Theodor Adorno, *In Search of Wagner*', review, *Nineteenth-Century Music*, 8/1.

Deliège, Célestin (1988), 'Moment de Pierre Boulez: sur l'introduction orchestrale de *Répons*', *InHarmoniques*, 4.

—— (1989), 'On Form as Actually Experienced', tr. D. Dusinberre, *Contemporary Music Review* (Music and the Cognitive Sciences), 4.

De Man, Paul (1979), *Allegories of Reading: Figural Language in Rousseau, Nietzsche, Rilke and Proust* (New Haven: Yale University Press).

—— (1983), *Blindness and Insight: Essays in the Rhetoric of Contemporary Criticism* (London: Methuen).

—— (1986), *The Resistance to Theory* (Minneapolis: University of Minnesota Press).

Derrida, Jacques (1974), *Of Grammatology*, tr. G.C. Spivak (Baltimore: Johns Hopkins University Press).

—— (1978), *Writing and Difference*, tr. Alan Bass (London: Routledge).

—— (1982), *Margins of Philosophy*, tr. Alan Bass (Brighton: Harvester Press).

Dews, Peter (1987), *Logics of Disintegration: Poststructuralist Thought and the Claims of Critical Theory* (London: Verso).

Dibelius, Ulrich (1984), 'Ligetis Horntrio', *Melos*, 45.

—— (1988), *Moderne Musik II, 1965–1985* (Munich: Piper).

Eagleton, Terry (1985), 'Capitalism, Modernism and Postmodernism', *New Left Review*, 146, July/August.

—— (1990), *The Ideology of the Aesthetic* (Oxford: Blackwell).

—— (1991), *Ideology* (London: Verso).

Eimert, Herbert (1958), 'What is Electronic Music?', *die Reihe*, 1.

Francis, John (1976), *Structure in the Solo Piano Music of John Cage*, Ph.D. thesis, reproduced by University Microfilms International.

Frobenius, Wolf (1981), 'Die "Neue Einfachheit" und der bürgliche Schönheits-begriff', Otto Kolleritsch (ed.) *Zur "Neuen Einfachheit" in der Musik*, (Vienna and Graz: Universal Edition).

Gerzso, Andrew (1984), 'Reflections on Répons', *Contemporary Music Review (Musical Thought at IRCAM)*, 1/1.

Griffiths, Paul (1978), *Boulez* (Oxford Studies of Composers, XVI) (Oxford: Oxford University Press).

—— (1983), *György Ligeti* (London: Robson).

Habermas, Jürgen (1983), 'Theodor Adorno – The Primal History of Subjectivity – Self-Affirmation Gone Wild', *Philosophical-Political Profiles*, tr. F.G. Lawrence (London: Heinemann).

—— (1984), *The Theory of Communicative Action*, 1, tr. T. McCarthy (Cambridge: Polity Press).

—— (1985), 'Questions and Counterquestions', R.J. Bernstein (ed.) *Habermas and Modernity* (Cambridge: Polity Press).

—— (1987), *The Philosophical Discourse of Modernity*, tr. F. Lawrence (Cambridge: Polity Press).

—— (1989), 'Modern and Postmodern Architecture', *The New Conservatism*, tr. S.W. Nicholsen (Cambridge: Polity Press).

Hanslick, Eduard (1986), *On the Musically Beautiful*, tr. G. Payzant (Indianapolis: Hackett Publishing Company).

Harvey, David (1989), *The Condition of Postmodernity* (Oxford: Blackwell).

Hegel, Georg (1977), *Phenomenology of Spirit*, tr. A.V. Miller (Oxford: Oxford University Press).

Hill, Malcolm (1992), 'Rihm, Wolfgang', B. Morton and A. Collins (eds) *Contemporary Composers* (Chicago: St. James Press).

Hirschbrunner, Theo (1985), *Pierre Boulez und sein Werke* (Laaber: Laaber Verlag).

Hodge, Joanna (1989), 'Feminism and Postmodernism: Misleading Divisions Imposed by the Opposition between Modernism and Postmodernism', Andrew Benjamin (ed.) *The Problems of Modernity* (London: Routledge).

Holloway, Robin (1989), 'Modernism and After in Music', *The Cambridge Review* (Symposium: What is Postmodernism?), June.

Huyssen, Andreas (1986), *After the Great Divide* (London: Macmillan).

Jack, Adrian (1974), 'Ligeti', *Music and Musicians*, xxii/11.

Jameson, Fredric (1991), *Postmodernism, or the Cultural Logic of Late Capitalism* (London: Verso).

Jameux, Dominique (1984), 'Boulez and the "Machine": Some Thoughts on the Composer's Use of Various Electro-Acoustic Media', tr. N. Osborne, *Contemporary Music Review* (Musical Thought at IRCAM), 1/1.

—— (1991), *Pierre Boulez*, tr. S. Bradshaw (London: Faber).

Jay, Martin (1973), *The Dialectical Imagination* (London: Heinemann).

—— (1984a), *Adorno* (London: Fontana).

—— (1984b), *Marxism and Totality: the Adventures of a Concept from Lukács to Habermas* (Berkeley: University of California Press).

—— (1985), 'Habermas and Modernism', R.J. Bernstein (ed.) *Habermas and Modernity* (Cambridge: Polity).

Jungheinrich, Hans-Klaus (1987), 'Die "Ästhetische Theorie" – wiedergelesen: Fragmentarische Annäherungen an ein Fragment', Hans-Klaus Jungheinrich (ed.) *Nicht versöhnt: Musikästhetik nach Adorno* (Kassel: Bärenreiter).

Kaufmann, Harald (1964), 'Strukturen im Strukturlosen', *Melos*, 31.

Kompridis, Nikolas (1993), 'Learning from Architecture: Music in the Aftermath to Postmodernism', *Perspectives of New Music*, 31/2.

Kostelanetz, Richard (ed.) (1970), *John Cage* (London: Allen Lane The Penguin Press).

—— (ed.) (1988), *Conversing with Cage* (New York: Omnibus).

Kramer, Lawrence (1995), *Classical Music and Postmodern Knowledge* (Berkeley: University of California Press).

Kristeva, Julia (1986), Toril Moi (ed.) *The Kristeva Reader* (Oxford: Blackwell).

Kropfinger, Klaus (1973), 'Ligeti und die Tradition', R. Stephan (ed.) *Zwischen Tradition und Fortschritt. Über das musikalische Geschichtsbewusstsein*, (Darmstadt: Veröffentlichungen des Instituts für neue Musik und Musikerziehung, 13).

Ligeti, György (1960), 'Pierre Boulez: Decision and Automatism in Structures 1a', *die Reihe*, 4.

—— (1961), 'Some Remarks on Boulez's 3rd Piano Sonata', tr. Leo Black, *die Reihe*, 5.

—— (1965), 'Metamorphoses of Musical Form', *die Reihe*, 7.

—— (1967), 'Zustände, Ereignisse, Wandlungen', *Melos*, 34.

—— (1971), Notes to score of *Melodien*, (Mainz: Schott).

—— (1975), Notes to recording of *Melodien*, The London Sinfonietta, Atherton (London: Decca).

—— (1978), 'On Music and Politics', tr. W. Blomster, *Perspectives of New Music*, 16/2.

—— (1983), *Ligeti in Conversation*, tr. Gabor J. Schabert, Sarah E. Soulsby, Terence Kilmartin and Geoffrey Skelton (London: Eulenburg).

—— (1988), 'On my Etudes for Piano' and 'On my Piano Concerto', tr. S. McLauchlan, *Sonus: a Journal of Investigations into Global Musical Possibilities*, 9/1.

—— (1992), 'Form' in R. Katz and C. Dahlhaus (eds) *Contemplating Music: Source Readings in the Aesthetics of Music*, 3 'Essence', (New York: Pendragon Press).

—— (1993), 'Ligeti at 70', Interview with Anthony Burton on BBC Radio 3, broadcast 2 June.

Lyotard, Jean-François (1984), *The Postmodern Condition: A Report on Knowledge*, tr. G. Bennington and B. Massumi (Manchester: Manchester University Press).

Mann, Thomas (1968), *Doctor Faustus*, tr. H.T. Lowe-Porter (Harmondsworth: Penguin).

Marsh, James (1983), 'Adorno's Critique of Stravinsky', *New German Critique*, 28, Winter.

Mellers, Wilfred (1993), 'Arvo Pärt: Te Deum; Silouans Song; Magnificat; Berliner Messe', review, *The Musical Times*, December.

Mertens, Wim (1983), *American Minimal Music*, tr. J. Hautekiet (London: Kahn and Averill).

Metzger, Heinz-Klaus (1960), 'Just Who is Growing Old?', *die Reihe*, 4.

Middleton, Richard (1990), *Studying Popular Music* (Buckingham: Open University Press).

Moravec, Paul (1992), 'An Interview with David Del Tredici', *Contemporary Music Review (New Tonality)*, 6/2.

Morgan, Robert P. (1991), *Twentieth-Century Music* (New York: Norton).

—— (1992), 'Rethinking Musical Culture: Canonic Reformulations in a Post-Tonal Age', Katherine Bergeron and Philip V. Bohlman (eds) *Disciplining Music: Musicology and its Canons* (Chicago: University of Chicago Press).

Nattiez, Jean-Jacques (1989), *'Répons' and the Crisis of Communication in Contemporary Music*, tr. Katharine Ellis, unpublished manuscript. Later version, 'Boulez et l'age Postmoderne: Le Temps de *Répons*', Nattiez (1993), *Le Combat de Chronos et d'Orphée* (Paris: Christian Bourgois Editeur).

—— (ed.) (1993), *The Boulez-Cage Correspondence*, tr. Robert Samuels, (Cambridge: Cambridge University Press).

Neubauer, John (1986), *The Emancipation of Music from Language* (New Haven: Yale University Press).

Nicholls, David (1990), *American Experimental Music 1890–1940* (Cambridge: Cambridge University Press).

Norris, Christopher (1982), *Deconstruction: Theory and Practice* (London: Methuen).

—— (1988), *Paul de Man: Deconstruction and the Critique of Aesthetic Ideology* (London: Routledge).

—— (1989), 'Utopian Deconstruction: Ernst Bloch, Paul de Man and the Politics of Music', Christopher Norris (ed.) *Music and the Politics of Culture* (London: Lawrence and Wishart).

—— (1990), *What's Wrong with Postmodernism: Critical Theory and the Ends of Philosophy* (Hemel Hempstead: Harvester Wheatsheaf).

—— (1993), *The Truth about Postmodernism* (Oxford: Blackwell).

Osborne, Peter (1989), 'Adorno and the Metaphysics of Modernism: the Problem of a "Postmodern" Art', Andrew Benjamin (ed.) *The Problems of Modernity*, (London: Routledge).

Osswald, Peter (1985), 'Als Chiffre von Freiheit', D. Rexroth (ed.) *Der Komponist Wolfgang Rihm* (Frankfurt am Main: Schott).

Paddison, Max (1993), *Adorno's Aesthetics of Music* (Cambridge: Cambridge University Press).

—— (1996), *Adorno, Modernism and Mass Culture: Essays on Critical Theory and Music* (London: Kahn and Averill).

Pasler, Jann (1993), 'Postmodernism, narrativity and the art of memory', *Contemporary Music Review*, 7.

Potter, Keith (1987), programme note to performance of *Roaratorio*, Sunday 19 July, Royal Albert Hall, BBC Proms.

Pritchett, James (1988), 'From Chance to Choice: John Cage's Concerto for Prepared Piano', *Perspectives of New Music*, 26/1.

—— (1993), *The Music of John Cage* (Cambridge: Cambridge University Press).

Puffett, Derrick (1994), Editorial, *Music Analysis*, 13/1.

Reiprich, Bruce (1978), 'Transformation of Coloration and Density in György Ligeti's Lontano', *Perspectives of New Music*, 16/2.

Riese, Utz (1992), 'Postmodern Culture: Symptom, Critique, or Solution to the Crisis of Modernity? An East German Perspective', *New German Critique*, 57, Fall.

Riethmüller, Albrecht (1983), Notes to recording of *Sub Kontur*, tr. J.B. Robinson, *Deutscher Musikrat: zeitgenössische Musik*, vol. 8, 1970–1980 (Heidelberg: HM/DMR).

Rihm, Wolfgang (1985), 'Musikalische Freiheit', D. Rexroth (ed.) *Der Komponist Wolfgang Rihm* (Frankfurt am Main: Schott).

—— (1992), Notes to *Gesungene Zeit*, tr. M. Whittall (Hamburg: Deutsche Gramaphone GmbH).

Roberts, David (1991), *Art and Enlightenment: Aesthetic Theory after Adorno* (Lincoln and London: University of Nebraska Press).

Rochberg, George (1992), 'Guston and Me: Digression and Return', *Contemporary Music Review (New Tonality)*, 6/2.

Rochlitz, Rainer (1989), 'Language for One, Language for All: Adorno and Modernism', *Perspectives of New Music*, 27/2.

Sabbe, Herman (1987), *Musik Konzepte 53: György Ligeti* (Munich: text + kritik).

Salmenhaara, Erkki (1969), 'Das Musikalische Material und seine Behandlung in den Werken *Apparitions, Atmosphères, Aventures* und *Requiem* von György Ligeti' (Regensburg: *Forschungsbeiträge zur Musikwissenschaft*, 19).

Samson, Jim (1991), 'Music and Society', Jim Samson (ed.) *The Late Romantic Era* (London: Macmillan).

Schäfermeyer, Michael (1990), 'Zur Hörspielarbeit John Cages', H-K. Metzger and R. Riehn (eds) *Musik-Konzepte* Sonderband "John Cage II" (Munich: text + kritik).

Schmidt, James (1979), 'Offensive Critical Theory? Reply to Honneth', *Telos*, 39.

Schöning, Klaus (ed.), (1982), *John Cage: 'Roaratorio'* (Königstein: Athenaeum).

Soja, Edward (1989), *Postmodern Geographies* (London: Verso).

Stahnke, Manfred (1979), 'Struktur und Äesthetik bei Boulez', *Hamburger Beiträge zur Musikwissenschaft*, 21 (Hamburg: Karl Dieter Wagner).

Stoianowa, Iwanka (1964), 'La Troisième Sonata de Boulez et le projet mallarméen du Livre', *Musique en Jeu*, 16.

Stravinsky, Igor (1936), *Chronicle of My Life* (London: Simon and Schuster).

—— and Craft, Robert (1961), *Dialogues* (London: Faber).

Street, Alan (1989), 'Superior Myths, Dogmatic Allegories: The Resistance to Musical Unity', *Music Analysis*, 8, 1/2.

Subotnik, Rose Rosengard (1978), 'The Historical Structure: Adorno's "French" Model for the Criticism of Nineteenth-Century Music', *Nineteenth-Century Music*, 2/1. Also in Subotnik, (1991), *Developing Variations: Style and Ideology in Western Music* (Minneapolis: University of Minnesota Press).

Taruskin, Richard (1980), 'Russian Folk Melodies in the Rite of Spring', *Journal of the American Musicological Society*, 33/3.

Trenkamp, Anne (1976), 'The Concept of "Aléa" in Boulez's "Constellation-Miroir" ', *Music and Letters*, 57/1.

Ulmer, Gregory L. (1983), 'The Object of Post-Criticism', Hal Foster (ed.) *Postmodern Culture* (London: Pluto Press).

Weber, Max (1958), *The Rational and Social Foundations of Music*, tr. and ed. D. Martindale, J. Riedel and G. Neuwirth (Carbondale: Southern Illinois University Press).

Wellmer, Albrecht (1985a), 'Truth, Semblance, Reconciliation: Adorno's Aesthetic Redemption of Modernity', tr. M. Cooke, *Telos*, 62, Winter.

—— (1985b), 'On the Dialectics of Modernism and Postmodernism', *Praxis International*, 4/4. Unabridged version in Wellmer, (1985), *Zur Dialektik von Moderne und Postmoderne: Vernunftkritik nach Adorno* (Frankfurt am Main: Suhrkamp).

—— (1985c), 'Reason, Utopia, and the "Dialectic of Enlightenment" ', R.J. Bernstein (ed.) *Habermas and Modernity* (Cambridge: Polity Press).

Williams, Alastair (1989), 'Music as Immanent Critique: Stasis and Development in the Music of Ligeti', Christopher Norris (ed.) *Music and the Politics of Culture* (London: Lawrence and Wishart).

—— (1991), 'Mimesis and Construction in the work of Boulez and Cage', A. Benjamin and P. Osborne (eds) *Thinking Art: Beyond Traditional Aesthetics* (London: Institute of Contemporary Arts).

—— (1994), '*Répons*: Phantasmagoria or the Articulation of Space', Anthony Pople (ed.) *Theory, Analysis and Meaning in Music* (Cambridge: Cambridge University Press).

—— (1995), 'Modernism, Functionalism and Tradition: The Music of Friedrich Goldmann', *Tempo: A Quarterly Review of Modern Music*, 193.

—— (1997), 'Technology of the archaic: wish images and phantasmagoria in Wagner', *Cambridge Opera Journal*, 9/10.

Wolin, Richard (1982), *Walter Benjamin: an Aesthetic of Redemption* (New York: Columbia University Press).

Wood, David (1985), 'Differance and the Problem of Strategy', R. Bernasconi and D. Wood (eds) *Derrida and Differance* (Coventry: Parousia Press).

Zeller, Hans Rudolf (1964), 'Mallarmé and Serialist Thought', tr. M. Shenfield, *die Reihe*, 6.

Zenck, Martin (1979), 'Auswirkungen einer "Musique Informelle" auf die Neue Musik zu Theodor W. Adornos Formvorstellung', *International Review of the Aesthetics and Sociology of Music*, 10/2.

—— (1980), 'Entwurf einer Soziologie der musikalischen Rezeption', *Die Musikforschung*, 23.

Zuidervaart, Lambert (1991), *Adorno's Aesthetic Theory: The Redemption of Illusion* (London: MIT Press).

Name and Title Index

Subject Index